E Pluribus Unum

E Pluribus Unum

*How the Common Law Helped Unify
and Liberate Colonial America, 1607–1776*

WILLIAM E. NELSON

OXFORD
UNIVERSITY PRESS

OXFORD
UNIVERSITY PRESS

Oxford University Press is a department of the University of Oxford. It furthers
the University's objective of excellence in research, scholarship, and education
by publishing worldwide. Oxford is a registered trade mark of Oxford University
Press in the UK and certain other countries.

Published in the United States of America by Oxford University Press
198 Madison Avenue, New York, NY 10016, United States of America.

© Oxford University Press 2019

Library of Congress Cataloging-in-Publication Data
Names: Nelson, William E. (William Edward), 1940– author
Title: E Pluribus Unum : how the common law helped unify and liberate
colonial America, 1607–1776 / William E. Nelson.
Other titles: how the common law helped unify and
liberate colonial America, 1607–1776
Description: Oxford [UK] ; New York, NY : Oxford University Press, [2019]
Identifiers: LCCN 2018017155 | ISBN 9780190880804 (hard cover) |
ISBN 9780190880828 (epub)
Subjects: LCSH: Law—United States—History. | Common law—United
States—History. | United States—History—Colonial period, ca. 1600–1775.
Classification: LCC KF361 .N45 2019 | DDC 349.7309/032—dc23
LC record available at https://lccn.loc.gov/2018017155

1 3 5 7 9 8 6 4 2

Printed by Sheridan Books, Inc., United States of America

To my students

CONTENTS

PART III   ALTERING EMPIRE TO DEFEAT FRANCE, 1689–1750

PART IV   THE COLLAPSE OF EMPIRE, 1750–1776

ACKNOWLEDGMENTS

I have dedicated this book, which is being published largely for student use, to my students, who have contributed so much to my life and my scholarship over the past half century of my teaching. Nearly ten of them have gone on to distinguished careers as academic legal historians and have produced important publications. Innumerable others have enjoyed successful careers as law professors in a wide variety of fields. Some have even served time (and I use these words advisedly) as law school deans. I thank my past students for all these contributions and trust that future students, who I unfortunately will not get to know as they read this book, will enjoy equal success.

As always I have accumulated many debts in writing this book. I am indebted to Cornelia Dayton and Jeremy Kessler, the readers for Oxford University Press, for their comments and suggestions as well as to Professor Thomas Mackey, who teaches legal history survey courses both to undergraduates and to law students at the University of Louisville and who read an early draft of the book and helped me try to make it suitable for both groups of potential readers. I am also indebted to numerous other historians who have written books, dissertations, and articles or published collections of archival material on which I relied in the four volumes of *The Common Law in Colonial America* (New York: Oxford University Press, 2008–17), of which this book is a summary; the works I used are referenced in the bibliography to this volume and in the extensive endnotes in the four volumes of *The Common Law in Colonial America*. Finally, I acknowledge the generous permission of law reviews and journals in which I pre-published various sections of the four volumes to reprint those sections; the specific articles are referenced in the acknowledgments to the four volumes and in the extensive endnotes. Readers searching for the most detailed available references should consult the footnotes in those articles.

I thank the Filomen D'Agostino and Max E. Greenberg Faculty Research Fund of New York University School of Law for its support and Deans John

Sexton, Richard Revesz, and Trevor Morrison for providing research leaves and funds for purchasing microfilm and for travel expenses. I acknowledge the invaluable research assistance of Ronald Brown, Elizabeth Evans, and Gretchen Feltes, all reference librarians at the New York University School of Law library, and of Jeffrey Mason, a now retired reference librarian at the Hewlett-Woodmere Public Library. Most of all, I thank all the members of the Legal History Colloquium for their multiple readings of the work underlying this book over the last fifteen years.

Finally, I need again to thank my wife, Elaine, and my children, Leila and Gregory, for their continued support.

Woodmere, New York
December 2018

E Pluribus Unum

Introduction

The study of government and politics in colonial America has long been engulfed in obscurity. But government matters, and historians commit a grave mistake in ignoring its workings. One of the main duties of historical scholars is to teach people how government at times has worked to help them but at other times has done them harm. People need to understand how government can function both for and against their interests because when people lack such an understanding, they cannot make intelligent decisions about whom to place in positions of power.

Traditionally historians have studied the workings of American government by focusing on national politics. But that approach has left the profession without a paradigm for the colonial period, resulting in history without a narrative line. Colonial political historians typically have written about the many trees they encountered in doing their research, but they have not offered an appealing picture of the forest. Even as able a scholar as Woodrow Wilson went into his colonial history exam "crammed with one or two hundred dates and one or two thousand minute particulars about the quarrels of nobody knows who with an obscure Governor, about nobody knows what." As Bernard Bailyn wrote half a century ago, historians of colonial America had at the time of his writing "touched on politics incidentally, and when they had, had conveyed to their readers only . . . [a] sense of triviality and boredom."[1]

As a result, many colonial historians have turned over the past half century to writing intellectual and social rather than political history. Great books have been published on the ideological origins of the American Revolution, on the theology of Puritans, on New England dissent, on the Virginia gentry, on slavery, on issues of women and gender, and on numerous other matters. But the history of government—of the institutions through which power is channeled—has received less emphasis than it merits. This book seeks to explicate how government worked in continental British North America from 1607 to 1776.[2] Its ultimate aim is to point future scholars toward analyzing how different structures of governance worked for the benefit of different individuals and different social groups; regrettably this book cannot even begin to offer such a sociopolitical analysis. The limited aim of the volume is merely to offer a new narrative about colonial government by focusing on law and constitutional development and de-emphasizing politics. The hope is that the new narrative will open up new ways of thinking for at least some other scholars.

Four major themes will emerge in the course of the narrative. First is the theme of *e pluribus unum*. The thirteen American colonies that became the United States, like others of the more than twenty British Atlantic colonies, were founded by different groups—indeed, by different nations—for many different purposes. Because law reflects the societal conditions under which it operates, significant differences existed among the legal and governmental cultures of the early colonies. As Part I shows, Maryland and Massachusetts and the other New England colonies were founded for religious ends—as havens for victims of religious persecution or as models of political and religious rectitude. The religious purposes of these colonies profoundly influenced their early law. Maryland, for reasons that will be explained, quickly adopted the common law, whereas Massachusetts and the other New England colonies turned to the word of God as a foundation for much of their law.

New Netherland and Virginia, in contrast, were founded by trading companies. New Netherland, which succeeded as a mercantile outpost, adopted the Dutch law of its parent company. Virginia initially was governed by military law, but when it failed as a trading and exploration venture and turned to agricultural production of a staple crop, tobacco, it needed different law. Like neighboring Maryland, it turned to the common law, although somewhat more gradually. Thus, by the mid-seventeenth century, three different legal systems were in place along the North American east coast—the common law in the Chesapeake, Dutch law in New Netherland, and law having a biblical foundation in New England.

How did the law of these diverse colonies come together? Examination of the theme of how a common legal culture emerged out of the diversity of the initial settlements begins in Part II, where the second of four major themes—the theme of reception of the common law—also emerges. Much has been written about reception, but the writing has been driven by the perspective of lawyers. The focus has been on what parts of English law were received and what parts were not received. Legal writers have paid little attention to differences among the colonies in what law was received, to the temporal pace of reception, or to why reception occurred.

Part II takes a different approach. It begins with the restoration of Charles II to the English throne in 1660 and with the English conquest of New York in 1664. These two events created a problem for Charles. How could he govern his discrete colonies and turn them into a coherent empire when he lacked a standing army, a bureaucracy, and money? The answer that he and James II, his brother and successor, developed was to use the legal profession, which brought the common law with it, as the mechanism of governance.

Part II examines the nearly century-long process by which the Crown imposed the legal profession and the common law on colonies that did not always want them. The imposition proved successful at least in part because of the common law's amorphous nature. Did the common law comprise all of the law of England, including the rules of canon law and equity? Or did the common law consist only of the body of rules administered by King's Bench, Common Pleas, and the Court of Exchequer? Were acts of Parliament included within the common law? Did the common law require its adherents to administer substantive rules of law, or was it merely a set of procedures adumbrated in various writs and forms of action? Over time some of these questions would be resolved. But in the late seventeenth and early eighteenth centuries, when authorities in England were demanding adherence to the common law, those authorities never defined precisely what law they were imposing. As a result, although every colony had to grant some degree of governance power to lawyers, each colony had a good deal of freedom as to what elements of the common law itself the colony accepted. Still, the process of reception in the end transformed radically diverse legal cultures into a coalescing, albeit variegated system—but a system in which lawyers had weighty influence everywhere.

Part III addresses the third theme of the volume—the unfolding and maturation of localism. As Part III shows, the Crown faced pushback to its efforts to impose common law, as many localities sought to govern themselves in their accustomed, diverse ways. After the Glorious Revolution of 1688–89, a new king, William III, and his successors, who needed colonial support for their wars against France, often yielded to these localist pressures, with the result that for some seventy years real power in the colonies lay mainly in local government. William III did, however, have one important goal that shaped local law—the encouragement of Protestant religiosity—and Part III examines how that goal affected colonial legal development.

It seems odd to twenty-first-century lawyers to conceive of the common law and the legal profession, as Charles II and James II did, as effective mechanisms of top-down governance. We are aware of a long history, going back at least as far as Sir Edward Coke, in which lawyers have opposed and prevented the imposition of executive policies. Part IV addresses how in the middle of the eighteenth century many members of the legal profession ceased serving as agents of royal government and instead became opponents of Parliament and the Crown. Part IV shows that these lawyers gradually developed a constitutional ideology empowering local judges and juries to determine the law's directions, how that ideology matured into the doctrine of judicial review of the constitutionality of legislation, and how by the time of independence in 1776 the American public had come to accept that doctrine. Ultimately Part IV suggests how courts and lawyers used the rule of law to amass substantial influence and power throughout the post-Revolutionary history of the American republic so as to check and balance government's more democratic legislative and executive branches.

Several additional issues and themes emerge periodically in various segments of the book. One theme concerns the differences between Chesapeake and New England slavery; the focus is on why New England law recognized but Chesapeake law destroyed the humanity of slaves. Another recurrent theme is that until 1775 Britain governed its empire through informal accommodation and compromise, and that when Parliament in the Intolerable Acts actually exercised its claim of sovereignty, royal government collapsed. A third minor theme focuses on the role of colonial courts in facilitating debt collection, mainly through default judgments, and thereby preserving lines of credit, while a fourth focuses on the legal system's efforts to regulate and stimulate colonial economies.

As noted above, a main theme of this book is that power in colonial America was intensely local. Of course, authorities in London—initially the king and his ministers and later the Crown in Parliament—possessed substantial power. But much power also lay in the colonies, where law was applied and administered. When the colonies were first settled in the seventeenth century, provincewide institutions governing a few square miles of territory mattered: provincial governors and legislatures made law for each colony as a whole. But once colonies grew and their populations spread out, power became fragmented, and local institutions—County Courts, Courts of Common Pleas, and Courts of General Sessions—took control. To understand colonial government, it is essential to study not just provincial legislatures but above all local institutions—that is, local courts. The study of government thus becomes the study of law, and legal understanding rather than efforts to synthesize colonial legislative politics becomes a potential basis for comprehending how colonial government worked.

This book, in sum, aims to offer one possible alternative to traditional political history as a means to understanding the workings of colonial government. I offer this alternative because I doubt that a persuasive narrative of colonial politics can ever be formulated. But a different narrative about colonial government is possible. That narrative, which forms the spine of this book, begins with a recounting of the diverse legal cultures of the early colonial settlements. It continues with the decision of the Crown to rely on the common law and its lawyers as instruments for creating and governing a coherent North American empire. It then shows how eighteenth-century Americans received the common law, but only on condition that it be administered locally to further local interests and policies. Finally, the narrative ends by showing how lawyers grew independent of the Crown and transformed the common law from an instrument of Crown governance into constitutional arguments pointing toward the rule of law—arguments in support initially of local governance, later of American independence, and ultimately of restraint on the political branches of government.

PART I

THE INITIAL SETTLEMENTS
1607–1660

The Chesapeake

Virginia

The English settlers who arrived in the Jamestown colony in 1607 brought with them a legal and political order radically different from the one under which Americans live today. They were not independent individuals but employees of the Virginia Company, the founder and governing entity of the colony. Planting and maintaining the colony required enormous and continuing investment, and thus whatever profits materialized had to be reserved for investors in England, whose continuing flow of cash was essential to keep the colony from extinction.

For this reason, the Virginia Company adopted three policies. First, it decided to retain ownership and total control of all assets, including all land, in Virginia. In 1613–14, the company did grant every settler a garden plot of three acres, but these grants did not reflect any change in the company's governing economic vision. The grants were designed to alleviate shortages of food by encouraging the settlers to grow their own and thereby reduce the need for the company to import food from England. Second, the Virginia Company regulated all economic transactions minutely. Sir Thomas Dale's *Lawes Divine, Moral and Martial*, the code promulgated in 1611, prohibited, for example, the selling of provisions at "unconscionable" prices;[1] in particular it was unlawful for a man to buy something at one price and resell it at a higher one.

Third, with the profit motive and the motive of acquiring land unavailable as devices to induce settlers to labor, the Virginia Company turned to coercion to induce the workforce to work. It may have had little choice given the composition of Virginia's early population, which consisted overwhelmingly of young men who were mostly impoverished, uneducated, and undisciplined. Worst of all, the young men who came to Virginia died at an appalling rate. The colony was, in fact, a death trap for most immigrants.

Such conditions did not encourage the men who populated Virginia either to work hard or to obey societal norms. Opportunities for misbehavior were abundant. Sloth was effortless. Beer, cider, and other alcoholic beverages calmed fears and made hardships temporarily disappear. Opportunities for theft, particularly of company property such as pigs, which could be quickly consumed, were ever present. And why should young men not enjoy sexual pleasure, either with the few women who lived in the colony, with each other, or with animals?

For nearly everyone in early Virginia, life was barbarous, savage, and vulgar. Dale's laws responded in a harsh fashion. The code imposed the death penalty for innumerable crimes; other punishments were whipping, galley service, tongue piercing, cutting off ears, and tying wrongdoers' neck and heels together. More extraordinary was the substance of the laws. After making provision for divine worship and for crimes against religion, such as blasphemy, the code also addressed such offenses as treason, murder, sodomy, adultery, rape, and perjury, all of which were punishable by death, as were most forms of theft. Next, it provided punishment for anyone who disobeyed the commands of any public officer, who spoke against the king or royal authority, or who slandered the council of the colony resident in England or its agents resident in Virginia. The code also contained stringent public-health provisions, such as a requirement that everyone "keep his house sweet and clean."[2]

Historians have disagreed about the significance to be attributed to Dale's *Lawes*. One view is that the *Lawes* fit readily with antecedent English and Virginia legal traditions. Another possibility is that Dale's laws were never enforced in Virginia. All we know for sure is that the code was published in England. Perhaps its main purpose was not to maintain order or to promote discipline on the ground but merely to reassure English investors that the Virginia Company was doing all that it could to secure labor from its workers. Nevertheless, the logic of Dale's *Lawes*, which proclaimed that Virginia was organized on a corporate, military model rather than on a civilian, free-market one, directed the small group of Virginia Company officials who exercised judicial authority to decide disputes in ways that maximized the company's power, not to do justice among the parties.

But Sir Thomas Dale's draconian rules remained on the books for only seven years. Beginning in the late 1610s, change began to occur. What drove the change was a transformation of the colony's economy from one based on trade and exploration to one based on the production of a staple crop, tobacco. Emergence of a tobacco-based economy affected Virginia's legal system in two profound respects. The first was to localize jurisdiction and power. As the tobacco economy expanded, growers needed more and more land. In addition, because the cultivation of tobacco rapidly exhausts the soil and Virginians did nothing to replenish it, growers frequently moved their plantations to new locations. The resulting demand for land quickly dispersed settlement to locations increasingly distant from the colony's center at Jamestown.

The original plan for Virginia was to give a General Court, consisting of the governor and council sitting in Jamestown, jurisdiction to adjudicate all disputes.

But the dispersal of settlement made it impractical for many litigants to come to Jamestown. To accommodate these litigants, county courts were created over the course of the 1620s and 1630s with original jurisdiction over many criminal and most civil cases, subject to a right of appeal to the General Court. However, in view of distances to Jamestown and of other expenses involved in taking appeals, many litigants did not bother to take that action; the result was that final adjudicatory jurisdiction often rested in the county courts. Because the General Court heard relatively few cases and the colonial government in Jamestown had no bureaucracy to enforce law locally, county courts quickly became the main source of government power.

The second impact of tobacco cultivation on Virginia law was privatization of the economy, which entailed the institutionalization of private property, adherence to the rule of law, and the development of mechanisms of credit and debt collection. Privatization began when the Virginia Company in 1616 offered fifty acres of land to anyone who had subscribed or would subscribe £12.10s to its funds. Then, in 1618 the company instituted what became the headright system, whereby anyone who transported himself or another to Virginia received fifty acres for every person transported. Finally, the company began issuing patents to groups of settlers who proposed to found entire communities.

With the arrival of a new governor, Sir George Yeardley, these early steps toward change became part of a package of reform that involved a wholesale transfer of power from the company directors in London to planters living in Virginia. Upon landing in April 1619, Yeardley issued a proclamation freeing all men who had resided for at least three years in the colony from working for the company and authorizing them to choose a dividend of land "to possess and plant upon." It also confirmed the abrogation of Dale's *Lawes* and provided for future government "by those free laws which his Majesty's subjects live under in England." Finally, Yeardley's proclamation directed the calling of an assembly, the House of Burgesses, so that the inhabitants "might have a hand in the governing of themselves."[3] This distribution of property and commitment to self-government under the laws of England had the obvious purpose of encouraging Englishmen to settle in Virginia.

The process of reform proceeded slowly, however, and did not lead immediately to a free-market, capitalist legal order. Even after the repeal of Dale's *Lawes*, the Virginia Company, and later the royal government of Virginia, continued to regulate the economy extensively. For example, both the company and the subsequent royal government persisted in regulating prices and in forbidding most resales of goods at a higher price than the first purchaser had paid. Legislation also required landowners to plant specified amounts of corn.

Indeed, the most pervasive regulatory schemes were introduced after the Crown took control of the colony in the mid-1620s. For over a decade, the

House of Burgesses sought to prevent declines in the price of tobacco by limiting the amount individual planters could grow, setting minimum prices at which crops could be sold, and establishing markets in which sales were to take place. The Burgesses also sought to fix the charges of millers and prevent the export of scarce commodities such as corn and female cattle. The strictest regulation of all was put in place in 1626 by Governor Yeardley. It sought to deal with the problems that arose when a few individuals bought up all the commodities that people needed and then resold them at oligopoly prices. Under Yeardley's regulation, the people of every locale selected a man who became known as the storekeeper of the common store; the storekeeper made all purchases for the locale but then was required to distribute goods to all people as equally as possible. Yeardley's regulation proved unpopular, however, and the General Court suspended its operation.

Harsh, coercive mechanisms for maintaining public order and obtaining labor from settlers also remained in place even after 1618 when Dale's *Lawes* ceased to be in force. In that year, for example, when some citizens of Bermuda Hundred went on strike and refused to perform assigned work tasks, the then-governor imposed military discipline on the community. In 1619, the year in which the Virginia Company announced its reform package, the company also reaffirmed the spartan nature of the colony's criminal justice system when it instructed the Governor and Council to appoint a master for anyone living in idleness and directed that drunkenness be punished severely, even by degrading the guilty individual to servile or bond status.

Why did the Virginia Company continue to engage in detailed economic regulation and to govern through harsh, coercive law even after proclaiming its 1619 reforms? In part, it acted out of habit rooted in long-standing English legal practices. The explanation also lies, however, in the inconsistency among the company's post-1619 policies. On the one hand, the company sought to attract settlers by promising them profits and opportunities to better their lives by coming to Virginia. On the other hand, the company remained under an obligation to produce profits for its English investors. Maintaining the company's investment lifeline, which had kept its colony afloat, required maintenance of conditions on the ground at war with the 1619 reforms. Hence the company proclaimed its reforms while also continuing frequently to follow its older, oppressive policies.

A liberal, free-market legal order based on private property, self-government, and the rule of law, at which the Virginia Company had hinted in its 1619 reforms, simply could not come into existence while the company retained control of the colony. But that control ended in 1624, when the Court of King's Bench in London, pursuant to a suit brought by the Crown in the previous year, vacated the charter of the Virginia Company. The next year, on the death of

James I, his son and successor Charles I, incorporated Virginia into the royal demesne. Virginia thereupon became a royal colony, with a governor appointed by the Crown.

The revocation of the Virginia Company's charter ultimately transformed the colony from one in which settlers were coerced into working for an absentee monopolist to one based on local self-government and rule under stable principles of law. This transformation was not, however, a Whigish one in which Virginians escaped from tyranny in search of freedom, liberty, and a constitution founded on the people's consent. Tyranny, liberty, and consent are the wrong concepts through which to understand why the legal and political system of seventeenth-century Virginia changed. Although some of the substantive law changes about to be addressed ultimately may have promoted liberty, there is no evidence that such was their purpose. Profit and the accumulation of wealth, not the attainment of liberty, were the highest aspirations of seventeenth-century Virginians and of the Englishmen who invested in Virginia. Those aspirations, and the need to facilitate the investment that would foster them, drove change in the colony's political and legal system.

The Virginia Company, which had been set up to maximize the profits of English investors through exploration and trade, was always searching for a stroke of good luck, such as the discovery of some precious metal, to find a secure, profitable basis for the colony. But luck never materialized. Instead, tobacco saved the colony. At the outset of the seventeenth century, smoking was a luxury reserved for wealthy Europeans; no one could produce tobacco cheaply enough and in sufficient quantity to bring its price within reach of the masses. Virginia did.

Tobacco cultivation, however, was not a great help to the Virginia Company. It had never intended to engage in large-scale agricultural operations and lacked a bureaucracy capable of supervising sizable numbers of workers on widely dispersed plantations; independent, property-owning planters performed those tasks more efficiently. Thus, when it became plain in the mid-1620s that the company would neither profit from tobacco nor produce any return on its old investments, it lost the ability to raise further funds. Change then became essential. The revocation of the company's charter, the institution of royal government, and the transformation of the colony's legal system accordingly are best understood as analogous to a modern Chapter 11 bankruptcy reorganization that facilitated future investment from other sources, namely, independent planters in the colony and merchants and other individuals in England who were willing to lend the planters capital.

Once Virginia had been reorganized, its law changed to induce the planters and those with whom they dealt to stake their lives and fortunes on Virginia's future. First, the ownership of land was privatized. Next, Virginia adopted the rule of law—that is, the adjudication of disputes by neutral and impartial, and ultimately professional, decision makers pursuant to established norms—an approach to decision making that was essential to stabilize the private property system and enable entrepreneurs to plan their investments. Then, the law of debt was articulated to encourage investors to advance money by promising them repayment. Finally, the law of servitude was elaborated to induce Europeans to immigrate and to coerce labor from them after their arrival.

To establish the rule of law, Virginia's leaders, it will be recalled, had proclaimed in 1619 that henceforth they would govern by the laws of England. It was a proclamation they kept repeating. Five years later, a sitting councilor proclaimed "that he thought that the Governor always governed for the King, for in all things he governed according to the King's laws,"[4] and four decades later the policy remained, "as near as the capacity and constitution of this country would admit, to adhere to those excellent . . . laws of England."[5]

The General Court also began acting as if it were bound by the rule of law when, in a series of cases beginning in the mid-1620s, it insisted that judges and litigants follow proper rules of procedure. By 1640, the General Court of Virginia had clearly committed the colony to governance under the rule of law. But the commitment remained fragile, although, as the years progressed, the judicial system's commitment to deciding cases under stable legal norms continued to grow stronger.

An important case was *Inhabitants v. Cololough*, in which residents of Northumberland County, including four members of the county bench, brought a proceeding against George Cololough, another member. That left only two members of the county court to take depositions. Adhering to the rule of law, those two members wrote, "In regard that we find no law extant for the taking of depositions before two Commissioners & being ambiguous whether or not the said interrogatories may be sworn unto in this case [and] finding no law to admit thereof or authorize us, we think not fit to take those depositions."[6] The two thus made a political judgment—whether or not to proceed against a fellow member of the bench—by appealing to an established legal rule.

Intertwined with the judiciary's growing reliance on rule-of-law norms in civil litigation was a concern for proceeding by law in criminal cases. Perhaps the earliest manifestation of this concern occurred when several drinking companions of Captain William Epps reported that after they had gone to sleep in a single room, Mrs. Alice Boise "lay down upon the bed besides Capt. Epps" and that thereafter "there was a great stirring & motion in the bed" on several occasions during the night. There was testimony that on two occasions Mrs. Boise said, "Oh, my leg"; that on another she said, "I pray let it alone while the morning"; and that when she got out of bed, her clothes "were raised to a great height." But the witness who testified in greatest detail was "not able to say that

Captain Epps was upon the said Mrs. Boise." On considering, weighing, and debating all the testimony, the court therefore concluded that it was "not proved or manifest . . . that Captain Epps and Mrs. Boise ha[d] offended the law."[7] Here was another occasion when a court turned to the forms of law in a case involving a politically significant member of the community.

The Virginia judiciary, in short, came to understand that reliance on the formalities of the law, or what one case called "the power of justice,"[8] was sometimes a better tool than physical coercion to maintain social order. As a result, courts began to deal less harshly with subjects who affronted them or challenged their power. Courts also began to deal more leniently with violations of religious norms, such as heresy or marrying a couple without a license. Similarly, offenses against sexual morality—a form of offense against religion—were rarely prosecuted, and, when prosecutions were successful, punishments were minor. Of course, women, mainly female servants, who gave birth to illegitimate children were routinely whipped, fined, made to serve additional time to compensate their masters for the costs of pregnancy, and sometimes forced to confess before their local church congregation. Similarly, men guilty of bastardy could be sued for child support and might also be required to do public penance during divine service. But there were almost no prosecutions for clandestine sexual offenses, whether heterosexual or otherwise, however sinful they may have been, if they did not result in the birth of a child.

The significance of Virginia's shift to the rule of law emerges with singular clarity in the case of *Confession of Willmote*,[9] a bastardy prosecution for which an unusually comprehensive record remains. The case was against a servant girl Anne Willmote, who had accused Argoll Yardley, her master and a longtime justice of the county court, of being the father of her expected child. One day, when John Stringer, the county sheriff, was walking past her lodgings, he heard Anne groaning and "immediately went in" and "demanded how she did." Willmote answered that "she was very ill," to which Stringer replied, "Thou has brought thyself to a fair pass. And all through thine own wickedness." On this cue, Willmote inquired what she should do, and Stringer, knowing that his high rank required Willmote to heed his advice, instructed her, "I would have thee to acknowledge thy offenses to God. And be sorry for thy bad course of life thou has hitherto run, and confess who is the true father of the child thou goes with (not wronging any man)."

Willmote must have understood what Stringer expected of her, but she could not bring herself to do it. She promised to confess, but requested "leave" until she was "somewhat better," to which Stringer responded, "Thou will do well in so doing. And God will the sooner forgive thee, for the truth will shame the Devil." He then departed.

He returned the next day and asked, "What sayest thou to that business that thou told me of yesterday?" "I will tell you," she answered; "it is Owen the Irishman that got me with child. He has lain with me several times. He lay with me that day my mistress was buried & several times since." That was all Willmote confessed that day, and accordingly Stringer departed.

On the third day, Stringer returned again, this time with a witness named Lucas, and inquired "whether she were still in the opinion that it was Owen the Irishman his child." Willmote responded, "It was no man else, for he lay with me a month (or thereabouts before my mistress died). And that day she was buried . . . and several times since. Notwithstanding diverse fallings out, . . . we were sure together above a year & half." Then Lucas demanded in Stringer's presence, "Then why would thou wrong thy master so much and in his absence?" Fully appreciating what Stringer and Lucas wanted to hear, Willmote "replied that she was advised unto it by that base fellow Owen, who told me (after I had told him I was with child by him) I doubt whether it be mine or not (although I have had to do with thee). And I know the Esquire has lain with you wherefore put it upon him. And I will marry thee & free thee." Thereafter, Owen "had often lain with" Anne, but "now [that] he has done all the injury he can (thinking he is quite cleared) has cast me off."

In the end, Owen Scott was not cleared; on the basis of Anne Willmote's ambiguous statement, he was prosecuted for fornication, convicted, and made to serve his and Anne's master for one additional year. Willmote herself was never prosecuted, perhaps because the court was satisfied that by accusing Scott she had exonerated Yardley, even though she did not deny that Yardley had had intercourse with her and thus had not fully eliminated the possibility that Yardley was the father of her child. To have prosecuted her thus would have reopened the possibility that she would again accuse Yardley.

We should pause to take stock. We should not imagine that the advent of the rule of law put an end to coercion. Officials, such as Sheriff Stringer, remained quite capable of administering the rule of law coercively. The advent of the rule of law did not end coercion and manipulation, for law ends neither; the advent of the rule of law merely created mechanisms that could be used without bloodshed by those with the capacity to coerce and manipulate. Anne Willmote, for one, succeeded in manipulating the law to achieve the result she wanted—no prosecution of herself. The minions of the law likewise used their powers of coercion to protect one of their own—Justice Argoll Yardley—from prosecution and punishment. But the rule of law often has its victims—the poor and powerless, in this case, Owen the Irishman.

Such an understanding of law's malleability and power is especially important in connection with the rise of commercial litigation and new forms of capital flow. Sometimes law was needed to facilitate the rise of a market economy by clarifying who owned what and thereby rendering ownership of property secure. At other times, specific rules were needed to encourage investors to advance funds by assuring them that their funds would be returned. But often it did not matter what rule the courts adopted: what was important was only that fixed rules of law be present so that various commercial actors could try to take advantage of them. Thus, many of the doctrines adopted by the General Court simply laid down background norms around which parties could, if they wished, negotiate as long as the norms were transparent.

By the 1640s, the judges had come to understand that entrepreneurs, which is what the free men of Virginia had become, needed to know the law to maneuver against each other, enter into contracts, and thereby make profits and accumulate wealth. Indeed, by the 1640s, the hallmark doctrine of market capitalism—"that free trade be allowed to all the inhabitants of the colony to buy and sell at their best advantage," however unjust and detrimental to the weak, the poor, or the witless free trade might be—had been enacted by statute.[10] Consider, for example, the 1643 case of a seaman on a Dutch vessel who sold his goods at an agreed price, later learned that his shipmates had sold similar goods at a higher price, and then tried to get out of his contract. The court responded austerely: it "ordered" that the seaman "shall perform his bargain or else" a judgment against him would be enforced.[11]

Regulatory laws also collapsed with the emergence of freedom of contract and free-market capitalism. Thus, in the midst of England's Civil War, King Charles I issued a proclamation prohibiting Virginians from shipping tobacco to London, the center of Parliament's domain, even if a shipment were in repayment of a debt. Virginians, on the whole, favored the king over Parliament, but by the 1640s loyalty to the Crown had become less important than repaying debts in order to ensure that loans and investments would continue. Given this balance of priorities, the presiding judge of the Northampton County Court not surprisingly directed one planter to ship to London, "saying God forbid we should refuse to pay [even] Turks or Jew for what we have received."[12] A week later, in response to "doubts" expressed by Londoners, the House of Burgesses "pledg[ed] the faith of the colony for a continuance of a free and peaceable trade to them."[13]

As they embraced the idea that they should rule by law, Virginia lawmakers turned to their English legal heritage, especially to the common law. They turned, that is, to what they knew from experience. A further reason for turning to the common law was that its writ system—the ancient body of procedure that pigeonholed all litigation into precise categories, each commenced by a particular writ and governed by fixed rules of practice—provided familiar forms of action, particularly the actions of debt and assumpsit, to facilitate debt collection and thereby encourage English merchants to lend money to Virginians.

Attracting loans became the main task of Virginia's legal system in the decades after 1625. Once English investors had ceased giving money to the Virginia Company, which, in turn, had used it to buy goods needed to sustain the colony, a new way had to be found to induce those investors to give the money directly to Virginia planters, who could then use it to buy the goods they needed. Investors were not prepared to advance money against promises to pay uncertain profits in the future; they had advanced money to the company on such terms, and profits had never materialized. Surely, individual planters presented a greater risk than the company. Vague resolutions on the part of the General Court that "the people shall pay their debts this year"[14] might help, but investors needed more, especially when the court also proclaimed at a time of falling tobacco prices that in dealing with debt it would "proceed according to equity and justice & pass by the law when too rigorous."[15] Potential lenders of money needed remedies that would give them the means to recover sums lent, with interest, at specified times in the future.

The common law provided such remedies. Virginia also enacted other legislation to facilitate debt collection. In particular, statutes provided procedures for recording mortgages, for controlling debtors who sought to depart from Virginia while indebted, for payment of debts due in England, and for regulating imprisonment for debt, including the terms of release from imprisonment. Judges finally provided sympathetic forums for creditors.

Most significantly, the central concern of courts changed after 1625. Judges began to spend proportionately less time coercing labor and controlling deviance. After 1625, the judiciary and its subordinate officials spent most of their time assisting creditors in the collection of debts. Anyone who examines Virginia court records from the 1640s and later decades will find what all historians have observed about eighteenth-century American records—namely, that entries about debt collection vastly exceed entries for every other category of case combined. Debt collection became a routinized process, with all the efficiencies that routinization brings, although it did not always make debt collection easy.

Judicial efforts to control servants did not, however, come to a complete end. Indentured servants did not benefit nearly as much as did free people from Virginia's move toward the rule of law. Harsh treatment of servants, as a means of coercing them to work, remained the norm throughout the middle years of the seventeenth century. But the same forces that pushed Virginia as a whole toward the rule of law—the need for certain and predictable rules that would induce people to invest their wealth and energy in the colony—also operated, albeit to a lesser extent, in connection with the law of servitude. Young men and women willing to migrate voluntarily from England to Virginia needed reassurance that the promises made to them when they departed England would be honored when they subsequently lived and worked in Virginia. Thus, the law of servitude needed to protect the expectations of volunteer servants while retaining enough harshness to frighten them into working.

Much harshness did remain. Judges dealt sternly, for example, with runaway servants. The law was especially harsh on servants who spread scandalous statements or behaved violently toward their masters as well as on servants who, after claiming that their masters abused them, failed to prove their claims. Even a servant who proved a claim of abuse would not be freed but merely protected against retaliatory abuse or, at best, transferred to a new master. The same was true for at least some servants who claimed freedom but failed to establish it.

On the other hand, the courts did deal fairly with servants who proved they had completed their term of service; courts would order such servants to be freed. Legislation also prohibited harsh usage, such as imposing sexual demands on unwilling servants or assigning apprentices to tasks other than those for which they had been apprenticed. Courts also required masters to provide servants with needed medical attention and with food, clothing, and other necessities. Finally, masters were required to give corn and clothes to former servants on the expiration of their terms.

A final element of the law of servitude was slavery. Soon after the arrival of the first Africans in Virginia in 1619, small steps were taken toward transforming servitude for blacks into slavery. Black servants were denied the right to bear arms, and if they ran away, they were punished more severely than white servants who did the same. Illicit sex was punished with special severity if it was interracial. Most significantly, blacks were presumed to be servants for life rather than for a term of years. But some blacks, especially those who converted to Christianity, could obtain their freedom and even acquire landed property and hold other slaves. Moreover, slavery was not statistically or economically important in Virginia's early years: it did not develop fully until after 1660, and therefore it will be discussed in a later chapter.

With the development of the law of servitude, along with the privatization of property, the institutionalization of the rule of law, and the protection of creditors' rights, the legal order of Virginia no longer functioned to advance company, Crown, or other public policies. Instead, courts and sheriffs lent public power to individual entrepreneurs and to investors and moneylenders. The law, that is, no longer provided central direction to society; rather, it became a system that individuals could commandeer to advance their own interests and pursue their own profits.

Maryland

Maryland was founded as a refuge for upper-class Roman Catholics when in the spring of 1634, sixteen Catholic gentlemen, accompanied by their families and by two Jesuit priests, established the colony as a haven for the persecuted members of their faith. From the beginning, though, the Catholics were outnumbered by the Protestant laborers and servants who accompanied them. Lord Baltimore strove to ensure Catholic control by granting vast quantities of land to his Catholic followers and by turning to the common law, as early as the late 1630s, to protect their titles.

Nonetheless, Catholicism's hold on Maryland was always tenuous. At the outset, the Maryland colony was governed by Leonard Calvert, the younger brother of the proprietor, Cecilius Calvert, Lord Baltimore, whose title rested on a charter from Charles I. Governor Calvert immediately encountered opposition from William Claiborne, who occupied Kent Island, which was located within Maryland's territorial boundaries, but which Claiborne sought to keep as part of Virginia. Nonetheless, in 1637 Calvert was able to obtain possession of the island.

But the onset of the Civil War in England emboldened Maryland's Protestants, and Claiborne, burning with revenge, retook Kent Island in 1644, at the same time that another Protestant rebel, Richard Ingle, angered at his arrest for treasonable words against the king, took control of St. Mary's, the colony's capital. But by 1648, Governor Calvert regained full control over his brother's colony, after his brother had staved off an attempt in England to revoke his charter. Leonard Calvert then went to England, and in an effort to reach out to Protestants, Lord Baltimore replaced him with William Stone, Maryland's first Protestant governor.

Until Stone's appointment, Maryland's Catholic rulers had had to struggle with indigenous Protestants, Protestants from Virginia, and Protestants in England to retain their control. Stone complicated matters when in 1649 he invited a group of some 500 Puritans to settle what is now Annapolis. He soon found himself on the defensive when the Commonwealth government in England appointed the Puritan leader at Annapolis, two Protestant sea captains, and Maryland's old enemy Claiborne to obtain the submission of the Chesapeake colonies to its authority. Claiborne and the Puritan leader went to St. Mary's in 1652, ejected Stone from the governorship, and sought to establish a new administration under their control. When Stone, under orders from Lord Baltimore, resisted, they appointed William Fuller as governor, and in 1655 civil strife broke out. The Puritan faction quickly won a decisive victory.

Meanwhile, back in England, Lord Baltimore petitioned Oliver Cromwell's government for help. The regime directed the Maryland adversaries to come to an agreement, and they did. Baltimore regained full control of his province, and in 1657 he appointed Josias Fendell as the new governor, with instructions to forgive the past deeds of all parties and to treat them fairly and equally in the future. Fendell, however, proved disloyal when early in 1660 he resigned his commission as governor and accepted a new commission from the assembly; Lord Baltimore, with the support of Charles II and assistance from the governor of Virginia, promptly replaced Fendell with his younger brother, Philip Calvert.

The law of early Maryland reflected the colony's Roman Catholic origins, the chaos resulting from Puritan efforts to subvert Catholic rule, and the proximity of its huge neighbor, Virginia. The central question in Maryland's seventeenth-century history was whether Maryland would develop in some distinctively Catholic fashion, pattern itself on Puritan New England, or copy Virginia's law.

From the outset, Lord Baltimore had understood that if he wanted the Roman Catholic minority to be tolerated in Maryland, he in turn would need to tolerate Protestants. Accordingly, he aspired to create a colony where Catholics and Protestants could live side by side in peace. The principal foundation of his program was the Act Concerning Religion, personally drafted by Baltimore and promulgated in 1648. It provided "that no person whatsoever professing to believe in Jesus Christ [should] be molested for or in respect of his or her religion or the free exercise thereof."[16]

The act remained an important one. In one key case—where the defendant was prosecuted for treason, sedition, and rebellious speeches, in that he "endeavor[ed] to seduce & draw from their religion the inhabitants assembled" at a militia muster, threatened to force a council member and his family to attend his church, and, as a result of his speeches, "caused several inhabitants of this province to refuse to appear at musters"—the Maryland Provincial Court upheld a demurrer to an indictment based on the 1648 act. It agreed that "preaching & teaching is the free exercise of every churchman's religion" and that it constituted "neither rebellion [nor] mutiny to utter such words as is alleged."[17] Similarly, when Protestant servants complained that their Catholic master had called Protestant ministers and Protestant books "the instruments of the devil," the court fined the Catholic master and required him to enter into a peace bond not to "offend the peace of this colony or of the inhabitants thereof by injurious & unnecessary arguments or disputations in matter of religion."[18]

But there were limits to the policy of toleration. Jews were one group outside those limits. Quakers were another. More important, Lord Baltimore's policy of toleration was not always followed during the periods of time when Baltimore himself was not in charge. In those occasional years when the Puritans ruled Maryland, they prosecuted people for such religious offenses as missing church or otherwise profaning the Sabbath. Puritans also instituted the practice of prosecuting bastardy—a practice that continued thereafter. But prosecutions against fornicators in Maryland, unlike those in New England, were not about morality and thus would usually be dismissed once it became clear that the public would not be chargeable with support of the bastard child. And, although a woman's oath would stand against whomever she accused of fathering her child, men were not without defenses. Typically, they would suffer no penalty at all if they could prove they did not have intercourse with the woman at issue: at least one court held there could be "no proof of a carnal copulation" without "sufficient evidence that had seen them Rem in Re."[19] Even when intercourse was admitted, a man might go unpunished. Thus, in one case, Lucie Stratton came to Arthur Turner's "bed & put [her] hand under the cloths & took [him] by the private parts" and made a "faithful promise unto him to be his wife," which "made him act what he did." But then she refused to marry him because "she could not love him," saying "that he was a lustful man, a very lustful man, & that she never could be quiet for him." On these facts, the court ruled that she "ought to provide for & maintain the said child herself."[20]

From 1642 to 1660, the period of the Civil War and Commonwealth in England, Maryland suffered significant religious and political strife, and that strife found its way into the courtroom. However, when in the winter of 1657–58 Lord Baltimore was restored to full authority over his colony, he took steps to restore harmony. Baltimore promised to pardon everyone's past actions, to grant land to all applicants without discrimination, and to abide by the Act Concerning Religion, which granted toleration to all Christians. His agents in the colony abided by his promise and thereby brought an end to Maryland's political and religious strife and enabled the colony's legal system to move forward in a more coherent way.

Ultimately, though, neither religion nor civil strife dictated the course of Maryland's legal development. What ultimately determined its direction was the presence of the neighboring colony of Virginia. Maryland's neighbor to the south was much larger in area, population, and economic significance. Maryland was dwarfed by Virginia. Thus, one Maryland case, in which title depended on a judgment in Virginia that, one litigant claimed, had been obtained unlawfully by the arbitrary power of the then-governor, was remanded to the courts of the larger and more powerful colony to prevent "clashing or contradictory orders, or otherwise to engender any breach or just distaste between the two governments."[21] Moreover, Maryland was a quarter-century younger than Virginia, and its early settlers could look to Virginia's experience for precedents with which to answer many problems that arose. Most important, Maryland's economy took a direction virtually identical to Virginia's. With tobacco as its principal export crop, Maryland faced the same economic pressures that had determined how Virginia's law had evolved. The pressures of the marketplace, for example, propelled Maryland's debtor-creditor law to follow the same directions as Virginia's. Like the planters of Virginia, Maryland planters needed capital to obtain new land, to purchase additional servants, and to obtain manufactured goods that both enhanced tobacco production and improved their standard of living. They had to borrow, and the prerequisite to borrowing was a legal system that facilitated creditors' collection of debts. Thus, in Maryland as in Virginia, the central concern of courts by 1660 was assisting creditors in the collection of debts. As the provincial court explained a few years after 1660, it was essential not to leave any creditor "remediless in the recovery of a just debt, which neither law nor equity can or will permit";[22] indeed, any "design of keeping" creditors "out of [their] debt[s]" would be "to the great discouragement of trade in this Province."[23]

With cases such as these, the function of law in Maryland was transformed. Religious issues that had provoked conflict at the colony's founding and during the time of England's Civil War began to fade into the background. The same economic policy issues that drove Virginia's law transformed Maryland into a parallel legal polity.

2

New England

Massachusetts

Unlike Virginia, the Massachusetts Bay Colony was not founded to generate profits either for investors who remained at home in England or for colonial leaders who crossed the Atlantic to America. Although the profit motive was not absent, the founders' foremost goal was to establish a utopian polity. The founders of Massachusetts were striving to build the best possible society on earth—a society that could serve as a model polity, if not for the entire world, at least for the English-speaking parts of it. But Massachusetts was not utopia as either Thomas More or we today would understand the concept. It sought to be a Puritan utopia, and thus it is necessary to begin this chapter by outlining the essential beliefs of those Puritans who settled Massachusetts.

Puritanism was both a theology and a political theory. Puritans strove to comprehend the relationship between divine sovereignty and human free will as well as to structure a government that balanced hierarchical authority with liberty. Their goal was to avoid what they viewed as two evil extremes. The one extreme was Roman papacy and European monarchy, in which a small upper class, itself controlled through a hierarchy led by one man, either king or pope, dominated the masses by keeping them in ignorance. The other evil was radical antinomian Protestantism, in which every person blessed with faith (and who does not ultimately think she is so blessed?) could receive divine revelation of the truth and rely on that revelation as the basis for disobeying the commands of those in authority. Puritanism represented a balanced and complex effort, both in the search for divine truth and in the structuring of human government, to reconcile liberty with hierarchy through ordered community.

The conceptual basis for this reconciliation was self-restraint. The Puritans knew, as John Winthrop had told them during their 1630 transatlantic voyage, that God had created a world in which "some [were] high and eminent in power and dignity; others mean and in submission." But God had not given any man power "out of any particular and singular respect to him . . . , but for the . . . common good of the creature, man." In Winthrop's view, "every man" had "need of others" so that they could be "knit together" in community "as one man." Accordingly, Winthrop urged both the strong and the weak to act by "moderating and restraining them[selves], so that the rich and mighty should not eat up the poor nor the poor and despised rise up against and shake off their yoke."[1]

In the words of John Cotton, a leading Boston minister, "all power that is on earth" had to "be limited." "Let there be due bounds set," he proclaimed, whether in the state, the church, or even the family. Although some might think it "a matter of danger to the state to limit prerogatives . . . , it is a further danger, not to have them limited: They will be like a tempest, if they be not limited."[2] The powerful had to restrain themselves through "love, mercy, gentleness, [and] temperance," while at the same time "the poor and inferior sort" were expected to behave circumspectly with "faith, patience, obedience."[3]

Immigrants typically came to Massachusetts as families, and once in Massachusetts, the law required them to live as families. A husband who did not live with his wife would be ordered to return to her, even if his wife was in England. He was not excused from returning because his business in Massachusetts was not yet done. Wives living apart from their husbands would receive public assistance in rejoining them, and a man or woman without a spouse would be directed to settle in some orderly family since Puritan judges understood that a person who lived alone contrary to the law of the country was subject to sin and iniquity, the frequent consequences of a solitary life.

Massachusetts differed demographically from Virginia in one other important respect. Tobacco drove the Virginia economy, and tobacco is a crop that quickly exhausts the soil. As a result, Virginia planters needed new land every few years, and they spread far out from Jamestown and from one another's plantations to obtain it. Moreover, because they were constantly on the move, the planters built few permanent buildings in Virginia's early years. In contrast, the Bay Colony required families to settle in towns, with fields typically fanning out from a town center in which residents lived within walking distance of their church. Indeed, when one man raised objections about the difficulty of farming in towns that were so densely settled, he was hauled before the Court of Assistants and made to acknowledge his error. As a result of this policy, Massachusetts towns had a permanence about them that Virginia's plantations lacked, and they soon became centers of culture and societal power for which Virginia had no equivalents.

The preservation of the religious establishment was the most important town function. The colony's government exerted considerable effort in support of religion. Much of what its leaders did was commonplace throughout the English-speaking world. But other governmental activities were more unusual, and, in some cases, unknown elsewhere.

Throughout most of the seventeenth century, the word of God was part of the law of Massachusetts. Major issues arose as early as 1641, when three servants of John Humfry had non-forcible intercourse with Humfry's three daughters, all under the age of ten. Many people demanded the death penalty. Intercourse with such minors was a capital offense at common law in England, but the 1641 Body of Liberties provided that no one could be prosecuted criminally except under some express law enacted by a General Court, or, in the absence of an express law, by the word of God. The General Court concluded that the word of God prohibited both forcible rape and intercourse with a female under the age of consent but did not make either offense capital, nor did any express law of Massachusetts. Accordingly, the court sentenced the defendants to corporal punishment, but not to death.

The legislature promptly enacted a law making conduct like that of Humfry's servants a capital offense, and that law remained on the books until 1648, when it was dropped from the codification of that year, apparently because the Bible did not justify capital punishment in such a case. Thus, when, some two decades later, Patrick Jeanison had intercourse with an eight-year-old girl, there was no statute prohibiting his act: rape had been made a crime only when a female was at least ten years of age. In the absence of applicable legislation, however, the General Court still remained empowered to determine cases by the word of God, and it interpreted the Bible differently from the way it had in 1641, found Jeanison guilty of rape, and sentenced him to death. Similarly, when Richard Gardiner brought a writ of case against Richard Nevard "for deflowering his daughter" and the jury returned a special verdict finding Nevard liable in damages if "the word of God . . . be a sufficient ground for a jury to act upon . . . where there wants an express law," the court held Nevard liable.[4]

Judicial efforts to protect the dominion of religion were ongoing. Thus, people received corporal punishment or were banished if they spoke against the church's rule or disputed its religious teachings. Anne Hutchinson and Roger Williams were merely the most notorious of them. Many other people were regularly punished for missing church or otherwise profaning the Sabbath.

Perhaps the most infamous case after the 1630s was that of William Ledra, a Quaker who on pain of death was banished from Massachusetts Bay in 1660. He returned in 1661, called the colony's ministers "deluders" and its magistrates "murderers," and declared "he owed no subjection to the wicked laws of this jurisdiction."[5] He was promptly hanged. Three other Friends—Mary Dyer, William Robinson, and Marmaduke Stephenson—likewise were banished and, when they returned, executed.

The Bay Colony's actions against the Society of Friends were harsh indeed. But they were not totally unrestrained. The Quakers, who carried antinomianism to its limits, threatened to bring social disorder and religious chaos to Massachusetts. They disrupted Puritan worship services, for example, by interrupting sermons and strolling naked down the aisles. Nor did the magistrates proceed initially with corporal punishment. First, they tried to persuade Quakers to alter their ways. When persuasion failed, Puritan leaders turned to other punishments such as jail and banishment. Death was the final punishment, used only when a Quaker like William Ledra returned and denied the authority of the Bay Colony's government. Indeed, Mary Dyer, who had first been banished in the 1630s as a follower of Anne Hutchinson, returned as a Quaker in 1659, was banished again, returned a second time and was sentenced to death, was reprieved and banished a third time, and finally executed only after she returned yet again.

In any event, these Quaker cases are unsurprising. The founders of the Massachusetts Bay Colony never intended to tolerate religious dissent, and their successors never deviated from their initial policy. Not only was Puritanism the colony's established religion; to the extent that the leaders of the colony could control events, they strove to make it the only religion.

The leaders also sought to make their church a united and harmonious one, and that was a far more difficult task. Puritanism contained strong centrifugal forces within it: the congregational system of church governance ensured that if factions developed within a congregation, no superior entity within the church's governing structure could impose one faction's will on another. A council of neighboring clergy could be called to mediate a dispute, but such councils had no binding authority and thus often proved ineffective. Only the state—with its control over the fisc and its system of appeals from individual magistrates to the county courts, then to the Court of Assistants, and ultimately to the General Court—contained mechanisms for bringing cases up to central authorities and sending orders supported by coercive sanctions back down.

But Puritan judges did not turn readily to coercion. Thus, when Edward Woodman was prosecuted for announcing in a Newbury town meeting that one town minister was "an intruder, brought in by craft & subtlety," and another "an apostate & backslider from the truth," two magistrates voted to convict him of making a false and scandalous statement and to require him to apologize publicly. But two others dissented. They "[stood] for the congregational way of church government & discipline" and did not think that the court should take sides in a parish dispute.[6] The tie prevented the court from acting.

The people of Newbury then called a church council but failed to heed its recommendations, and the dispute lingered, only to return to court two years later. By the time of the return, the court had lost patience. It found "Mr. Woodman & his parties"—the minority faction—guilty of "dishonor to the name of God [and] to religion here established" and also of "scandalizing of a venerable pious and loving pastor." It thought that they "deserv[ed] severe punishment," but it "was willing to exercise as much lenity as the case" permitted. Fines were imposed on some forty individuals.[7]

Even the clergy occasionally could find itself subject to judicial discipline. For example, when one minister spoke "against the court and diverse other persons," he "was sharply admonished to forbear to vent his distemper to the scandal of persons and dishonor of God" and warned that "if he should find himself unable to demean himself more soberly and Christianlike, as becomes his office, they 'do think it more convenient for him to surcease from the exercise of any public employment.'"[8]

Judicial intervention in ecclesiastical affairs also occurred in *Mansfield v. Hathorne* and *Longley v. Hathorne*.[9] The cases began when Hathorne at a church meeting accused Longley and Mansfield of breaking the ninth commandment by bearing false witness in depositions in a civil suit. The church voted to censure them, to which Longley and Mansfield responded by suing Hathorne for slander. The jury then returned verdicts for the plaintiffs, finding, in effect, that they had not lied. At that point, the court wrote a somewhat restrained letter to the church, noting that it was "much to be desired that contrary judgment in one & the same case may be prevented if possibly it may be." The court therefore gave "the church the opportunity & cause to change their mind & reverse censures so far as concerns the particular case in question." When the church refused to follow the court's suggestion, however, the judges sent another letter expressing their sorrow that their "endeavors ha[d] not produced that effect we hoped" and warning that "no cause [was] so purely ecclesiastical but the civil power may in its way deal therein." Judgments for Longley and Mansfield were thereupon entered in the two cases and affirmed by the Court of Assistants.

Judicial intervention in religious affairs, even if only of a gentle sort, was simply inevitable if a united church was to receive public support. Consider, for example, the 1657 case of *Giddings v. Brown*,[10] in which a taxpayer brought trespass against a tax collector who seized the plaintiff's pewter dishes when he refused to pay a tax in support of giving the town minister a residence in fee simple, at public expense, rather than as a life estate. A life estate was clearly authorized by statute, but it was unclear whether a fee simple was authorized. *Giddings*, which arose out of a town political conflict, was especially interesting because the judge who initially decided it wrote an opinion relying on common law rules of precedent and statutory construction and holding the tax void. In the end, it became a run-of-the mill statutory interpretation case in which the General Court ultimately decided that the statute did authorize a tax for a fee simple. But because the case was about taxation, it clearly was one that only the courts and not the church could resolve.

None of this was new, nor was it indicative of Puritan declension. Throughout the charter period, the churches of the Bay Colony needed and received the judiciary's support, on terms set by the judiciary, to maintain an outwardly religious society in which there was no place for dissent —a society in which a visiting ship captain, who was "an atheist believing that there was neither God nor devil, hell nor heaven, . . . dare not speak what I think here or in this country."[11]

Similar interplay between civil and church authorities had occurred during the 1630s, and the power of the General Court and the Court of Assistants had proved essential in dealing with the key schismatics of that decade —Roger Williams, John Wheelwright, and Anne Hutchinson. Similarly, in the 1640s a Salem Quarterly Court had admonished a minister for seizing a writ that a parishioner had obtained and throwing it in the fire to stop judicial proceedings. Throughout the charter period, the courts of the Bay Colony worked with the colony's churches and gave them their support, but they insisted on the judiciary's supremacy.

The Puritans gave their name to an attitude toward sex outside marriage and toward various other trivial pleasures that remains with us today. The naming is appropriate. Throughout the mid-seventeenth century, the government of the Massachusetts Bay Colony worked continuously to restrain sexual sin and other sinful pleasures. But even here, magistrates typically acted with restraint.

The most common sexual offense for which people were prosecuted in the Bay Colony was fornication. It must be emphasized, however, that the gravamen of the offense was not the birth of an illegitimate child who might require public support but sex outside the bounds of matrimony. Fornication was a sin. Accordingly, hundreds of single women were prosecuted for becoming pregnant, and many young couples were punished for having a child less than nine months after they were married. Similarly, a young man was whipped for bragging of his conquests, even though no pregnancies resulted.

Adultery, for which the penalty was death, was another commonly prosecuted crime, although few adulterers were, in fact, executed. Death was also the penalty for bestiality, although here too execution often was avoided as judges and juries showed self-restraint. One defendant, for instance, was found innocent, and another found guilty only of an attempt to bugger a cow. Homosexual behavior also was punished. Even masturbation was a crime, for which one man received six lashes.

Finally, there were minor offenses against morality dealing with alcoholic beverages, cards and dice, singing, fiddling and dancing, smoking tobacco, and violating the sumptuary laws. And there were the odd cases—of a man whipped for spying into the chamber of his master and mistress and for reporting what he saw, and of a man charged with singing a lascivious song.

Moral values not only denied certain pleasures to the people of Massachusetts Bay; they also affected the way people worked and did business. Puritans took seriously the notion of just price—a medieval concept that all goods had a fair price and that selling them for more than that price was extortionate. Unlike Virginia, Massachusetts did not quickly embrace in its law the idea that all its inhabitants should be allowed to trade freely and to buy and sell to their best advantage. Price regulations were enforced, at least periodically, through most of the seventeenth century. Although just price was a complex concept not completely unrelated to the concept of market price, its very complexity legitimated the regulation of market price. Thus, the Bay Colony's legislators felt comfortable enacting various price controls throughout the 1630s, including one provision specifying that imported commodities could not be sold at 33 percent more than their market price in England. In addition, the Court of Assistants warned all merchants not to exceed the bounds of moderation, and in a famous case, the prominent merchant Robert Keayne was censured for making excessive profits on the sale of goods. The legal system also regulated the quality of goods and services.

Then, there was wage and labor regulation. Following up on earlier legislation, the Laws and Liberties of 1648 authorized town meetings to set wages and to prosecute those who took excessive wages. Moreover, all adults, both men and woman, were required to work; when Mary Boutwell lived idly and took others' food, she was sentenced to be whipped, although after receiving clemency she was merely admonished. Legislation prohibiting idleness was adopted as early as 1633, and a number of people were prosecuted for violating the law.

Along with wage and labor regulation, the law of the Bay Colony demanded that servants, women, and others who lacked power be treated humanely. Although Massachusetts like other colonies severely punished servants who ran away, stole, spoke against, or physically threatened their masters, laborers also received a variety of protections. Masters were not permitted to assign servants to work for a different master for more than a year and were liable for abuse of servants. The law was especially solicitous of children who were servants. Thus, a female apprentice who was neglected was returned to her mother, and another child who had been treated well, but was left alone in bed some evenings, was ordered returned to its father. An apprentice also could obtain release from his indentures if a master failed to teach the trade he had agreed to teach and was compensated for his costs.

From the time of initial settlement, Massachusetts servants were different from Virginia servants. The Virginians were overwhelmingly lower-class immigrants who arrived in the Chesapeake with no protection from kin or other ties. They were at the mercy of their masters and of the legal system their masters controlled; their only hope was freedom at the end of their period of service. In contrast, few servants in Massachusetts were immigrants: the law discouraged immigrant servants by imposing on them a presumptive nine-year term, substantially longer than the customary four- to seven-year term in Virginia.

Instead, Massachusetts servants tended to be children of nearby townsmen who were in the vicinity and ready to protect their kin through the legal system they controlled.

Finally, came women. Women were not legally equal to men in the Massachusetts Bay Colony. Only eldest sons, not eldest daughters, inherited a double portion from parents who died without wills. Although, as the century progressed, some females received some education in town schools, they received less than males, and, of course, they could not attend Harvard College. In addition, the rules of coverture remained in effect for married women, and children remained firmly under their father's control.

Nonetheless, the Puritan concern for self-restraint required husbands and fathers to act with moderation, and the law accordingly generated some important rules protecting women and children. One allowed women to obtain divorces if their husbands deserted them or were impotent. In at least one case, a wife received custody of the couple's children following their divorce. Another rule protective of women, a result of legislation in 1641 and 1650, made it a crime for their husbands to beat them. Similarly, if a woman could establish that her husband had abused her, she would not be punished for refusing to live with him.

What made the law of Massachusetts Bay distinctive was its emphasis on protecting the religious institutions and moral values of Puritanism. That was not all, however, that the colony's judicial system did. It also had to perform most of the usual functions of courts and government in the English-speaking world, such as preserving authority and punishing crime.

However, Puritanism affected the law of the Bay Colony in a profound respect. It kept seventeenth-century Massachusetts from becoming the debt-ridden outpost of British imperialism that Virginia became. Like Virginia, Boston became part of the transatlantic commercial economy, but Boston's merchants, unlike Virginia's planters, were not deeply in debt. The rest of seventeenth-century Massachusetts, consisting of small towns of self-sufficient yeoman farmers, never became part of the transatlantic economy, and debt-collection litigation never became the dominant concern in seventeenth-century Massachusetts courts that it was in Virginia's. Indeed, legislation discouraged such litigation by prohibiting arrest and imprisonment for debt unless a plaintiff could show that his debtor was secreting assets; indeed, by making debt collection difficult, the legislation probably discouraged lending and credit, which, as shown in chapter 1, was a mainstay of the Chesapeake economy. Rather than focus on debt collection, the Massachusetts judiciary concentrated on building the infrastructure of the interior towns that would enable them to prosper over time. Hundreds of cases dealt with recording land titles, building roads, opening schools, erecting mill dams, and otherwise creating public goods. Unlike Virginia, Massachusetts had the infrastructure for civilized community living in place within a few years of its settlement.

But we must not think of seventeenth-century Massachusetts as an agrarian paradise; it was not one. Developers busily bought up land, and entrepreneurs sought profit. Nonetheless, the law did point the Bay Colony in a different direction from that taken by its Chesapeake neighbors to the south. The law inclined Massachusetts away from unbridled entrepreneurial capitalism and from the exercise of power unconstrained by anything but the forces of the marketplace and the formalistic black-letter rules that the marketplace demanded. It prevented those wielding political, economic, or social power from pressing their advantage and exploiting those under their control to whatever limits the market would permit.

By the end of the 1630s, in sum, the social landscape of Massachusetts differed strikingly from the landscapes of either England or Virginia. Above all, Massachusetts lacked the vast differences in wealth that characterized England and early Virginia. There were few landless men barely eking out subsistence through labor for others; land was plentiful, and any family head willing to work could gain access to it. Unlike the inhabitants of Virginia, Massachusetts residents lived in compact, permanent towns where they could participate in public life free from the sorts of domination that great magnates exercised in most rural communities of England. In their small, ordered communities, the people of Massachusetts thus possessed power that common people lacked almost everywhere in Europe. And, to the extent that Puritans learned to read and write so as to extract truth from the Bible, without which salvation was impossible, they also empowered themselves politically. The high level of literacy in Massachusetts created a polity in which the governing class could not monopolize control over the flow of written information between localities as it could in most of the world. Ordinary people in Massachusetts, by gaining the ability to communicate with each other just as effectively as elites could, were empowered in all colonial institutions, not merely in their own towns.

But Massachusetts Bay was not a democracy as we understand the concept. Popular power was not unchecked. The royal charter of the Massachusetts Bay Company, which everyone assumed to be the Bay Colony's governing document, had important aristocratic characteristics.

On its arrival in Massachusetts in 1630, the government consisted of twelve magistrates who constituted the Court of Assistants, and initially they alone governed the new colony. In the spring of 1631, however, the Court of Assistants decided to reconstitute the General Court, which had fallen into desuetude with the Puritans' departure from England. The new General Court consisted initially of the Court of Assistants together with all freemen—that is, all adult men who were full members of one of the colony's local churches.

The General Court was not a democratic body by modern standards; membership was highly restricted by a religious test and in no way represented a cross section of the Bay Colony's population. But the freemen who sat in the Court were more representative of ordinary people in the towns than were members of the aristocratic Court of Assistants, and they promptly began exercising political power.

First, in 1631, the freemen began electing the assistants, who once elected tended to serve for lengthy terms, and in 1632, the governor and deputy-governor as well. Two years later, a group of freemen demanded to see the charter; upon seeing it, they learned that the General Court possessed plenary legislative power, which they then insisted on exercising. The assistants caved in, reconstituted the General Court for most purposes as a representative body of deputies elected by freemen rather than a plenary body of freemen, and conceded its role as a major organ of government with full legislative and adjudicative power.

But although the assistants were willing to concede a major role to the representatives of the freemen, they were unwilling to concede unlimited control or anything approaching democratic self-rule. The assistants' goal was a polity that balanced local, popular liberty, on the one hand, and aristocratic authority, on the other, through the restraint of both. Relying on language in the charter, the assistants accordingly claimed power to cast a negative vote to veto any legislation pending in the General Court. On the whole, their claim met with success, especially when a law of 1644 provided that unless the deputies and assistants agreed otherwise, henceforth they would meet as separate bodies and that the concurrence of both would be required for the enactment of legislation. The magistrates also claimed a negative in matters of adjudication, but here the outcome was murkier.

With the organization of the General Court settled, the leaders of the Bay Colony turned to the creation of other institutions—in particular, institutions for the adjudication of disputes. Of course, the Court of Assistants, which was also the upper house of the General Court, remained. It possessed original jurisdiction in major cases and appellate jurisdiction in all others. Immediately below it were the Quarterly Courts, which later evolved into the County Courts. Jurisdictional bounds were not as clear, however, as this summary suggests. On the contrary, they were unsteady and flexible, as the General Court used available manpower to deal as best as it could with pressing needs, often on an ad hoc basis. Similarly, appeals, which usually were taken to the next highest court, at times were taken directly to the General Court, even from the lowest of courts.

The key point about institutional arrangements in seventeenth-century Massachusetts, in both the General Court and the lower courts, is their suppleness and adaptability. For the leaders of the Bay Colony, rules of jurisdiction and procedure had no purpose in and of themselves, serving only to advance the colony's substantive objective—the creation of a godly commonwealth in which self-restrained leaders restrained the sins of others.

Massachusetts was equally lax in its treatment of the common law. The common law served as a handy background norm when lawmakers needed to adopt a rule but lacked time to fashion it carefully. The Bay Colonists were equally ready to abandon the common law, however, when the needs of the colony so dictated.

They abandoned much of it through their adoption of a provision in the Body of Liberties of 1641 aimed at simplifying court procedure, as follows: "no summons, pleading, judgment, or any kind of proceeding in court, or course of justice shall be abated, arrested, or reversed upon any kind of circumstantial errors or mistakes, if the person and cause be rightly understood and intended by the court", and through the further provision that while litigants could "employ . . . any man" to represent them in court, they could give him "no fee or reward for his pains."[12]

A legal profession was one victim of these provisions; without fees, it could not exist. The common law writ system was another casualty. Although Massachusetts plaintiffs used writs, especially the action of case, to institute civil actions, they often used them incorrectly. But because of the lack of a legal profession and the goal of simplifying procedure, no one cared. The English legal heritage that the Puritans brought with them also embraced a vast body of local law and custom outside the common law that varied significantly from place to place in England. Finally, the Massachusetts courts and juries exercised considerable powers in equity, such as chancering bonds and ordering specific performance of contracts for the sale of land.

There is much that is praiseworthy in a legal system flexibly committed to customary norms and to principles of equity and justice. But such a system also raises problems. In the case of Massachusetts, where the ultimate standard of justice was the word of God, ordinary people feared that the magistrates might not interpret God's word consistently. Indeed, as seen earlier in the cases of Humphry's servants and of Patrick Jeanison, the General Court did not interpret the Mosaic law of rape consistently, and as anyone at the time observing the course of the Thirty Years' War in Germany and the Civil War in England knew, fundamental disagreement existed over the meaning of God's words. Moreover, even if the magistrates had acted consistently, those who had to know the law in order to obey it might have had trouble predicting what the courts would do.

As early as 1635, the townspeople of Massachusetts accordingly demanded that their law be reduced to a detailed written code that would be accessible to them. This movement for codification resulted from two separate though overlapping urges—first, the colonists' distrust of discretionary justice as administered by their betters, and second, the importance they attached to stable and written laws that they could readily ascertain and obey. An intense battle over codification lasted for thirteen years until Massachusetts achieved first, a partial code in the Body of Liberties of 1641 and finally, a fuller code in the Laws and Liberties of 1648.

The subjects that the 1648 code addressed, as well as those it left untouched, suggest, however, that the impetus for moving toward codification in Massachusetts was different from the impetus behind adopting the rule of law in Virginia. The Massachusetts code comprehensively reenacted all prior legislation intended to remain in force and also codified for the first time much public law, criminal law, inheritance law, and domestic relations law. These were critical matters for farmers concerned with providing for their families and worried that central authorities would intrude on their lives. The code, in contrast, did not deal with subjects that lawyers today would place in the categories of contract and tort—matters of special concern to mercantile and entrepreneurial types planning investment strategies. The inference to be drawn is that the impetus for the rule of law did not come, as it had in Virginia, from merchants and commercial farmers eager to attract investment; instead, the catalyst was a more popular form of pressure emerging from peripheral farming communities anxious to preserve an independent way of life.

But the 1648 code did not give popular forces all that they had wanted. Many of its provisions stated general principles that required interpretation in future cases and thus left people under a duty to deduce their specific obligations from general rules. Other provisions specifically conferred discretion on future adjudicators: for example, the section on fornication directed the sentencing of convicted defendants with fines, corporal punishment, an order that they marry, or any combination of those penalties, in whatever fashion was "most agreeable to the word of God."[13]

Thus, the 1648 code did not put an end to contention between magistrates seeking to preserve discretion in applying the word of God and townspeople intent on circumscribing the assistants' power. It merely transposed that contention to another locus where the people could rely on a method other than fixed and certain rules to control the magistrates—namely, the jury box.

From the earliest days of the Bay Colony, everyone had understood that powerful juries could rein in judges. Accordingly, the right to trial by jury received statutory protection in civil and criminal cases both in the 1641 Body of Liberties and in the Laws and Liberties of 1648. The courts almost invariably granted a jury trial when a litigant requested one, although occasionally they denied a jury and dealt with defendants severely when it suited their perception of the colony's needs. Before the right to trial by jury was codified in the 1641 and 1648 laws, for example, a number of individuals—Anne Hutchinson,

Thomas Morton, Phillip Ratliffe, Roger Williams, and John Wheelwright, among others—were banished by the Court of Assistants using procedures reminiscent of those used by the Star Chamber in England. Lower courts also disposed of hundreds of petty offenses without juries.

Meanwhile, in the cases that were tried by juries, there was an ongoing issue about the power of juries—an issue related, in turn, to the claim of the magistrates to a negative voice in matters of adjudication before the General Court and ultimately to the movement for codification. At a deeper level, the issue was about the proper balance between the power of people in local communities and the power of the colony's aristocracy.

We must begin with the provision in the 1641 Body of Liberties providing that any case in which trial judges disagreed with jurors about their verdict would be referred to the General Court for a final decision. The Laws and Liberties of 1648 contained a like provision, as well as a further one authorizing juries to request advice in open court from sources other than the judges—presumably the clergy. In the two decades following the 1640s codes, many bench-jury disagreements occurred, many of them political or religious in character. In one case, for example, a defendant was accused of blasphemy for calling God the devil and saying the only God he knew was his sword. When the jury found him not guilty of a capital offense, the magistrates rejected the verdict, but before the General Court could decide the case the defendant escaped. In another criminal case, in which a defendant was accused of gaming with dice, the jury found him not guilty of playing for money; when the assistants rejected the verdict, the General Court upheld them, finding the defendant guilty by his own confession.

What happened to cases such as these, often politically sensitive, when they arrived at the General Court? There too, representatives of local communities, on the one hand, and the Bay Colony's aristocrats, on the other, were sometimes in tension. The first conflict between the deputies, chosen as representatives of the freemen, and the assistants occurred in 1636 over Thomas Hooker's emigration to Connecticut. As a result of the conflict, the General Court adopted a statute providing that the court could not issue any order without the approval of both the majority of the deputies and the majority of the magistrates and that cases of disagreement between them would be decided by a committee consisting of equal numbers of deputies and magistrates and an umpire chosen by them.

Together with the magistrates' power to reject jury verdicts, the 1636 settlement evenly balanced the power of local communities and that of the aristocracy. Both the freemen, represented on the jury and by the deputies, and the magistrates, who presided over the county courts, constituted the Court of Assistants, and sat as assistants in the General Court, were required to agree to all judgments. If they failed to agree, the case went up to a next level—a committee staffed equally by deputies and assistants, who chose a mutually acceptable umpire to cast the decisive vote.

But the 1636 settlement quickly proved unstable. In 1644, a new statute provided that the General Court henceforth would meet in two separate chambers—the Deputies and the Court of Assistants. It is not clear whether the committee of umpires survived this establishment of full bicameralism. What is clear is that the General Court could not act effectively as the highest court of the Bay Colony, at least in cases that came before it as a result of bench-jury disagreements, if no procedure existed for reaching judgments when the deputies and magistrates were at odds. Giving both the aristocracy and the representatives of local communities a negative or veto could work in the context of legislation, but in matters of adjudication it was no way to run an efficient judicial system capable of resolving the disputes presented to it. Either the deputies or the assistants had to have the final say, or else appeals to the General Court would remain unresolved.

It was in the context of this need for finality, as well as the failure of the 1648 code to cabin fully the magistrates' discretion, that the General Court in 1649 again revisited the issue of the assistants' negative. An act of that year provided that in cases of disagreement between the deputies and the assistants the General Court would sit as a single chamber to hear the case and determine the case by majority vote. Further legislation in 1652 made it clear that the 1649 settlement applied only to judicial and not to legislative matters, where both bicameralism and the magistrates' negative survived throughout the colonial period. Nonetheless, the 1649 act meant that the deputies would have the controlling voice in adjudicatory matters because they outnumbered the magistrates by about three to one.

By giving the decisive voice to the deputies, the 1649 act gave the more popular branch of the legislature dominance over the aristocratic magistrates. The 1649 act thereby had the effect of reducing significantly the discretion that magistrates had retained pursuant to the Laws and Liberties of 1648: magistrates could exercise discretion when they found it necessary, but jurors could disagree with them, and when they did, discretion ultimately would fall to the representatives of the towns sitting in the General Court. Until the nineteenth century, this triumph of popular community power never would be challenged effectively.

In short, the Massachusetts Bay Colony developed a remarkable body of procedural law during the half century of its existence. Although Massachusetts procedure was influenced by the common law, it was not, in essence, a common law system. Nor, in essence, was it a religious system. The codes of 1641 and 1648 and the law of judge and jury and of the magistrates' negative, in particular, were indigenous growths that balanced popular communitarian concerns for the rule of law and aristocratic concerns for government by the word of God in an always changing mixture as realities on the ground changed. Initially, it balanced them equally, but in the end, it gave superior power to popular representatives. But even when popular forces had the edge, they acted with restraint and did not always choose to exercise their power.

Like Virginia, Massachusetts in the decades preceding 1660 thus moved in the direction of government by the rule of law. But the rule of law had a different meaning and the law itself retained a different substantive content in the two colonies. In Virginia, the turn to the rule of law entailed the importation of English common law concepts in order to establish fixed and certain black-letter rules that would facilitate entrepreneurial planning and thereby encourage investment in Virginia's economy. In Massachusetts, the purpose of the rule of law, which was advanced through legislation and the empowerment of local townspeople sitting on juries and in a mixed popular-aristocratic legislature, was to control the discretion of the governing elite and thereby prevent it from interfering unpredictably in the lives of ordinary people. Different societal interests propagated the rule of law in the two colonies, and its adoption accordingly served two very different purposes. Indeed, those purposes were so different that we should understand the concept of rule of law as being quite different in Massachusetts and Virginia.

Moreover, even after the turn to the rule of law, the substantive law of the two colonies remained dissimilar. The reason is that their law was built on different foundations—that of Virginia, on the underpinning of a spartan labor system, and that of Massachusetts, on the word of God. The foundations remained present after the rule of law was built atop them, for the core purposes of the two colonies—the maximization of investor profits and the creation of a Puritan utopia—did not change. The rule of law was designed only to provide a check on ruling elites to ensure that they did not treat arbitrarily the socioeconomic groups essential to each colony's success.

Connecticut, New Haven, Plymouth, and Rhode Island

These four additional settlements in New England in 1660 all were geographically small entities about the size that Rhode Island is now. Connecticut had been established as a sort of outpost of Massachusetts, and New Haven by settlers from England who were tied to the Puritan cause; both were in the Massachusetts orbit. Although Plymouth was founded a decade before Massachusetts, its law was strongly influenced by that of the Bay Colony. Rhode Island, which was settled by dissenters from the Massachusetts religious establishment who had been driven into exile as a result, was something of an outlier in New England, but even its law felt the influence of Massachusetts.

The religious values of the five New England colonies were similar. Although the churches of Plymouth and Rhode Island had governance structures differing from those of Massachusetts, Connecticut, and New Haven, they remained, in their theological beliefs, within the Puritan fold. The churches of all five colonies were non-hierarchical Protestant ones dedicated to purification of their people; even the Rhode Island exiles were far closer in their worldview to the ministers and magistrates of Massachusetts than to the planters striving to make money out of tobacco in Virginia.

Connecticut, New Haven, Plymouth, and Rhode Island all possessed, albeit some more than others, a distinctively Puritan legal regime. The law of the four colonies, in the main, copied that of the Bay Colony and gave New England, in most significant respects, a single, somewhat uniform legal system. The word of God was at the foundation of the legal system of every New England colony. As New Haven legislation declared, "the judicial laws of God, as they were delivered by Moses" were to be "a rule to all the courts,"[14] and all judges had a "duty to do the best they [could] that the law of God may be strictly observed."[15] Similarly, the Plymouth Colony made it a crime to "deny the scriptures to be a rule of life."[16] Except in Rhode Island, people were punished for disagreeing publicly with official theological dogmas. Others were fined in all four colonies for failing to fulfill religious duties, such as not attending church on Sunday, otherwise violating the Sabbath, or using profane language.

Quakers were a special problem. Viewing them as "subersi[ve] of the fundamentals of Christian religion, church, order, and the civil peace,"[17] the Plymouth Colony banished them, and the General Court set aside a day of fasting and humiliation to seek God's blessing in saving the colony from the "infection and disturbance" of those "fretting gangrenelike doctrines and persons commonly called Quakers."[18] Both Connecticut and New Hampshire prosecuted Quakers into the eighteenth century, and Connecticut brought criminal proceedings against the proto-Baptist Rogerene sect in the 1690s.

Judges also strove to help religious authorities eradicate sin. The sin they prosecuted most frequently was fornication. Significant numbers of single women were punished for getting pregnant, and many young couples were prosecuted for having a child less than nine months after they were married. Single men also were prosecuted for fornication. Another sexual sin prosecuted with some frequency was adultery, for which death was the official penalty in New Haven. Death was the penalty everywhere for bestiality, and some defendants were executed, although execution often was avoided as judges and juries showed self-restraint. The same pattern was true of sodomy, for which there were few actual prosecutions. More numerous prosecutions occurred for lesser offenses committed between persons of the same sex, among them a pros-ecution of two men for spilling their seed upon one another. Sexual offenses could be of such a great variety that Connecticut did not even try to codify them but merely authorized judges to use their discretion against the several ways of uncleanness, including masturbation.

The smaller New England colonies also joined Massachusetts in criminalizing such minor offenses as drunkenness, singing, fiddling and dancing, smoking to-bacco, and idleness. As in Massachusetts, moral values also led to regulations against unreasonable prices and excessive wages. New Haven, for example, allowed only a 25-percent markup of goods. The New England colonies ap-plied basic common law rules of servant discipline, although religious values led New Englanders to treat their servants, especially children, more gently than Virginians treated theirs.

Women, of course, were not legally equal to men in New England. As one Connecticut court declared, for example, in construing an ambiguous will, money was left so "that the sons shall have learning to write plainly and read distinctly in the Bible and the daughters so to read and sew sufficiently for the making of their own ordinary linen."[19] In a like vein, a New Haven court "reproved" a woman "for her forward disposition, remembering her that meek-ness is a choice ornament for a woman."[20] At the same time, religious precepts about self-restraint required husbands and fathers to act with moderation.

Acceptance of religious precepts created societies in the smaller New England colonies similar to that of Massachusetts. As in Massachusetts, people were ex-pected to live with families, and even a man who lived with his family remotely in the woods was ordered to move near some neighborhood. Land was plentiful, and any family head willing to work could gain access to it. Indeed, on one occa-sion in Plymouth, the General Court invited young men or others who wanted land to apply for it. The availability of land made the southern New England colonies, like Massachusetts, into agrarian communities inhabited mainly by yeoman farmers.

Like those in Massachusetts, litigants in southern New England used common law writs to institute civil litigation, but they often chose the wrong ones, and when they did, no one cared. For nearly two decades New Haven did not use writs at all. Courts also ignored other sorts of technical objections. In most respects, the law of the smaller New England colonies thus replicated that of Massachusetts.

But there were some differences. One was that the magistrates of the smaller colonies possessed more discretion and, at least on a few occasions, acted more aggressively than those in Massachusetts. They were more willing, for example, to assert their authority over local popular forces, as in one Plymouth case in which the General Court set aside an election and ordered a new one because it found the electoral victors "unmeete persons for such a place" and chosen "in contempt of the government."[21]

An important difference occurred with respect to juries. New Haven dispensed with juries altogether, and Connecticut, Plymouth, and Rhode Island left the judiciary's power over juries largely intact. Rhode Island courts, for example, set aside verdicts that were contrary to law, and Connecticut legislation provided that a court could grant a new trial if a jury returned a verdict contrary to the evidence, subject, however, to the right of either party to appeal the case to the General Court. Once a case came to the General Court, both the magistrates and the deputies had to concur in the judgment, although it is unclear what would happen if they did not.

Nonetheless, it is important not to exaggerate the authority and freedom of New England magistrates outside Massachusetts. All the colonies witnessed popular demands for codification, and by the 1650s all of them had published at least partial codes. In addition, Rhode Island limited the discretion of its magistrates by prohibiting anyone from being "molested or destroyed, but by . . . some known law, and according to the letter of it."[22] Thus, when a man was accused of "matters of very pernicious nature against the peace of the place: yet no particular law being found that is of force in the colony, which takes hold of the said offense," the Rhode Island court declined to proceed against him.[23]

To a significant extent, the law of the satellite New England colonies thus mirrored that of the Bay Colony. But on one important set of issues—the relationship between church and state—those colonies diverged from Massachusetts and from one another, although even here, convergence in the direction of uniform practice occurred. Connecticut and New Haven, like Massachusetts, used the coercive mechanisms of the law to keep local churches under control. But Plymouth and Rhode Island, which were founded by people who believed in separation of church and state, strove with differing levels of success to preserve a church/state boundary.

At the heart of government control of religion lies taxation. From the outset Connecticut imposed religious taxes and entertained suits by taxpayers displeased with their local churches. Many of these cases raised religious differences. Sometimes the courts supported dissidents, as in one case in which people who had been excommunicated were seeking a "way for the composing [of] their differences," and the court directed the church to find "some way that might effect the issuing [of] their sad differences."[24] But other times they did not. In some cases, indeed, judges disciplined both sides to a dispute. In return for financial support, the clergy accepted subordination. As one New Haven minister declared, "He did not judge it unlawful for a minister of the word to present his case to the judgment of the magistrate, for the determination of such civil controversies as may arise between themselves & others." Were it otherwise, the clergy would "be in worse case in that respect than other men."[25]

Rhode Island, in contrast, kept its churches entirely separate from government. Likewise, the leaders of the Plymouth Colony strove to set up churches independent of government. Rhode Island succeeded over time in maintaining the separation of church and state, but perhaps because Plymouth never progressed beyond being a poor, agrarian outpost, its religious institutions proved unable to maintain themselves without the aid of the state. When in 1655 the town of Marshfield, for example, petitioned for help in supporting the ministry, the General Court sent Miles Standish and John Alden to call a town meeting and direct its inhabitants to contribute according to their abilities. Two years later, the General Court by statute authorized the levy of taxes to support public worship, and two years after that, the General Court applied outright coercion to the town of Yarmouth, directing the appointment of four men who would levy religious taxes on those who refused to contribute voluntarily. With the 1657 act and its subsequent enforcement, Plymouth was well on the path toward becoming a religious polity nearly identical to that of its neighbor, Massachusetts Bay.

In sum, the law of the smaller New England colonies displayed a striking tendency to converge in the direction of the law of Massachusetts. In important respects, the five New England colonies shared the same law. Ultimately, that law was shaped by the Puritan aspiration, which dominated society throughout New England, that families live together in godly communities where the faithful could watch over one another to promote the spiritual and moral welfare of all. Throughout New England, this aspiration pushed the law toward punishing those who behaved sinfully or rejected community norms. Unlike Virginia, early New England was not an individualistic, highly mobile society of single, young men geared toward doing whatever was needed to make money. Virginia, not New England, was the first place in America where capitalism took root. New England's law, in contrast, provided early nurture to religious and moral values that still remain alive in America today.

3

New Netherland

During the same decade in which the English were establishing their colonies in Plymouth and Massachusetts Bay, the Dutch founded trading posts on Manhattan Island and at Albany that developed into the colony of New Netherland. A few years later, New Englanders settled Long Island, and Sweden established a colony in what is now Delaware. In 1664, England would conquer all of New Netherland, but before that occurred the Dutch had conquered the Swedish settlement and had exercised at least some authority over several of the Long Island towns.

New Amsterdam and the Hudson Valley

The legal system of New Netherland, derived as it was from the civil law system of the fatherland, differed profoundly from the legal systems of England's colonies. First, the New Netherland system possessed a more centralized institutional structure than did the common law, especially as that law had been transferred to England's North American colonies. Second, Dutch judges did not use juries as fact-finders; instead, they turned to oaths, confessions, and sometimes torture as they relied on their own judgment to find facts. Third, Dutch courts, as they were replicated in the New World, were descendants of local European medieval courts that dealt with all the myriad problems and disputes of the communities they served rather than central courts with jurisdiction limited by writs, formulated, as the common law writs had been, to address only matters of special concern to the king and his central government. Accordingly, courts in New Netherland enjoyed much broader substantive jurisdiction and remedial flexibility than did their English colonial counterparts. In all, the judges of New Netherland, especially the governor and his councilors at the top of the judicial hierarchy, were far less restricted by black-letter rules than were their counterparts in English North America.

During the first two decades of New Netherland's history, justice was administered mainly by a single, central court established by Director Peter Minuit in 1626. Consisting of Minuit and his council of five, assisted by a schout, an official who possessed the powers of a prosecuting attorney combined with those of a sheriff or marshal, the court possessed jurisdiction over all civil and criminal cases.

When Peter Stuyvesant arrived as director-general in 1647, he replaced the old court with a new one; rather than presiding over the court himself, Stuyvesant appointed Lubbertus VanDincklagen, who held a degree of doctor of laws. This court, like its predecessor, possessed jurisdiction over all cases whatsoever. Nonetheless, Stuyvesant reserved his capacity to intervene in the activities of the court as he sometimes sat beside VanDincklagen and at other times decided important questions referred to him by VanDincklagen.

Over time, local courts also were established, first for the patroonship of Rensselaerswyck in the 1630s, then for English towns on Long Island, and finally for outlying Dutch towns, such as Albany, from which it was difficult to travel to Manhattan, and for Brooklyn. As late as the early 1650s, however, no local court existed for New Amsterdam, and Stuyvesant came under intense pressure from its inhabitants to create one in order, they claimed, to prevent "the establishment of an arbitrary government among us." Arguing that "the laws of nature" gave people the right to act together for "the maintenance and preservation of the[ir] freedoms, privileges and property," Stuyvesant's adversaries opposed government by "one or more men" claiming "exclusive power to dispose, at will, of the life and property of any individual . . . under pretense of a law . . . which he or they might enact without the consent . . . of the whole body or its agents." They demanded "laws and orders, not transcending, but resembling as near as possible those of the Netherlands."[1] In so arguing, they echoed earlier demands that judicial matters be resolved "according to law" by "neutral and impartial men having legal knowledge."[2]

In 1653, under direction from the West India Company, Stuyvesant finally set up a Court of Burgomasters and Schepens in New Amsterdam, modeled on the courts of old Amsterdam. By 1664, New Netherland had a total of seventeen local courts. These courts, except for those in English towns, routinely applied local Dutch law and custom, typically that of Amsterdam but in one instance that of The Hague.

Although there is no evidence that a formal legal profession existed in New Netherland, many magistrates and other court officials were trained in Dutch law; at least two had doctorates in law from Dutch universities and several others had practiced in the homeland. As a result, the colony's local courts displayed considerable expertise in Dutch law, often citing specific authorities.

In establishing local courts, however, the director-general and council, a consultative body appointed by the director-general, explicitly reserved their capacity "to enact any ordinances or issue particular interdicts, especially those which tend to the glory of God, the best interests of the inhabitants, or will prevent more sins ... and crimes, and properly correct ... transgressors."[3] Stuyvesant also retained control over the appointment of lower court judges and put in place a clear appellate structure, with the director-general and council at the top.

Surviving minutes fail to indicate when customary law, on the one hand, or Peter Stuyvesant's views of public policy, on the other, determined outcomes before the director-general and council. But the ease and frequency of appeal make it plain that Stuyvesant's agreement to establish local courts did not, in and of itself, preclude his continuing to use his colony's centralized legal institutions to exercise his power to promote whatever he saw as the glory of God and the best interests of its inhabitants. Both the people of New Netherland and their local magistrates were constantly reminded that the director-general and his council determined the law in New Netherland, subject only to possible review by authorities in the Netherlands.

There were profound differences between Dutch procedure, which was derived from continental civil law, and that of the common law. A core difference was that the courts of New Netherland functioned without juries; this difference, in turn, gave rise to many others. Juries relieve judges of the difficult task of weighing evidence by delegating the task to a group of laymen, who are sent into a back room until they come out agreeing which litigant has the more credible case. To perform this task effectively, juries need to be given not complex cases but narrow issues for resolution, and accordingly classic common law procedure—the writ system, in particular—was obsessed with finding means to narrow the issues in every dispute. In contrast, civil law procedure must, and the procedural law of New Netherland did, focus on developing tools for considering claims in often vaguely presented, unstructured cases.

The most important such tool in New Netherland was the oath. A litigant's swearing of an oath typically led to judgment in his or her favor, whereas refusal to take the oath led to judgment for the opposing party. The magistrates, however, had considerable discretion in deciding who should take an oath. This discretion to decide which party had the burden of proof gave magistrates considerable power.

The lack of assistance from juries forced the courts of New Netherland to assume even greater power in criminal cases—especially investigative power that might uncover solid proof of guilt. A favored form of proof was a confession by the accused—obtained by torture, if necessary. Torture was a legal proceeding derived from Roman law and typically carried out under judicial supervision. Torture might be invoked when an accused's answers were inconsistent or because he protested his innocence. It might be used to discover a defendant's accomplices. Lesser means of coercion, such as fines and imprisonment, were also used, as with one witness who was fined when he was asked to give the name of a culprit and "answer[ed] that he [was] not an informer."[4]

Magistrates and other prosecutorial officials also exercised broad powers of search. Still other significant power devolved on prosecutors when the magistrates permitted them to put those accused of petty offenses in irons and rejected defendants' claims that they could not be prosecuted for a single offense in two different courts.

Yet another tool for dealing with difficult problems of proof was arbitration. Here magistrates avoided determining the burden of proof by referring even criminal cases to arbitrators or referees, who typically were directed to conciliate the parties if possible or report failure to the court. Cases could be referred to arbitrators at the request of the parties or over the opposition of one of them. But the main reason for a reference almost always was to avoid lengthy or complex litigation, especially in cases that were obscure or doubtful.

Nonetheless, magistrates had to consider some hard cases, in which their discretion and power were on display. In such cases, they developed rules for proceeding, under which they determined results by majority vote and with a statement for the record of individual reasons for their decision. Dissents were publicly noted, and the presiding magistrate cast a double vote in case of a tie. The statements for the record make it clear that decisions often turned on disputed rules of evidence that sometimes were unsettled because of competing visions of public policy.

As already noted, the law of New Netherland, unlike the common law, did not require litigants to narrow issues before presenting disputes for adjudication. Litigation was not shoehorned into fixed categories of the sort represented by the common law forms of action within which particular, established remedies, and only those remedies, were available. Instead, litigants typically came before magistrates seeking human solutions to human problems, for which remedial relief could be structured as individual cases required. The fact-finding power and freedom to decide cases as they wished, which New Netherland judges wielded in unstructured litigation, emerged especially in cases where the magistrates had to consider various excuses that defendants offered to avoid criminal liability. Courts generally were unmoved by pleas of necessity, of youth and extreme poverty, of a defendant's stealing only from the English at a time when the Dutch and English were at war, and of a woman's being in the last days of her pregnancy. They also rejected a plea that a defendant engaged in crime because others had openly acted as he did; the court responded "that one should not sin on account of the example of others."[5] On occasion, however, courts did exercise discretion in favor of defendants.

Criminal law was not the only area in which magistrates' broad investigative powers, fact-finding discretion, and freedom to structure remedies as needed gave them considerable power. Nothing better illustrates the problem-solving approach and hence the power of New Netherland judges than the law of contract.

The merchants of New Netherland traded widely. From its founding, the colony had a commercial economy that relied on the use of advanced commercial practices and sophisticated commercial instruments. But it is difficult to find black-letter law in contract cases because the courts resolved disputes with great flexibility, as litigants came before them seeking human solutions to human problems rather than narrow, pre-established forms of legal relief. In one case, for example, a lessee of a farm that had produced "a small yield of grain" was allowed to remain in possession "because it [was] not right, in the first year of the lease, to take a farm from the lessee because he is not able, owing to poor crops, to pay the rent."[6] It is essential, however, to recognize that cases such as this did not reflect pro-debtor bias; on the contrary, they constituted practical compromises to keep the economy functioning and thereby ensure the ultimate payment of debts. In other cases, creditors were the beneficiaries of judicial rulings, such as one requiring the payment of debts in beavers, which could be traded in Europe for specie, rather than wampum, which could be traded only to Native Americans for more beaver.

Together with what has come before, the contract cases make possible an interim summary of the main points of this chapter. The open-endedness and remedial flexibility of the Dutch litigation process imposed an arduous fact-finding burden on magistrates but also gave them immense fact-finding discretion. Discretion to find facts, in turn, often was intertwined with power to determine public policy; deciding to believe whether a man was the father of an illegitimate child was not easily separated, for example, from the policy of ensuring support for the child from a source other than the public fisc. Similarly, deciding to believe whether parties had agreed to payment in beaver or wampum was not easily separated from the policy issue of which would be the superior reserve currency for the colony. Policy issues often lie in the interstices of fact-finding, and thus fact-finders often possess political power, potentially of great magnitude. In English colonies, local juries wielded much of that power. But given the appellate structure of the New Netherland legal system, which lodged ultimate fact-finding discretion in the director-general and council, ultimate power inevitably resided in the same place.

One other element remains to be discussed. As already noted, the courts of New Netherland were descendants of local European medieval courts that dealt with all the myriad disputes and governance issues of the communities they served; everything lay within their jurisdiction. They heard the usual sorts of criminal cases and also heard cases involving disrespect of officials and challenges to authority, some raising matters of high politics, as when Adriaen van der Donck, one of the two men in the colony who held a doctorate in law, wrote statements allegedly defaming officers of the colony, or when a minister of the Reformed Church, Everardus Bogardus, scattered abuse against the colony's government from the pulpit.

In addition to hearing the usual sorts of cases, the courts of New Netherland also exercised jurisdictional authority that led them far beyond functions in which most colonial American courts engaged. They thereby became enmeshed in controlling the details of their subjects' lives.

Like courts in New England but unlike those elsewhere in early English North America, Dutch criminal courts, for example, took steps for the prevention of sin. People were prosecuted or punished for blasphemy, for violating the Sabbath, or for working during divine service; one such case involved Abram de la Sina, "a Jew" who "kept his store open during the sermon, and sold by retail." This case apparently prompted the director-general and council to make a decision "that the Jews, who came last year from the West Indies and now from the Fatherland, must prepare to depart forthwith,"[7] but authorities in Amsterdam overruled them and the order exiling Jews never was carried into effect.

Jews were not the only religious minority that local authorities treated harshly. The council, for example, fined and banished one Flushing, Long Island, resident for leading Baptist services in his house and another for harboring Quakers, all in violation of an Ordinance against Practising any Religion Other Than the Reformed. When residents of Flushing protested the treatment of dissenters and stated that if any believing "in Christ Jesus . . . whether Presbyterian, Independent, Baptist, or Quaker . . . come in love unto us, we cannot in conscience lay violent hands upon them," a number of them were arrested immediately.[8] Similarly, the magistrates of Albany took an oath to maintain the reformed religion according to the Synod of Dordrecht and not to tolerate any other sect, and, pursuant to their oath, prosecuted a man who held a Lutheran service at a private house.

The legal system of New Netherland interfered in the day-to-day lives of its residents even more through intensive economic regulation. Dutch courts were deeply enmeshed, for example, in regulating trade with Native Americans. Probably the most common charge for which inhabitants of New Netherland were prosecuted was selling alcoholic beverages to Indians, but inhabitants also faced prosecutions for selling sugar cake to Indians, for cheating Indians, for giving rather than selling commodities, for trading at locations other than those designated for trade, and for sending Indian brokers to trade with Indians in the woods.

Regulation of Indian trade, moreover, was merely the beginning of trade regulation. The magistrates regulated the price and quality of nearly everything, beginning with wampum, one of the colony's principal circulating mediums. They
fixed the price and weight of loaves of bread; prohibited bakers from including
sugar, currants, raisins, or prunes in bread; set prices on beer, wine, and other
alcoholic beverages; and limited what butchers could charge for slaughtering
animals as well as inspecting meat for contamination. Despite threats of an
embargo and claims that denying trade a free course would lead to a decrease
of commerce, the council set prices on common imported goods and fixed at
20 percent the markup that importers could charge over the price at which they
had purchased more unusual goods in Europe. They also regulated wages, probably at rates lower than the labor-starved free market would have borne, and the
conditions of labor. Finally, magistrates regulated land use and controlled who
could settle and remain within various cities and towns.

Dutch magistrates also tightly controlled family life. One activity, in which
courts everywhere in America engaged, was supervising the intergenerational
transfer of wealth. New Amsterdam had one special institution, however—the
Orphan Chamber. Run by orphan masters, who monitored the care with which
curators, guardians, and the like performed their duties and had standing to
challenge such people's performance in court, the Orphan Chamber enhanced
the knowledge and hence the power of magistrates. By accumulating assets of
estates, it also created a capital investment fund that existed nowhere else in
America and gave the chamber substantial influence over the economy.

Even more peculiar to New Netherland was the extraordinary level of regulation of marriage, which began with regulation of the process for entering
marriage. Couples wishing to marry began the process by seeking court permission to have the banns of marriage proclaimed in the locations where they lived.
Once the banns had been proclaimed three times and no lawful impediments
found, parties were required to solemnize their marriage within one month.
A couple entering the process of marriage was required to proceed forward unless they publicly released each other. Couples who did not follow these rules,
like one youth who did not wait for parental approval but married against the
prohibition of his legal guardian and without previously publishing banns,
might have their marriages annulled and be ordered to separate and live apart
under penalty of being punished under the law against concubinage.

Even after couples were married, courts continued to interfere in their
relationships. Thus, one husband brought a proceeding against his wife demanding to know why she would not live with him; apparently she had good
reason because the court ordered him kept in confinement until she had had
time to leave the colony. But it appears that courts were loath to put an end
to marriages even when wife-beating was involved; one wife, accused by her

husband of drinking too much, was told to live in peace with her husband so that no more complaints should be heard of her, while a wife- beater, accused by his wife of touching another woman's breasts and putting his mouth on them, was ordered to live, eat, drink, and sleep with his wife as is befitting an honorable husband. Divorces were granted only under exceptional circumstances—to one man whose wife had run away nine years earlier with another man, with whom she had had several children, and to a second man who had married a new wife in the mistaken belief that his first wife was dead; when the first wife appeared, the court divorced him from his second wife with that wife's consent.

The marriage cases are important because they display again the approach to law that gave the magistrates of New Netherland extraordinary power. Marriage cases did not arise, as common law cases do, because a plaintiff sought some specified form of relief, such as a divorce, for which legal standards established by a form of action listed in the Register of Writs had to be met. Instead, they arose because someone had a problem for which he or she sought the magistrates' help: a man suddenly found himself with two wives or a woman found herself with a husband sexually involved with other women. Listening to human stories and uncabined by inflexible rules of procedure or evidence, the magistrates tried to fashion practical, human solutions, not to administer fixed remedies in favor of those who met preexisting, fixed standards. To the extent they succeeded in imposing their solutions, Dutch magistrates exercised a level of power and flexibility that later New York common law judges never would have.

The marriage cases also illustrate the breadth of the New Netherland courts' jurisdiction; the magistrates heard all sorts of disputes, not only those that could be shoehorned within the narrow confines of some common law action. Finally, the lower courts functioned under an ever-present prospect of an appeal to the director-general and council, which had reserved the power to interpret legislation and fill in gaps—that is, the power to determine as a matter of public policy whether law should be changed.

Contemporaries—for instance, those in New England discussed in the preceding chapter—fully appreciated the dangers of concentrating discretionary power in judges, especially high court judges, as they sought to limit the law through codification and to assign whatever discretion remained in the hands of jurors rather than judges. The people of New Amsterdam showed similar appreciation when they demanded the creation of local courts in addition to a single central one in order, as they said, to prevent the establishment of arbitrary government. But New Netherlanders had little choice. They needed law to preserve public peace and order and to provide the foundation for the colony's vibrant commercial economy. Director-General Stuyvesant and his council gave them that law.

Long Island

The Dutch were not the only people to settle in New Netherland. Puritan Englishmen, originating mainly in New England, also settled on Long Island and Staten Island and along the Connecticut-Westchester border. The Dutch government in New Amsterdam claimed jurisdiction over all these Puritan towns, which had been settled sometimes with and sometimes without Dutch permission. But New Amsterdam rarely succeeded in establishing effective control over the island towns.

Southampton, which was founded on the east end of Long Island in 1638, was the first Puritan settlement. When Southampton was settled, its founders did not imagine that they were establishing an insignificant town or even a summer spa for wealthy residents of New Amsterdam. On the contrary, they thought they were establishing a sovereign polity, comparable to the Plymouth Colony, the New Haven Colony, or the Massachusetts Bay Colony. Like those other New England colonies, Southampton was to be governed by a General Court, with plenary power to enact law and to adjudicate all civil and criminal cases.

Like their New England compatriots who were fearful of judicial discretion, the people of Southampton insisted that their magistrates govern not arbitrarily or randomly but according to laws established by the General Court. That law was set down in "An Abstract of the Laws of Judgment as given Moses . . . that is of perpetual and universal Equity."[9] But this religiously driven code was never seriously enforced. Under pressure from more populous Indian tribes and Dutch claims of sovereignty, the tiny settlement of Southampton voted in 1644 to become part of Connecticut, and after the merger, Connecticut law rather than the Abstract of Universal Equity apparently governed Southampton.

With the exception of one prosecution for carnal filthiness between two servants, both of whom received corporal punishment, all the criminal cases of the 1640s involved irreverent speech toward magistrates. Indeed, the town meeting was obsessed with controlling speech. In the interest of maintaining peace and unity among the inhabitants of the town, legislation imposed a fine on anyone who spoke contentiously about grievances tending to the disquiet of the town. The town meeting also criminalized private agitations—that is, lobbying. Finally, it ordered that no person except a magistrate speak at a meeting without removing his hat and then only when the matter he was addressing was in hand and prior business had been completed.

The bulk of litigation before 1664, however, was not criminal but civil. Here there was no legislation, but only local English custom and the common law. Perhaps to distinguish themselves from the Dutch and perhaps because they came through New England from various places in old England, the people of Southampton turned to the common law. But they applied it in a rudimentary, untechnical fashion, as one would expect in a town that had no lawyers and in which, as the grammar and spelling in the town records suggests, many residents were at best only semi-literate.

A striking difference between the work of the court in Southampton and the work of Dutch courts in New Netherland was the relative absence of regulatory matters from the Southampton docket. Like every other court, that of Southampton administered estates and appointed guardians for minors. Of course, magistrates prohibited the sale of guns to Native Americans and controlled the settlement of newcomers in the town. Later, they regulated the price of bread, corn, and cloth sold to Indians, while leaving merchants free to sell to Englishmen at such price as they could obtain. The only other noteworthy regulations occurred when the General Court set the fees of the town miller, required parents to whip children who stole fruit, and gave a particular individual a monopoly over the sale of liquor in an effort to keep it out of the hands of Indians and to preserve sobriety within the town.

At least in comparison with New Netherland, Southampton thus possessed an inactive government; individuals were constrained mainly by market forces and by whatever pressures their neighbors placed on them, either socially or through litigation. Courts intervened in daily life only in egregious criminal cases and in cases challenging the authority of government or in an arbitral role when neighbors sued each other. Even in their arbitral role, courts did their best to ensure nothing more than fair procedure and to leave decision of the substance of disputes to juries as representatives of the community. Unlike New Netherland magistrates, the judges of Southampton made no effort to ensure that individuals acted for the well-being of the community as a whole or of their less fortunate fellow-subjects.

Before 1664, English courts existed in at least four other locales in what is now New York: Flushing, Huntington, Newtown, and Westchester. Like their counterpart in Southampton, these four courts exercised limited criminal and regulatory authority and resolved civil disputes through application of a bastardized version of the common law.

In sum, by 1664 the English settlements surrounding New Amsterdam, operating independently of their Dutch neighbors, had put in operation a rudimentary, untechnical, common law legal system reflecting New England values and ideals. Although Long Island courts were responsive to Puritan religious concerns, their records were fragmentary and carelessly kept, with the result that there is no evidence of the same religious sophistication in addressing legal issues that characterized the New England mainland, especially Massachusetts Bay. Unlike the Massachusetts judiciary, the judges of Long Island do not appear to have struggled under the watchful gaze of the world with great issues of constitutional power; they merely adjudicated those disputes among their residents that the residents brought to their attention. In doing so, they, like their New Netherland counterparts, appear to have served adequately the legal needs of their communities.

Delaware

A small colony in what is now Delaware also was part of New Netherland. Initially settled by Swedes and then taken over by the Dutch in 1655, it contained a mixture of Swedish, Dutch, and English settlers who were governed by Dutch law administered by a combination of Dutch and Swedish officials.

The mixed character of Delaware's early jurisprudence emerges most clearly in the records of two early courts—the first at New Castle, slightly south of modern Wilmington, Delaware, and the second at the small village of Upland, on the site of what is now Chester, Pennsylvania. Since the records of both courts are extant only from 1676, they allow only a faint glimpse of pre-1660 law. At the time of their openings, the Upland court had six justices, none of them with English surnames, whereas the New Castle court had five whose names suggest an ethnic mixture.

The judges of both courts paid little attention to legal niceties or to any other formalities. They focused instead on the rich details of everyday human endeavor and strove to resolve, in a just but non-coercive fashion, the inevitable human conflicts that those details revealed. For example, in *Helm v. Oolsen*,[10] one of the first cases to be recorded, the plaintiff, one of the justices of the Upland court, accused the defendant of "beat[ing] & strik[ing]" him "in a most abusive and malicious manner," and, when the defendant failed to appear, the court warned him that "in case of further default, judgment . . . [would] pass against him according to law and merit." When Oolsen finally did appear, the sheriff asked that the court "not suffer that a justice of peace shall be so abused," and the court, in response, fined Oolsen 210 guilders. But it remitted 150 guilders of the fine, "considering that the said Oole was a poor man with a great charge of children." In another case from the same term that also was about fighting, the court postponed consideration and meanwhile "recommend[ed]," as Dutch courts in New Netherland often did, that "the parties . . . compose the difference between them."[11] The court, it appears, was hesitant about issuing orders that might prove difficult to enforce.

By far the most common sort of case in the jurisdiction of both the New Castle and the Upland courts involved the collection of debts. In these cases, the courts did come to decisions, typically entering judgment against the debtor. In one case, however, the court examined the plaintiff's books, found his suit unjust and vexatious, and ordered him nonsuited.

Even after the English conquest in 1664, the New Castle and Upland courts continued to function in an informal, un-English fashion through their final terms in 1681. The Upland court was terminated by a letter dated July 21, 1681, in which authorities in New York thanked the justices for their good services and informed them that thereafter they would reside under the jurisdiction of William Penn, to whom Charles II had just granted Pennsylvania.

In short, from the time of its founding, New Netherland, soon to become New York, possessed a pluralistic legal order. On the one hand, part of the colony operated under a Dutch civil law system with a centralized institutional structure, broad substantive jurisdiction, and remedial flexibility that relied on oaths, confessions, and sometimes torture to determine facts. On the other hand, Long Island was governed under a loosely controlled common law system with narrow categories of substantive capacity and limited remedial freedom, where much lawmaking and all fact-finding remained in the hands of local communities represented by juries. And Delaware, to the extent later records provide us a glimpse, had a rudimentary, untechnical body of law administered largely independently of authorities in New Amsterdam.

PART II

THE FORGING OF EMPIRE
1660–1750

4

The Crown's Imposition
of the Common Law and
Colonial Resistance

With the restoration of monarchy in 1660, English policy toward its North American empire began to assume some coherence. In the reigns of James I and Charles I, policy had been haphazard. The first two Stuarts, for example, had permitted New England to be settled by religious zealots seeking, in the case of Plymouth, to escape and, in the case of Massachusetts, to reform the English religious establishment. Charles I then failed to halt further religious splintering as Connecticut, New Haven, Rhode Island, and Southampton spun off. No uniform or explicit imperial vision, in short, undergirded the settlement of New England. The same was also true for Maryland, founded as a haven for Roman Catholics. In contrast, the behavior of the merchant adventurers who founded Virginia manifested at least a hazy vision of empire. But those adventurers acted largely on their own, with little royal support or interference. Only when the Virginia colony failed financially and something had to be done did the monarchy step in and assume control.

Because of the lack of imperial control and the resulting diversity of purpose underlying settlement of the early Chesapeake and New England colonies, substantial differences existed in their initial legal systems. In particular, the common law assumed very different roles from colony to colony. From the outset, common law was central to Lord Baltimore's plans for Maryland's legal order. Virginia, on the other hand, ignored the common law during its first decade and thereafter received it gradually during the course of more than another decade. In New England, common law was always present in the form of background norms to which lawmakers could turn when they lacked the time or inclination to think carefully about what they wanted their law to be. But, especially in Massachusetts, a main impetus behind law was religious, as the General

Court strove with great sophistication to work out the tension between Puritan communitarianism and Puritan biblicism.

The coherence of post-Restoration policy must not, of course, be overstated. A coalition of diverse political, religious, and economic interests had brought Charles II to the throne, and he had to listen, at least to some extent, to all. As a result, it is not always easy to find a coherent vision beneath the Crown's behavior toward its growing North American empire.

Nonetheless the reach of the Crown increased during the reigns of Charles II and James II, as various institutions of English government sought to recover previously delegated authority and to assume an increasingly direct role in the administration of England's overseas territories. This growing reach manifested itself in two main respects.

First, the Crown reversed the practices of James I and Charles I of granting colonial charters to religious dissidents and independent merchant groups. Although Charles II did not himself undertake to establish new entities as royal colonies under his direct control, he did insist that all new proprietary grantees be close confidants and supporters of his regime. Thus, one of the first newly created entities, New York, was granted to the king's brother and heir apparent, James, the Duke of York. Another proprietary grant was of the Carolinas to a group of eight mostly high officials, including Edward Hyde, the Earl of Clarendon, at that time the Lord Chancellor; the Earl of Albemarle, who as General George Monck had facilitated the return of Charles II to the throne; and Sir Anthony Ashley Cooper, who would become Earl of Shaftesbury and Lord Chancellor two years after the founding of Charleston. A third colony, New Jersey, was granted by the Duke of York to two of the Carolina proprietors, Lord John Berkeley, one of the principal officers of the navy, and Sir George Carteret, treasurer of the navy and vice-chamberlain of the royal household. Even the proprietor of Pennsylvania, William Penn, despite his position as a Quaker leader, was the son of one of Charles II's leading admirals, to whom the king owed a large financial debt, and his brother, the Duke of York, owed strong personal debts; the younger Penn himself became an advisor to the duke after the latter had ascended to the throne as James II.

Second, the Crown imposed significant legal restrictions on the post-1660 colonies. The sole restriction imposed in 1629 on the Massachusetts Bay Colony, for instance, was that its laws not be "contrary to the laws . . . of England."[1] Likewise, the only restriction on Maryland was that its laws "be consonant to reason and be not repugnant or contrary, but (so far as conveniently may be) agreeable to the laws . . . of England."[2] The 1663 Carolina charter contained similar language. Charles II's 1664 grant of New York to his brother, the Duke of York, contained yet another provision, authorizing an appeal to the king from any judgment rendered in New York. And the charter granting William Penn the province of

Pennsylvania contained still further restrictions tying the proprietor's hands more tightly than hands had been tied in any prior North American colony. It required that Pennsylvania be governed "by the general course of the law in our kingdom of England" until that law was duly altered by Penn and the freemen of his province;[3] the Pennsylvania charter, that is, imposed the common law until such time as altered by legislation. It further required that all legislation adopted in Pennsylvania be submitted to the Privy Council, which received authority to adjudge it void and thereby keep the common law in place. Collectively, these provisions reflected a pivotal policy of the regimes of Charles II and James II—to ensure that the colonies would be governed by the common law and by the lawyers who administered it.

New York

Late in the summer of 1664, Colonel Richard Nicolls, the first English governor of New York, arrived off Manhattan Island in command of a fleet of five vessels that was transporting an army of a few hundred men with the goal of conquering the Dutch colony of New Netherland. On the fleet that Nicolls led into New York harbor, he also brought three lawyers who had attended the Inns of Court. What purpose did these lawyers serve as a component of a conquering army? Why did Colonel Nicolls bring them with him?

The key fact about New Netherland was that significant European settlement had occurred before it became, as a matter of conquest and law, an English colony. When the Duke of York took control in 1664, New York was in reality three separate entities—Manhattan; the Hudson Valley, a part of the Dutch commercial empire; and Long Island, a part of New England demographically, culturally, and economically. The duke, however, made a choice to govern it as a single entity. Because techniques of government that worked in one part of the colony often did not work in other parts, the duke's choice would have a negative impact on the effectiveness of New York's government throughout the colonial period.

Why did the duke make that choice? The answer goes back to the reasons that had induced Charles II to seize the colony from the Dutch and give it to his brother James at the outset of the second of three Anglo-Dutch wars between the 1650s and the 1670s. Essentially, the wars were about regime stability. Cromwellian England had first fought the Dutch, who were aiding and abetting the Stuart cause, in order to obtain full recognition as the legitimate successor of the government of Charles I.

This first Anglo-Dutch war steered the Netherlands in a more republican direction, and when Charles II was restored in 1660, he had reason to fear that the now republican Dutch might undermine his regime. Although the Dutch colony of New Netherland had only minor significance in the larger Anglo-Dutch conflict, it did pose two particular concerns for the restored Stuart monarchy. The first was that Dutch vessels out of Manhattan traded widely along the Atlantic seaboard and in the Caribbean in violation of the Navigation Acts; their trade deprived the Crown of customs duties estimated as at least 1 percent of the permanent revenues that the Restoration Parliament had bestowed on the king. The second concern arose out of New England's republican leanings, which were manifested in the anti-Stuart activities of New England Puritans during the English Civil War and in Connecticut's postwar harboring of the regicides who had signed Charles I's death warrant; a republican Dutch colony adjacent to republican-leaning New England posed a threat, as a potential source of renewed revolution, to the stability of the Restoration settlement. Although we now know that Charles II remained securely on his throne until his death in 1685, he could not have been confident about that outcome in 1664, and hence, it made sense for him to take preemptive action against the threat, however trivial in retrospect it may have been, that the Dutch on the Hudson posed to his rule.

But if a purpose of capturing New Netherland was to strike a blow against New England republicanism, it made no sense to add the Puritan settlements in the colony to Connecticut or to create an additional, separate republican-leaning New England entity. It was important instead for the king and his brother to govern their newly acquired New York colony from Manhattan in a monarchical fashion. Unfortunately for them, they could not destroy either the Puritan legal heritage of Long Island or Dutch resistance to English rule in the Hudson Valley, and thus they were able to impose fully effective government only in Manhattan.

Colonel Nicolls faced yet another difficulty: he had to govern his disjointed New York colony without the help of a bureaucracy and with only a small army. One way to do that would have been to assemble representatives of the Dutch and English towns together in a legislative body, coax them to hammer out a compromise system, and employ them, together with local officials chosen with their consent, to go back home and enforce it. But Nicolls's master, the autocratic and Catholic James, Duke of York, would have nothing to do with Reformed Protestant legislatures; thus, the governors of New York had to rule without legislative help until 1683.

Nicolls accordingly had no choice but to try to oversee his disparate domain through another option—reliance on lawyers. In the fleet that Nicolls led into New York harbor, he accordingly brought with him the three lawyers. His plan was to give those lawyers government jobs while simultaneously permitting them to practice on behalf of private clients. Apparently, the underlying idea was that government jobs would secure the loyalty of the three attorneys and give them leverage to persuade private clients, from whom they would receive most of their income, to support government policies. For the regime of Charles II, which had no money to hire either soldiers or bureaucrats, and of his brother, the Duke of York, who was unwilling to rely on elected legislators, the appointment of lawyers to fill the small number of government posts that in any event had to be filled and the use of those lawyers to inform subjects of the requirements of the law and to obtain their obedience to it seemed the cheapest, most effective way to rule.

A huge problem existed with this approach, however. In the articles of surrender that had brought Nicolls a bloodless conquest, he had promised to preserve, at least in part, the sophisticated Dutch judicial system in place on Manhattan Island and in the Hudson Valley. It would have been very much in Nicolls's interest to preserve the Dutch system because that system would have given him, as it had his Dutch predecessors, control of law in the Dutch settlements. But preserving the Dutch system would have required Nicolls to engage in a problematic gambit: he would have had to retain at the highest levels of the judiciary some of the few existing Dutch residents of New York learned in Dutch law and somehow induce them to serve his English masters with loyalty as he strove with their aid to negotiate the gap between Dutch custom and English policy. Instead, he relied on English-trained lawyers who knew nothing of Dutch law that governed the cases that came before them on appeal. That was, in fact, as counterproductive a move as Nicolls could have made. It cut the appellate link between local Dutch courts where Dutch residents remained in control and central, English authorities in New York City, thereby leaving the Dutch courts in the Hudson Valley effectively free to govern their local communities with little real supervision from officials in the colonial capital.

Meanwhile, in the Puritan sections of New York, locally elected judges, local juries, and town meetings had assumed plenary power to make and repeal laws. Nicolls did not even know what those institutions had enacted and decided. To exercise dominion effectively over his Puritan subjects, Nicolls accordingly had first to learn what Puritan law was and then to decide whether to enforce or overturn it. It is doubtful whether the three lawyers he brought with him had either the time or the capacity to undertake such a task; in any event, they never tried.

Nicolls's effort to govern his New York colony with only a handful of lawyers from England produced only mixed success, and then only in the short run; ultimately the policy had anarchical consequences. For a while Nicolls did succeed in using existing Dutch elites to govern Albany and Kingston, and he appeared to gain some minimal control over the English towns of Long Island, Staten Island, and Westchester. Over time, however, the English towns remained in large part independent, and the Dutch communities of the Hudson Valley became increasingly so. In the long run, Nicolls was most successful in Manhattan, which, as discussed later in the chapter, proved to be unique; its uniqueness forced Nicolls and his successors, along with lawyers on the ground, to reform the law in ways that anticipated an American future that none of them could have foreseen.

Along the Upper Hudson, local courts in Albany and Kingston continued to function into the 1680s and even later largely as they had under Dutch rule. Despite the availability of appeals to the English Governor and Council, and after 1683, to the newly established Sessions Courts, old practices such as reliance on oaths and recourse to arbitrators remained in place. Indeed, Dutch family and inheritance practices continued in some parts of New York well into the eighteenth century.

The most significant innovation the English introduced was trial by jury. The procedure first appeared in Albany in February 1672/73 in a trial in which two Native Americans were convicted of murder and sentenced to death. But the use of juries was rare. Moreover, the procedure proved irregular and problematic as old Dutch ways persisted. Typically, instead of returning a simple but opaque verdict, such as guilty or not guilty, responsive to narrow, precise issues framed by common law pleadings, juries returned complex, detailed conclusions of fact and left to judges the task of fashioning the facts into a judgment. Often the judges acted as Dutch courts had by facilitating some sort of compromise.

How can one account for the willingness of the English Governor and Council to delegate to the conquered people of New Netherland power to govern themselves pursuant to their customary Dutch law? In part, the answer lies in the near impossibility of governing by any other means. Many people in the upper Hudson region proved resistant to English assertions of authority. When the English, for example, sent small garrisons to Albany and to Kingston to occupy the towns, the garrisons created more problems than they solved. They needed to be housed and fed, and the military accordingly quartered troops in private homes. In response, the local court in Kingston "absolve[d]" itself of "all responsibility for possible calamities."[4]

In the end, the English were forced to compromise in order to keep law and government functioning. With compromise, English officials in New York City obtained something vitally important—acceptance of England's ultimate sovereignty by Dutch leaders in the upper Hudson region. In return, the Crown allowed local authorities to govern by locally acceptable, established Dutch law. Superficially, Long Island, Staten Island, and Westchester were totally different from the Hudson Valley in that they governed themselves by English common law, not Dutch customary law. But the underlying pattern that Governor Nicolls adopted to rule them was quite similar.

As was suggested above, Governor Nicolls faced a problem in this region of not knowing what the law was, and his few lawyers probably lacked the capacity to find out. As a result, he decided to promulgate by fiat a new code to govern the English regions of the colony. In March 1665, at Hempstead, he accordingly published the Duke of York's Laws.

Nicolls understood that his code had to be acceptable to the people it would govern, and for that reason, he derived it largely from the New England law that he assumed they already were using. It took the form of the Massachusetts Code of 1648—an alphabetical arrangement of titles. Its substance also mirrored either the Massachusetts code or existing local New York practices of which Nicolls was aware, and, as a result, the Duke's Laws were largely familiar and unobjectionable. After establishing a Court of Assizes to meet annually in New York City, the Laws took note, for example, of the familiar common law forms of action as well as the familiar crimes prosecuted in New England courts.

The Duke's Laws displayed special solicitude for the New England way in two key provisions. The first required sheriffs to make the initial selection of jurors from among the overseers of the various towns, who, in turn, were elected by the freeholders of those towns, thereby ensuring jury responsiveness to local electorates. The second authorized the governor to license as ministers anyone ordained by a Protestant bishop or minister; directed that no Christian should be molested, fined, or imprisoned for differing in judgment in matters of religion; and provided that no congregations should be disturbed in the time of prayer, preaching, or other divine service. As a result, transplanted New Englanders were assured that they could retain existing clergymen and obtain new ones and that they could continue to practice their Puritan faith.

On the other hand, the Duke's Laws contained two other provisions that must have rankled those familiar, as Long Islanders appear to have been, with debates in Massachusetts over the discretion of magistrates. The first recognized that it was "almost impossible to provide sufficient laws in all cases, or proper punishments for all crimes," and prohibited lower courts from hearing cases where there was "not provision made in some laws." But then it granted jurisdiction over such cases to the "Court of Assizes where matters of equity shall be decided or punishment awarded *according to the discretion of the bench.*" The second provision specified that judges were to "direct[] the jury in point of law" and the jury was only to "find the matter of fact";[5] the Court of Assizes interpreted this provision to give judges power to set aside verdicts when the jury had undertaken to find the law by itself. The Court of Assizes, aided by a nascent legal profession, also strove with considerable success to abide by the forms of common law pleading and to prosecute the usual run of criminal cases.

Taken together, the enactment of the Duke's Laws with their establishment of the Court of Assizes with the governor as presiding judge, the reservation of lawfinding and lawmaking power to the court, and the early steps taken toward founding a legal profession to assist the court and regularize its practices suggest a new approach to colonial governance on the part of English authorities: reliance on a central court under gubernatorial control and a legal profession beholden to the court. Examined from the perspective of those who administered the central court, the policy appeared moderately successful.

However, the Court of Assizes faced pushback when it attempted to prosecute political offenders. An even greater failure occurred when the court proved unable to accomplish what Governor Nicolls most needed it to do: to control and ultimately change the course of adjudication in the local courts of Long Island, Staten Island, and Westchester, as those courts continued after 1664 to pursue their rudimentary, untechnical, customary New England ways as if the Court of Assizes and its lawyers did not exist.

In the end, it is necessary to ask, as it was in connection with the Dutch towns along the upper Hudson, why the colonial administration was only partially successful in projecting its power into the English settlements surrounding New York City. The chief reason was that the Court of Assizes and the lawyers who attended it, the vehicle Nicolls created to exercise control, did not ride circuit. Litigants accordingly did not institute their suits in the court, nor was it worthwhile for most of them to bother taking an appeal. As a result, the colonial administration continued to have limited knowledge of the law that local courts were applying and little capacity to impose its own law.

Manhattan was different, however, from the rest of New York. In the city, the common law began to assume primacy within a year of the English conquest. The presence of lawyers and of other Englishmen sympathetic to the Crown's policies probably accounts for the common law's vitality. Lawyers continued to arrive in the colony along with other Englishmen, all of whom joined the significant English minority already living in New Amsterdam. As the governing class, those Englishmen found themselves lumped together with the Dutch majority, whose law the English had agreed to respect, into the first melting pot in American history. As the pot cooked, Dutch law slowly melted away and the common law, under the guidance of an ever-present legal profession, became New York City's law.

One week after writing to the directors of the West India Company to inform them of New Amsterdam's surrender to England, the Court of Burgomasters and Schepens met in City Hall to conduct business as usual. Over the next several sessions, the court handled routine cases and dealt with important ministerial questions arising out of the transfer of power, such as from whom to obtain salaries for the clergy, the schoolmaster, and former Dutch soldiers. The Dutch magistrates were not cowed by the English conquest or garrison, for when on October 14 Governor Nicolls directed them to take an oath of allegiance to King

Charles and the Duke of York, they refused. They feared that taking the oath might nullify rights reserved to them under the Articles of Surrender. Nicolls responded four days later in a letter assuring the magistrates that the oath would not nullify their rights, and when he agreed to place his seal on the letter, the magistrates on October 20, 1664, took the oath.

The English military occupation of New York was not easy on the city's residents or on its courts. Governor Nicolls insisted that troops be quartered in private homes, and when residents objected, the city had to raise a substantial tax to pay homeowners to accept the soldiers. Soldiers also misbehaved by groping women, using force to compel residents to provide them with liquor, and threatening people with displays of violence. And when soldiers violated the city's laws, by drinking on Sundays or after hours, for example, the magistrates could not punish them, although they did punish the Dutch residents who abetted them.

Meanwhile the magistrates continued doing their ordinary work in the ordinary fashion. But the Dutch system could not withstand the pressures that the presence of Englishmen, both the governor and lawyers from above and ordinary litigants from below, imposed on it. When one Englishman was arrested for smuggling, for instance, he demanded that justice be done in an English court where he could confront his accusers. Less than two months later, in June 1665, Governor Nicolls closed the Dutch courts and directed a newly formed corporation of the City of New York to govern by English law and by other laws necessary for the good of the corporation. Nicolls ensured a blending of English and Dutch law by appointing an English army captain as mayor while continuing the old schout as sheriff and appointing sitting burgomasters as two of the five new aldermen. At least two of the remaining three aldermen were old Dutch residents of New Amsterdam.

The common law immediately worked its way into the practice and proceedings of the new Mayor's Court. Thirteen days after the new court had been established, the first jury verdict was rendered. And by the end of the year, common law actions of debt, case, and slander were being filed. By 1670 the Mayor's Court was on the cusp of becoming a common law court. But that did not happen for several more years, as the court did not force the Dutch majority of the city to accept law for which the Dutch were not yet ready. Rather, it continued to govern New York City effectively but gently through a mixture of Dutch and English law.

Gentle government ended, however, in 1673, when a Dutch fleet reconquered New York. The new Dutch governor immediately abolished the Mayor's Court and reinstated the Court of Burgomasters and Schepens, and for over a year Dutch customary law alone governed New York. The Dutch West India Company did not really care about retaining New York, however, and accordingly ceded it back to England in 1674.

Massachusetts

With the restoration of Charles II in 1660, the aspiration of Massachusetts to serve as a city on a hill revealing the path to moral and righteous governance came to an end. Indeed, the existence of Massachusetts as a distinct entity with an independent approach to religion and politics was threatened, as the Crown sought to compel the colony to conform to the Anglican and common law ways of the mother country.

The extent of the threat should not be minimized. For a quarter century, the Crown grappled with Bay Colony leaders as it continually questioned the colony's independent policies and Puritan religiosity, always under the prospect of revoking the 1629 Massachusetts charter. The administration in England objected repeatedly to the colony's refusal to tolerate religious dissent even on the part of Anglicans, to its restriction of the franchise to men who had been accepted to communion in local Puritan church congregations, to its denial of appeals from colony courts to the king in England, and to its adoption of laws based on religious norms rather than on the common law.

In connection with the common law, in particular, the king in a letter to the governor of Massachusetts demanded as early as 1662 "that all laws and ordinances made during the late troubles contrary and derogatory to the King's Government be annulled and repealed."[6] Charles II did not indicate whether the laws and ordinances requiring repeal included the entirety of the Code of 1648. Fourteen years later, the Crown sent Edward Randolph, one of its emerging cadre of civil servants, to Massachusetts to inquire, among other things, "what laws and ordinances are now in force there derogatory or contrary to those of England," to which Randolph responded that "no law" was in force "but such as [were] made by the general court" and that "where no law [had been] made by the general court, . . . the offender [was] to be tried by the word of God." He added that it was "accounted a breach of their privileges and . . . liberties . . . to urge the observation of the laws of England" and made a list of "the laws most derogatory and contradictory to those of England."[7] Although some leaders in Massachusetts were willing to compromise with the Crown on some of these issues, those who controlled the General Court persistently refused to yield to most demands. Their fear was that the loss of legal and constitutional independence would lead to the destruction of Puritanism.

The threat to Puritanism became especially plain in 1679, when the Crown separated what is now New Hampshire from Massachusetts and established it as a distinct royal colony. One set of incidents was particularly telling. In 1684, the royal governor of New Hampshire, Edward Cranfield, demanded that Joshua Moodey, the Puritan minister of Portsmouth, administer the holy sacrament to him pursuant to the rites of the Church of England. Moodey refused. Cranfield thereupon had him prosecuted under an act of Parliament requiring clergymen to perform such ministrations. Because Moodey admitted all the facts alleged against him in Cranfield's proceeding, trial was to the court, which Cranfield successfully pressured to convict him. After serving his time in jail, Moodey fled to Massachusetts. Cranfield then placed the same demand on the Puritan minister of Hampton, Seaborn Cotton, who promptly departed for Massachusetts. Massachusetts's ministers could legitimately fear that if some future royal governor placed the same demand on them, there would be nowhere to flee.

Cranfield also made a determined effort to enforce Parliament's Navigation Acts by coming to the assistance of Edward Randolph, by then the Crown's collector of customs. The first step was to hand pick New Hampshire juries in Navigation Act cases instead of having them elected by towns; Cranfield then frightened those jurors by threatening to attaint them—to punish them for perjury, that is, if they returned verdicts with which he disagreed. As a result, the Crown began to win customs cases in New Hampshire, although ultimately at the cost of driving shipping out of the colony. Cranfield also tried to impose taxes without legislative sanction, but typically he proved unable to collect them.

Puritan leaders were divided over how to respond to the Crown's pressures. At the heart of the predicament that Massachusetts faced after 1660 was the reality that its leaders could no longer preserve everything that its founders had created. The civil strife of 1640–60 had transformed England and its empire into a religiously pluralist world, and in an effort to save what mattered most in their lives and communities, the residents of the Bay Colony had to do what anyone living in a pluralist world must do: they had to cease insisting that everything be done their way and, with regard to matters of ancillary importance, learn to accept rules and approaches preferred by others. That is, they had to learn tolerance and compromise.

Many—in particular, those fearing religious declension—resisted such learning. But in the end, the people of Massachusetts did learn. Those in control of its law—by the mid-eighteenth century common law lawyers rather than Puritan political leaders and divines—gradually transformed the Bay Colony's legal order into a system similar to the legal systems of Britain's other North American colonies. They thereby made it possible for Massachusetts to play a leading role in the late eighteenth-century creation of a new nation and ultimately of a pluralist culture where tolerance and dissent are legitimate—the culture in which Americans, whether they like it or not, reside today.

Reception of the common law was one matter on which compromise was comparatively easy. During the first three decades after its founding, Massachusetts had not modeled its law on the common law. Common law rules had always been present as background norms to which judges and lawmakers could turn

if needed, but Puritan biblicism and communitarianism had been the controlling sources of Massachusetts law. After 1660, however, Massachusetts began,
gradually and with key statutory reservations, to receive the common law writ
system—the ancient body of procedure that pigeonholed litigation into precise
categories, each commenced by a particular writ and governed by fixed rules of
procedure. In light of the Crown's policy of ruling its North American empire
through the common law, reception of the writ system became a means to placate
at least some officials in London. But because the portions of the common law
that the Bay Colony adopted consisted of a set of procedures rather than a body
of substantive rules, reception did not undermine established Massachusetts
law. Reception affected mainly the manner in which those who administered the
law performed their professional tasks but had little impact on the daily lives of
most people.

Reception began with use of the common law forms of action. Although
litigants occasionally had used common law writs in cases brought before 1660,
they often had done so in a fashion that did not adhere to English form. They
also had ignored other technical objections that would lie against their common
law actions. After 1660, change began to occur. Use of common law writs became more frequent, although writs contrary to proper form continued to appear. Courts also began to consider and dismiss cases on the basis of common
law technicalities.

By the 1670s, the leaders of Massachusetts thus could assert that their colony
followed common law rules and that appeals to England, which the Crown was
demanding as a device to police the Bay Colony's adherence to English law, were
therefore unnecessary. They could excuse departures from the common law as a
product of the local bar's lack of skill. And with legislation that cleverly removed
lawfinding power from the General Court, where royal officials could readily observe its exercise, into the hands of local juries, where its exercise was largely invisible, they could display how they were disposed to follow the latest decisions
handed down by the common law courts in England.

In 1649, as discussed in chapter 2, the General Court had assumed power
to resolve bench-jury disputes in a fashion that left the lower-house deputies
in control. But a new issue arose in the late 1660s. It focused on the differing
oaths taken by magistrates and deputies: the assistants swore to act "'according
to the Laws of God, & of this land,'" whereas each deputy swore only to decide
cases "'uprightly & justly, according to my judgment & conscience.'" This vague
oath, the magistrates claimed, allowed the deputies to "'gratify the restless or
turbulent passions of some particular persons'"[8]—that is, to decide cases out of
sympathy, favoritism, or local interest. To rein in such behavior, the magistrates
in 1667 proposed that the deputies take the same oath as they did—to adjudicate by law.

The deputies rejected the magistrates' proposal, and for five years the conflict simmered. Finally, the General Court requested the clergy to arbitrate the dispute. Resting on an observation that juries, like the magistrates, took an oath to proceed according to law and evidence, the ministers proposed repeal of the legislation authorizing the magistrates to reject jury verdicts. In its place they recommended that magistrates be directed to accept jury verdicts and to grant judgment accordingly; if they judged a jury's verdict to be evidently contrary to law and/or evidence, the only remedy was to attaint the jury—that is, to summon a jury of twenty-four persons chosen by the freemen of the same county to review the verdict of the initial jury and to punish the initial jury for perjury if it disagreed with that jury's verdict. The General Court accepted the clergy's proposal and in 1672 enacted legislation adopting it, thereby abolishing appeals to the General Court in cases of bench-jury disagreement. In so doing, the legislature cleverly eliminated a procedure unique to Massachusetts law and brought that law into conformity with the latest developments in the common law in England, where *Bushell's Case*[9] had just upheld the power of juries in criminal cases to reject instructions from the court. More significantly, the 1672 legislation transferred ultimate lawmaking power from the provincial legislature, where Crown authorities could easily observe its exercise, to local juries, where its exercise was largely invisible.

Local power in Massachusetts thereby became dominant through the jury. Of course, juries had to act under procedures that required them to exercise self-restraint, to decide according to their understanding of law and the evidence, and if the court or the losing litigant thought they had not done so, to face bothersome proceedings (attaints). During the fourteen years after 1672 that the charter government remained in place, a number of attaints were brought in the Court of Assistants, even though the procedure was an expensive one. On the whole, however, attaint juries would return verdicts only against petit juries that had committed clear errors.

In the end, local communities were cooperating with each other to ensure that ultimate lawfinding power remained in their hands. First, they conferred that power on juries by statute. Second, they appear to have created communication networks by which the freemen who served on juries and attaint juries informed and supported each other in their claims of adjudicatory power.

The presence of ultimate power in juries does not necessarily mean, however, that juries used their power in a fashion adverse to the wishes of the bench. Most of the time juries acted with restraint and cooperated with the judges. Even when the bench and jury seemed at loggerheads, in fact, they may not have been. Consider, for example, a case brought by Edward Randolph as collector of customs against George Hutchinson, a merchant whom Randolph accused of smuggling. Randolph was not a popular man in Massachusetts Bay, and not surprisingly, the jury returned a verdict for Hutchinson. Then "the court sent out the jury once & again with the case further to consider of it. [A]t their coming in again they declared by their foreman they saw no cause to alter their verdict."[10] By so asking the jury to reconsider its verdict, the court performed its duty of supporting royal authority, and by adhering to its verdict, the jury did what the court probably wanted but lacked power to do—it undermined royal government.

In short, institutional arrangements in seventeenth-century Massachusetts were supple, adaptable, and ultimately political. If it was necessary to adopt common law procedure to placate enemies in England, so be it. Through all the procedural changes, however, Puritan substantive law persisted. At least into the 1670s, the word of God remained part of the law of Massachusetts, and judges continued to protect the dominion of religion.

None of this was new. Throughout the charter period, the judiciary supported the unity and dominance of the Bay Colony's churches. Although Massachusetts adopted common law procedure and followed the rule of *Bushell's Case* so as to confer lawmaking authority on juries, until the mid-1680s the law of the Bay Colony remained grounded in traditional Puritan values of biblicism and communitarianism, little changed from what it had been in the era of the colony's founding.

Connecticut, Plymouth, and Rhode Island

During the seventeenth century, the judges of the smaller New England colonies likewise continued to pattern their law mainly after the Puritan law of Massachusetts rather than after the common law of England. In addition to the standard sorts of criminal prosecutions, for example, the smaller New England colonies witnessed prosecutions for the sin of fornication and prosecutions of women for being common scolds, as well as prosecutions for many sexual offenses, such as adultery, bestiality, incest, rape, sodomy, and administering potions to women for the "purpose of exciting unlawful lust thereby to bring & subdue such females to his the said [defendant's] will."[11] Finally, a doctor was convicted of performing an abortion.

Connecticut, New Hampshire, and Rhode Island also punished other sorts of religious offenses, such as blasphemy, breach of the Sabbath, profanity and swearing, witchcraft, and defamation of the clergy. Except in Rhode Island, there also were prosecutions of religious dissenters, notably Quakers, and, in Connecticut, the Rogerene sect, a group of proto-Baptists. Rhode Island did not have an established church and practiced religious toleration, even of a small Jewish congregation in Newport founded in the late seventeenth century.

In the seventeenth century, documents initiating criminal prosecutions, whether indictments or informations, often were quite informal. This informality, however, did not reflect a lack of concern on the part of ordinary people for what we might now label civil liberties. On one occasion, for example, when a constable appeared at a house with a warrant of debatable legality, the occupants stated that "they would not come out, but were resolved to knock down any man that should pry in upon them for their house was their castle."[12]

The courts of Connecticut, New Hampshire, and Rhode Island also undertook to perform regulatory duties, such as supervising the probate of wills, the discipline of apprentices, and the building of infrastructure, similar to those performed by judges in Massachusetts—indeed, in all of England's North American colonies. The most important such duty was to watch over subordinate institutions, such as the militia and town officials, in the performance of their duties. When the criminal and regulatory duties of the judiciary are combined, it becomes clear that the lives of ordinary people in New England were strictly regulated. Early America had little or nothing in the way of bureaucracy, but local officials, especially judges, and through them local communities, were all-powerful. Connecticut, New Hampshire, and Rhode Island were not laissez-faire states: their residents were controlled by their local governments in the pursuit of communitarian values of Puritan lineage.

The development of civil procedure in the smaller New England colonies likewise followed patterns that had surfaced in Massachusetts. Throughout the seventeenth century, pleading remained informal in all those colonies. But there was one important difference in trial practice between Massachusetts and the smaller colonies. Everywhere in New England, juries chosen by local towns were central to the adjudicatory process. But, whereas after the 1672 legislation discussed above, judges in Massachusetts had no power to reject jury verdicts as contrary to law and evidence, judges in the smaller colonies, at least in the seventeenth century, could reject verdicts and did so with some frequency.

Finally, the substantive law of the smaller New England colonies tended to mirror the law of Massachusetts. New Hampshire, indeed, was a part of Massachusetts until the Crown made it a separate royal colony in 1679, and New Hampshire's first legislature provided that existing Massachusetts law should continue to govern the new royal colony after the separation. Similarly, the Connecticut Code of 1650 had borrowed many provisions from the Massachusetts Body of Liberties of 1641. Even Rhode Island, which had been founded by exiles from Massachusetts, adopted much of the Bay Colony's law. Two subjects on which there was noteworthy consistency throughout New England were land law and the law of servitude, especially in regard to slaves, who were treated more humanely in New England than in colonies farther south.

5

The End of Resistance and
the Triumph of the Common Law

New York

The Netherlands, it will be recalled, had reconquered New York in 1673, but then ceded it back to England in 1674. With that 1674 cession, the residents of New York City knew that the Dutch nation had forever abandoned its sovereignty over the colony and hence that Dutch customary law would never again be of major force. Their knowledge was confirmed by a poignant final order closing the Court of Burgomasters and Schepens in November 1674 and distributing the court's substantial library of Dutch legal materials into private hands. A common law Mayor's Court then replaced the old Dutch court.

Within five years of the reconstitution of the Mayor's Court a new legal order was born. The common law writ system and forms of action took hold, and new sorts of common law procedural motions appeared. The Dutch practice of permitting married women to appear in court ended, and common law rules of coverture limiting the legal capacity of married women were adopted. Finally, jury practice was regularized when the court insisted on unanimity for a verdict. In short, little more than a decade after their arrival in New York City, English lawyers had taken charge and had firmly implanted the common law, although occasional Dutch practices did survive. For several years, for example, the Mayor's Court retained the criminal jurisdiction of the old Dutch court until a common law Court of Sessions was established in 1683.

New York City's entrepreneurs readily accepted these changes because they needed England's aid to support their far-flung trade along the Atlantic coast and to the Caribbean, England, and even continental Europe. One form of help vital to the growth of the city's economy came from the royal navy, which in the early eighteenth century largely wiped out piracy by killing some leading pirates and bringing others to trial in England. More important, the city's entrepreneurs required stable commercial law consistent with that governing their major trading partners and stable property law to structure their exploitation of real estate, especially of land along the Manhattan shoreline, where they located their docks and piers.

The Crown responded to these needs by effectively delegating to the city jurisdiction both to administer commercial law and to control exploitation of the shoreline. After 1675, the mass of civil litigation in New York City, including innumerable commercial, maritime, and admiralty cases, was brought to final determination in the Mayor's Court, over which merchants as a class possessed great influence. New York also adopted a number of substantive rules of considerable benefit to the merchant class, such as the rule, common to other commercially oriented jurisdictions, making promissory notes negotiable—a rule confirmed by parliamentary legislation in 1704 that made most notes negotiable thoughout the empire. Promissory notes, along with bills of exchange, which had always been negotiable, thereby became a form of circulating currency in New York's specie-starved economy.

The Crown similarly gave the city control over land. The Montgomerie Charter of 1730 granted title to all lots along the shoreline to the city's Common Council, which already possessed title to all other land in Manhattan not in private hands. The council, which like the Mayor's Court was heavily influenced by the merchants collectively, then granted lots to individual merchants. These grants were always effectuated by deeds drafted by the council's lawyer—deeds that contained restrictive covenants and conditions authorized by the common law of property, providing in the alternative for damages or forfeiture to the city if an individual merchant did not use a lot consistently with city plans for development.

Thus, the Crown conferred on lawyers acting in its behalf, while at the same time counseling New York City's merchant class, almost unlimited power over the economic well-being of individual merchants, who would become pariahs if they failed to obey the rules that the Mayor's Court and the Common Council generated in their favor. Individual merchants, in turn, had vast control over the lives and economic opportunities of those with whom they dealt—tradesmen, artisans, laborers, and others, who, if they failed to deal with the merchants in accordance with the city's rules, would become paupers at best and outcasts at worst. In short, the city government had great power, functioning as it did under the influence, if not the domination, of a Crown-lawyer-merchant alliance, to formulate legal rules facilitating economic growth and wealth accumulation; this gave the city vast control over individuals of all classes, from the highest to the lowest, residing within it. In New York City, quick reception of the common law, in short, appears to have achieved what Charles II and his advisors had sought—an effective government, like most local governments in England, under elite control and loyal to the empire and the Crown.

But New York City was unique in the extent to which true common law quickly permeated the legal system and facilitated the city's effective governance. Elsewhere in the colony of New York, resistance to reception of the common law continued, and the role of the common law and its lawyers remained marginal as late as the 1680s. But thereafter, common law institutions expanded their jurisdiction over the entire colony, although it would remain unclear into the middle of the eighteenth century whether the colonial administration could rely on those institutions to be strong tools of governance.

Major events, some of them cataclysmic, transformed New York law and politics over the course of ten years starting in 1683. In that year, the Duke of York finally yielded to popular demand and authorized the calling of the colony's first legislative body. A few years later, however, as King James II, he reneged and merged New York into the Dominion of New England, which he hoped to govern despotically without any legislature whatsoever. Two years later, James was overthrown, and his lieutenant governor in New York returned to England. Jacob Leisler, assuming the duties of governor, ruled for two years, until a new governor arrived from England in 1691. The new governor promptly had Leisler tried and executed for treason.

Two important pieces of legislation, both of semi-constitutional stature, were adopted by the legislature around the time of this turmoil. One was the Charter of Liberties of 1683. After establishing the structure of government, it provided among other things that no freeman be imprisoned or deprived of freehold without the judgment of his peers, that no tax be levied without the consent of the legislature, that all trials be by jury, that no troops be quartered, and that no commissions of martial law be issued against civilians. It next provided that no Christian be molested or punished for his or her religious opinions and specifically conferred legal status on the Congregational religious establishment on Long Island and the existing churches of New York City. Although the Charter of Liberties never received the royal assent and accordingly lacked formal legal force, many still regarded it as a foundational element of New York law.

The other major law was the Judicature Act of 1691, as amended by the Judicature Act of 1692, which, in the main, continued in force until the Revolution. This legislation created countywide Courts of General Sessions and Common Pleas, Mayor's Courts in Albany and New York City, and a colonywide Supreme Court, with both original and appellate jurisdiction in cases of £20 or greater value. For cases in excess of specified values, further appeal could be taken to the Governor and Council and ultimately to the Privy Council. There was also a separate Court of Chancery, consisting of the Governor and Council or a specially appointed chancellor. One key difference existed between the 1691 and 1692 acts: the 1691 act provided that the Supreme Court would sit only in New York City, while the 1692 act directed it to ride circuit around the province.

Examination of the 1691–92 Judicature Acts along with a short-lived 1683 act setting up courts reveals what was at stake in the judiciary's structure. The issue was about local access to and popular control over the law, on the one hand, or centralized authority, ultimately that of the governor, on the other. There were two important differences between the 1683 and the 1691–92 acts. First, the 1683 act placed at the base of the judicial hierarchy town courts, elected by townspeople, rather than countywide courts with judges chosen by the governor. Second, the 1683 act gave jurisdiction over appeals from local courts to countywide Courts of Oyer and Terminer, consisting of one judge and four local justices of the peace, rather than to a colonywide Supreme Court, based out of New York City. The 1692 judiciary thus was far more centralized than that of 1683. Moreover, it was centralized in a fashion that its drafters undoubtedly hoped would make central control effective. Recall that the old Court of Assizes had been under the governor's complete control; he had presided over it. It also had broad jurisdiction, including full authority to overturn jury verdicts, over all cases decided below. However, as a result of its inaccessibility and deficiencies in its knowledge of local doings, the Court of Assizes had lacked effective power to control the law that lower courts applied. The 1692 Judicature Act sought to solve this problem by requiring the new Supreme Court to ride circuit. It would be accessible to the people of the counties, and it would learn, and thereby become able to control, the law those people were employing.

But in exchange for a highly centralized judiciary, the administration made two concessions, one in 1683 and one in the 1690s. The Duke's Laws, it will be remembered, gave the Court of Assizes over which the governor presided equitable discretion to make law whenever there was no clear preexisting rule; the Charter of Liberties, in contrast, made it plain that supreme legislative authority could be exercised only with the consent of the General Assembly and that the governor could govern only according to established laws. Meanwhile, the 1691 and 1692 Judicature Acts protected the role of juries, which represented local communities in the litigation process, by declaring explicitly that only juries could determine matters of fact. Those acts also limited the judicial role of the Governor and Council to hearing appeals in cases where the amount in controversy exceeded the large sum of £100 and to acting as a Court of Chancery in cases above the same jurisdictional amount.

In establishing a Court of Chancery a decade later, New York's governors did not rely on the 1691 and 1692 acts, but on their own prerogative power, specifically on ordinances of 1701 and 1704 and a gubernatorial proclamation of 1711. This claim to reliance on prerogative in and of itself raised constitutional objections to the court, which met only sporadically before 1711. The court met with greater regularity thereafter, but when Governor William Burnet used the court in the 1720s to collect quitrents, he exacerbated the situation, so much so that his successor, Governor John Montgomerie, who was allied with the anti-prerogative faction, declined to sit as chancellor.

Common law courts sitting with juries accordingly remained central to New York's system of justice. As a result, the distribution of power between judges and juries became an issue of substantial importance, although as late as 1730 little conflict between trial judges and juries had occurred. Juries returned their verdicts, and judges routinely accepted them. If juries had doubt about the law, they could return a special verdict, in which they found only the facts and left it to the court to apply the law to the facts; juries returned special verdicts with some frequency. And when conflicts arose in cases employing general verdicts, judges often granted post-verdict motions for new trials or in arrest of judgment. The most important jury-control device, however, was the demurrer to the evidence, by which one litigant at the close of the other litigant's evidence moved for judgment on the ground that the other side's evidence was insufficient as a matter of law to warrant submission of the case to the jury. Trial judges thus had ample procedures with which to control juries.

But it is unclear how frequently they were prepared to use those powers. Although one chief justice of the colony in an early eighteenth-century case instructed a jury that "if you will take upon you to judge of law, you may, or bring in the fact specially,"[1] almost no jury instructions before 1730 have been preserved, and thus it is impossible to know how often judges gave juries such free rein. Appellate courts, in turn, enjoyed substantially less freedom to review jury verdicts or otherwise control lower court decision making. The reason was that the writs of error and certiorari, the principal procedures for appellate review, brought only matters of record in a trial court to the attention of an appellate court and no evidence was reported in a trial court record.

The capacity to review the record did enable central courts, however, in conjunction with New York City's legal profession, to impose on localities common law procedural formalities, which are the main component of any common law record. And inasmuch as a good deal of substantive common law was embraced within the interstices of procedure, that substantive law, as will appear below, also triumphed gradually throughout the colony.

New York's criminal law, for example, came to resemble that of England, as judges processed standard crimes together with political offenses, such as treason, riot, sedition, and contempt of court. But prosecutions for sin, vice, and immorality, such as fornication, atrophied. More important, English criminal procedure superseded that of the Dutch. Local prosecutors representing the Crown in criminal proceedings were appointed at least from the outset of the 1700s, and the use of torture, placing people in irons, and multiple prosecutions for the same offense disappeared.

The turn to common law similarly narrowed the regulatory power that New York judges had inherited from the Dutch. The regulatory jurisdiction, especially of the Courts of General Sessions, became limited, and old Dutch patterns of intrusive regulation of the details of everyday life disappeared. English courts no longer used criminal law to regulate entry into marriage, and relations between husbands and wives became a private matter, not one for judicial scrutiny. Land use regulation likewise atrophied, as did other forms of economic regulation such as regulation of prices and wages. Long before the middle of the eighteenth century, New York courts had come to understand that "the price of goods . . . must be regulated . . . as parties on both sides can agree."[2] The common law also superseded Dutch law in the realm of civil procedure and private law more generally.

By the 1720s, in sum, the displacement of the Dutch legal system by English common law was nearly complete. What was the significance, however, of that displacement? Three points need emphasis.

First, as already noted, New York's law in its essentials became the same as that of England's twelve other mainland North American colonies. Whereas a lawyer from the Chesapeake or New England who came to New York in 1660 would have confronted a foreign legal order (which also may have been true for a Chesapeake lawyer coming to New England, and vice versa), it was feasible in 1735 for John Peter Zenger, when he was prosecuted for sedition, to retain a Philadelphia lawyer, Andrew Hamilton, to take over his case; Hamilton had to learn nothing fundamentally new when crossing jurisdictional boundaries. It is difficult to imagine how New Yorkers could have participated a mere four decades later in the American Revolution if they had not developed a legal and constitutional culture that they shared with their fellow rebels.

Second, the English common law's displacement of Dutch law produced an important change in the nature of record-keeping. The court records of New Netherland bring to life the rich detail of everyday human endeavor and the inevitable human conflict it produces. The historian of today can read a case record from New Netherland and make a judgment on the facts presented about how to resolve in a just fashion the conflict that those facts reveal. Governor Stuyvesant and his council, sitting in the fort in New Amsterdam, were able to do the same.

A common law record from the eighteenth century, in contrast, is much less revealing. In most cases that went to trial, the record contained no more than a writ directing a court officer to serve process, a declaration or formulary statement of the plaintiff's claim, a defendant's general denial, and an inscrutable jury verdict. The real matter in dispute and the evidence with which to resolve it were hidden. A few records contained more data—special pleadings, motions, and, in instances of demurrers to the evidence, the evidentiary allegations of the party whose claim was being challenged. But the additional data were not designed to enable a reader of the record, either the historian of today or the appellate court of the past, to comprehend the facts beneath a dispute. The point of pleadings, motions, and demurrers was to suppress many of the facts and thereby abstract from the complexity of life narrow issues of law and fact appropriate for judges and juries to decide.

Of course, a judge who presided over a trial would have known in rich detail what the case was about. He would have had the information necessary for a fair judgment about how best to resolve the dispute and would have had substantial power to influence or alternatively set aside an unfair or erroneous jury verdict. But transmission of the record alone did not give similar knowledge and power to the ultimate appellate judges—first, the colony's Supreme Court; second, the Governor and Council; and finally, the Privy Council. They would have had to obtain that power through some other means.

Third, the difference between Dutch and common law legal records helps us better understand why eighteenth-century Americans so readily accepted the concept of the common law as a guarantor of English liberty. As noted in chapter 3, both local and central courts of New Netherland had intrusively regulated the details of everyday life—economic life, family life, religious life. Moreover, the nature of Dutch record-keeping made local judgments readily and fully appealable to the director-general and council in New Amsterdam. It is only a slight exaggeration to observe that if a husband and wife were quarreling in Albany, nothing in Dutch law prevented Governor Peter Stuyvesant from directing them how to resolve their quarrel.

New York's common law, in contrast, restricted the power of government in general and of central government in particular. As was shown above, government's prosecutorial and regulatory powers were far more constrained in eighteenth-century New York than they had been in seventeenth-century New Netherland. Even more significant were the differences between Dutch private law and English common law. Dutch adjudicators appear to have been willing to entertain and adjudicate any dispute that private individuals brought to them and to decide it in whatever fashion their understanding of justice dictated. However, common law courts, perhaps because they originated in England as courts of limited, central jurisdiction, could hear only cases that could be shoehorned into one of the categories contained in the Register of Writs, and even the catch-all action of case failed to capture most categories of human conflict. Moreover, a court could only grant remedies authorized in a particular writ. The common law simply left vastly wider domains of human endeavor to private ordering and informal community regulation than Dutch law had done.

Moreover, even when the common law in theory authorized government intervention, Crown officials were restrained by the power of the jury. Ultimately, no major penalty could be imposed or significant civil judgment authorized without the interposition of a jury—representatives of local communities standing between the Crown and the subject. And whereas trial judges, as was shown above, possessed ample power to control juries, it still remained to be resolved—and would not be resolved until the end of the colonial period—whether the Crown could piggyback on that power to impose imperial policies on localities.

Of course, the liberty that the common law fostered was not an unmixed blessing. People of wealth and power are often better positioned than the poor and the weak to take advantage of their liberty, either in the private marketplace or in local forums of community governance. Sometimes, only institutions of central government have sufficient capacity to restrain the rich and the strong; for better or worse, the central institutions of New York's colonial government were too weak to assume such a role. As a result, especially in New York City, the rich and powerful, in alliance with a professional bar, used the power the Crown delegated to them to enhance their own wealth and power.

At the same time, the government in England appeared to obtain, at least in the city, what it most needed: competent governance that preserved the peace and did not challenge the mercantilist foundations on which the empire was based. Delegation to a merchant-lawyer elite eager to use delegated power to enhance its wealth thus was probably the most effective approach available for a penurious Crown. But, as will appear in chapter 13, the approach would entail risk when those to whom power was delegated developed interests beyond merely enhancing their own wealth—interests potentially adverse to the Crown.

Massachusetts

Reception of the common law was even slower in Massachusetts than it was in New York and so gradual as to be almost imperceptible. After a quarter century of conflict, the recalcitrance of the Massachusetts General Court led the Crown in 1684 to institute *quo warranto* proceedings for the revocation of the colony's 1629 charter. Within months the Crown had won its lawsuit, and two years later, in 1686, it incorporated Massachusetts Bay into the Dominion of New England. New common law judicial institutions—Courts of Common Pleas and General Sessions and a Superior Court of Judicature—replaced the old county courts and Court of Assistants. They functioned for three years until, on receipt of word of the Glorious Revolution, the Dominion of New England was overthrown, and the old charter with its old courts put back into operation. This interlude lasted until 1691, when Massachusetts received a new charter as a royal colony with a royal governor. Separate Courts of Common Pleas and General Sessions were again established with a Superior Court hearing appeals.

It was unclear, at first, what impact these revolutionary changes would have. Would a new royal governor try, as had the royal governor of New Hampshire, to wipe out Puritanism? Or would former Puritan ways of law and governance remain in place with only minimal changes? Would the result of the revolution be something in between and, if so, what?

It was in the midst of this uncertainty that accusations of witchcraft erupted in Salem Village. Witchcraft was not new at the time in Massachusetts; a number of cases had been prosecuted earlier in the seventeenth century. Nor were the accusations in Salem unique. Witches were prosecuted at the same time in Hampshire and Middlesex counties, and one servant was prosecuted for falsely accusing his mistress of witchcraft in Suffolk County. But the Salem prosecutions were more numerous and became infamous. It is not the purpose here to explain why the Salem accusations occurred; a vast body of scholarship has discussed that issue at length. But it is necessary to explain why the legal system reacted to those accusations as it did, with nineteen trials and executions, one defendant pressed to death for refusing to plead, and many others reprieved after they entered guilty pleas. The explanation lies in the policy of Crown officials, first announced by Joseph Dudley when he was appointed in 1686 to take charge of the new government of New England following revocation of Massachusetts's 1629 charter. That policy was to change almost nothing of significance in connection with the law.

In some counties, for example, the new courts of Common Pleas and General Sessions met together, effectively constituting an entity like the old county court, sometimes, as in the case of Hampshire, with a single trial jury as late as the 1750s. Even more significant was the continuity of personnel. For example, Dudley, the son of a former Bay Colony governor who had first been elected to the Court of Assistants in 1676, presided over the Court of Appeals initially established after the revocation of the 1629 charter. Later he served as chief justice of the Dominion of New England and between 1702 and 1715 served as Massachusetts's royal governor. William Stoughton, who became chief judge of the Superior Court in 1692, similarly had served on the Court of Assistants. In addition to Stoughton, two of the other four judges of the Superior Court, Samuel Sewall and Wait Winthrop, had served on the Court of Assistants. Winthrop, of course, had impeccable Puritan credentials: he was the grandson of founder John Winthrop. Similar continuity occurred on the lower courts.

This continuity in personnel led, in turn, to continuity in policy. The men named above, along with others who served in the various Massachusetts regimes from the mid-1680s into the mid-1690s, were not anti-Puritan. Before the revocation of the Bay Colony's 1629 charter, everyone serving in its government was Puritan. By the 1680s, the policy issue that divided the governing class was whether the best way to preserve Puritanism was unbending resistance to the Crown or compromise with royal authorities. Those who served in the various regimes during the decade of upheaval following revocation of the charter were the advocates of compromise. But recall that they advocated compromise because they thought it the best way to preserve Puritanism.

The Crown had little choice but to govern Massachusetts through those Puritan leaders who were willing to compromise. Like his brother Charles II, James II never had the resources to send a large bureaucracy or military force to the Bay Colony. He had to rely on local leaders. Perhaps, had he succeeded in remodeling England's government, he would have relied in the long run on English placemen to govern Massachusetts. But his reign was brief. And, as later chapters will show, his successor, William III, pursued a different set of policies. He did not fear New England's quasi-republican Puritanism as much as Charles and James had feared it, and he and his successors needed the support of Massachusetts in their wars against France. Depending on Puritan leaders who were prepared to compromise was the obvious way to obtain that support.

Thus, when Joseph Dudley first took charge of the Massachusetts government in the aftermath of the charter's revocation, he made clear the new regime's commitment to the preservation of Puritanism. In a 1686 speech, he declared that "if there be any so ill minded as to . . . think to allow themselves [to live] in debauchery," the king's "commands . . . to us are expressly to the contrary, and most agreeable to our own inclinations; and we . . . intend the suppression of all vice and ill-manners."[3] The new government also directed that all existing contracts with ministers and schoolteachers remain in effect, and it upheld the exemption of Puritan ministers from taxes. Later, in one of its first acts under the 1691 charter, the General Court adopted a resolution keeping in force all laws enacted under the old charter that were not repugnant to the laws of England, and several years later the Superior Court, consistent with the 1692 resolution, ruled that the old laws of Plymouth remained in force in the counties of the former Plymouth Colony that had been joined to Massachussetts.

This policy of continuity dictated the judiciary's response to the Salem witchcraft accusations. Witchcraft—specifically, entering into a pact with the devil—was a serious religious offense that could not be ignored and had to be prosecuted. When the first accusations were made in Salem Village in February, 1691–92, while the interim government under the 1629 charter was still in place, two magistrates serving under that government, Jonathan Corwin and John Hathorne, examined those who were accused and held them for trial.

The first royal governor, William Phips, arrived in Boston a few months later, in mid-May, and within two weeks he had appointed a special Court of Oyer and Terminer to try those being held. Two of the nine judges who sat on that court were Corwin and Hathorne, and four others, including the presiding judge, had served on the interim government's Court of Assistants. These Puritan judges were guided by the colony's Puritan leaders and clergy in regard to the most important legal issue they faced during the witchcraft trials—the admissibility of spectral evidence.

Initially, the Court of Oyer and Terminer heard testimony from victims that specters had taunted them. Several clergymen were uncomfortable with the testimony, however, and they met in mid-summer at Harvard College and persuaded the acknowledged leader of the Ministerial Association, Increase Mather, to draft a statement against spectral evidence. At the beginning of October, Mather presented his draft to the association. After thirteen other ministers had signed it, he presented it to Governor Phips and probably circulated it more widely as well. Several weeks later the General Court, by a narrow 33–29 vote, called for a day of fasting and a convocation of the clergy to lead the colony in the right way as to witchcraft. Three days later Phips directed the Court of Oyer and Terminer to cease sitting and thereby brought an effective end to the witchcraft prosecutions.

Little change occurred, in short, in the way that authority was exercised as a result of the royal takeover of Massachusetts. Both before and after the revocation of the 1629 charter and its replacement by the charter of 1691, central officials rarely acted without the guidance, support, or at least acquiescence of local communities, the clergy, or both. That is how they continued to act during the witchcraft episode. In Middlesex County, for example, the lawfinding power of juries under the 1672 legislation had been preserved by the General Court's 1692 resolution keeping all existing laws from the charter period in force, and when Middlesex juries returned not guilty verdicts in witchcraft cases, judges readily accepted their verdicts. But when defendants insisted, as some in Salem did, on going to trial and juries found them guilty, the judges were compelled to display their loyalty to Puritan law, at a time when the Crown's continued recognition of that law was at issue, by sentencing the defendants to death.

The judges, that is, merely did their duty and displayed their continuing commitment to preserving the Puritan legal order. One of the most important elements of the old order that post-1690 judges preserved was the lawfinding power of juries, which were selected by local town meetings in response to venires issued by the courts. Judges accepted that power by sentencing to death those whom juries found guilty and reprieving those found innocent.

An important foundation of the jury's power lay in the process of appeal from lower courts to the Superior Court. Litigants dissatisfied with a lower court decision could seek a writ of review, pursuant to which they would receive a new trial before a new jury in the same court. Alternatively, they could appeal to the Superior Court, where they also would receive a full trial *de novo* before a new jury. Mechanisms for bringing legal issues alone to the attention of the Superior Court, such as the writs of error and certiorari used in New York, were employed only on the rarest occasions. As a result, courts almost never sat without juries to resolve pure questions of law; legal issues were conjoined with factual issues and left to juries, which possessed the final word on how those mixed questions of law and fact would be decided.

More significantly, judges rarely challenged the verdicts brought in by juries. The rule of *Bushell's Case*[4] remained the law in Massachusetts in civil as well as criminal cases, even after revocation of the 1629 charter and under the new charter of 1691. Massachusetts courts acted strongly to protect the lawfinding power of juries. Thus, they denied motions in arrest of judgment made on the ground that a jury verdict was contrary to the evidence or to the law. They refused to allow litigants to interpose pleas in bar that would deprive juries of their power to determine the substantive legal issues in a case, and they did little to control the evidence that litigants presented at trial. There is no doubt that in the cases that were tried by juries, those juries at times engaged in jury nullification, refusing to apply the law and to reach the verdict directed by the court.

The transfer of lawfinding power from the General Court to local juries did not, however, leave the General Court without power to affect the course of ordinary litigation. Although it no longer sat at the apex of the appellate superstructure, it still could and throughout the eighteenth century did entertain and act on petitions from litigants to alter the course of ongoing litigation. But the occasional enactment of such special bills did not leave the General Court in day-to-day control of the legal process. That role was assumed instead by the Court of Assistants and, after 1692, by the Superior Court, which, sitting with its juries, became a significantly more powerful entity than the high courts of most other colonies.

Several factors are key to explaining the Superior Court's power. First, except in cases in which the Crown had an interest, it sat only as an appellate court rather than as a court of first instance. As a result, it did not waste time on routine matters that could be resolved by lower courts. The Superior Court also could conscript lower courts into enforcing its judgments; after deciding issues that required its attention, it routinely remanded cases for further proceedings in the lower courts or issued specific commands to lower courts or their officials.

The second factor is that the Superior Court rode circuit: it sat twice a year in major counties such as Suffolk, Middlesex, Essex, and Plymouth and traveled annually some hundred miles or more west to the Connecticut Valley, north to Maine, and south as far as Nantucket. All told, the court probably was in session for roughly half of every year and, as a result of many appeals and remands, knew what local courts were doing and whether they were following its directives.

Third, perhaps most important, the Superior Court did not function by itself. Instead, it functioned as part of a coherent system, together with the lower courts and with local juries and local communities, committed to the preservation of the Puritan legal order established in the seventeenth century.

One way that the Superior Court simultaneously enhanced its own power and preserved the Puritan legal order was through its supervision and control of the instrumentalities of local government. Even more important was its control over royal instrumentalities. Thus the court, in reliance on English common law precedents, issued a number of prohibitions to the Court of Vice Admiralty. The Superior Court also adjudicated many cases concerning maritime contracts, often protecting the rights of Bay Colony residents by holding, for example, that payment of seamen's wages had priority over penalties for forfeiture of a vessel for violating the Navigation Acts.

In *Savage v. Menzeis*,[5] one of the most important cases of the 1720s, the marshal of the Court of Vice Admiralty sued the judge of the court for giving him an order to sell a condemned vessel after the Superior Court had issued a prohibition against Vice Admiralty's exercise of jurisdiction over the case. The case was complex, with several pleas and numerous citations to English authorities. Ultimately, the court ruled that an inferior officer could not bring suit against a superior one for directing him to perform an unlawful act; the inferior officer's proper remedy, according to the court, was to refuse to obey the order.

The impact, if any, that this decision had on the relationship between common law courts and the Court of Vice Admiralty and on law enforcement more generally is unclear. Perhaps the decision weakened Vice Admiralty and others seeking to enforce unpopular laws by encouraging subordinate officials to disobey the commands of their superiors. Alternatively, the refusal to take action against the admiralty judge may have served as a substitute for a doctrine of judicial immunity and thereby strengthened all judges. What *Savage v. Menzeis* did make clear was the growing sophistication of the judiciary. It showed that judges understood that, at least with the aid of their juries, they could protect subordinate officials who disobeyed unlawful commands from efforts of their superiors to discipline them. On the other hand, it was unclear whether courts could enforce a judgment directing a royal judge or other high royal official to pay damages or to obey some other judicial order. In *Savage v. Menzeis*, the judges made a decision not to try.

As the sophistication of judges was advancing, so too was their reliance on the common law. Of course, as chief judge of the Dominion of New England's courts between 1686 and 1689, Joseph Dudley continued the old regime's compromise policy of gradual reception of the common law. So too did the restored old charter government of 1689–92 and the new judicial system under the charter of 1691. Reception of the common law remained haphazard into the 1720s, however, in part as a result of lack of learning on the part of the Massachusetts bar.

Use of common law writs continued to lie at the heart of reception. Often, though, lawyers continued to file writs that failed to follow proper common law form, and the courts did not care, even when defendants objected. The process of requiring plaintiffs to adhere to proper common law forms was a slow and gradual one, and it was not until the 1720s that the judiciary began routinely to dismiss cases in which plaintiffs brought actions not drawn according to the English Register of Writs.

Termination of lawsuits on other technical grounds also increased, albeit slowly, under all three regimes. Rather than seek to abate an action on technical grounds, a defendant alternatively could plead to issue and thereby seek a jury trial. It is noteworthy, however, that whereas pleas raising technical objections to plaintiffs' pleadings gradually grew increasingly sophisticated between 1690 and 1730, defensive pleading to issue on the merits remained highly informal. In the decades leading up to 1730, that is, courts increasingly required plaintiffs to get their pleadings right or face dismissal of their lawsuits, but defendants remained free until roughly 1730 to commit whatever pleading errors they wished without facing any penalties or costs.

Two factors might help explain why Massachusetts gradually adopted a practice of requiring plaintiffs to adhere to formal rules while leaving defendants free to ignore them. The first was the low level of sophistication of the early Massachusetts bar. Proper defensive pleading required a higher level of technical legal skill than a plaintiff's lawyer needed to select and fill in the blanks of a proper writ, and lawyers in Massachusetts were slow to develop the necessary skill.

The second factor may have been one of policy. Although there is no direct evidence, it is possible that as the Bay Colony slowly began to adhere to the common law, a policy judgment was made to discourage people from using the courts. After all, a vibrant ecclesiastical jurisdiction existed as an alternative vehicle for dispute resolution. One way to promote continued use of this alternative ecclesiastical jurisdiction, where the playing field was level, was to make it more difficult technically for plaintiffs to use the courts while leaving it easier for defendants to defend suits brought there.

In any event, as late as roughly 1730, defendants without objection routinely pleaded general issues that would have been incorrect under English common law. But in 1729 change began to occur. In that year, the Superior Court reversed a judgment given by the Barnstable County Court of Common Pleas and quashed the proceedings because the plea of the general issue filed by the defendant was an improper one. Of necessity, lower courts responded to the Superior Court's new approach by requiring defendants to plead properly.

But requiring defendants to plead properly still did not put plaintiffs and defendants on an equal footing. If a defendant pleaded properly, his or her case would go to trial in the lower court, where both parties would be forced to disclose their evidence, following which the losing party could appeal to the Superior Court and obtain a trial *de novo* before a new jury. If, on the other hand, a defendant did not want to disclose evidence, he or she could either default or plead improperly in the lower court, appeal to the Superior Court upon the entry of a negative judgment, and thereupon plead properly. Defendants, in effect, had a choice of whether to obtain pre-trial discovery before having a final trial in the Superior Court—a choice that plaintiffs lacked.

Not only did the Massachusetts system of pleading favor defendants over plaintiffs; because defendants often exercised their right to two trials, the system also was expensive and inefficient for the courts. Finally, in the early 1750s the Superior Court reformed it. The court preserved the capacity of defendants to avoid a trial in a lower court by defaulting or pleading improperly there and then filing a correct plea in the Superior Court. It gave plaintiffs a similar capacity by allowing them to demur to a proper plea in a lower court, have judgment entered against them, and then appeal to the Superior Court and withdraw their demurrer there. The result was that a case would go to trial in a Common Pleas court only if both parties agreed to try it there and disclose their evidence to each other; the ultimate result was that after the early 1750s, most cases went to trial only in the Superior Court.

With the gradual adoption of common law pleading in the decades following 1685, substantive doctrines of common law also began to emerge. One result of the rationalization of pleading rules was the evolution of substantive law, both in regard to defenses as well as more generally. Perhaps the most important area of substantive development was the law of debtor and creditor. In the mid-seventeenth century, the extension of credit and hence the collection of debts was significantly less important in Massachusetts than, for example, in Virginia, but by the mid-eighteenth century, debt collection had become the most frequent activity in which the courts engaged. A related area was the law of bills and notes, most of which became negotiable under Parliament's 1704 statute.

Tort law, especially the law of negligence, also broadened its reach. Much of it coalesced around the duties of jail-keepers, sheriffs, and constables. But cases of negligence spread beyond sheriffs and jailers. When a doctor on board a slaving vessel during a transatlantic voyage treated the slave cargo negligently and many slaves died, he found himself sued for £3,000. Hugh Hall similarly claimed damage to the timber at his sawmill when Martin Armstrong "for want of due care of his fire" "causelessly and negligently" burned the timber.[6]

The law of real property constituted a final subject of development, most importantly in connection with inheritance. Here Massachusetts received much of the common law, such as the fee tail and the common recovery as the means for docking an entail. But reception of the common law involved compromise, and on one important issue—the Bay Colony's rejection of primogeniture—the

Crown, as will be seen in chapter 8, ultimately permitted Massachusetts to pursue its traditional Puritan ways.

Legal practice in the Bay Colony also continued well into the eighteenth century to reflect the Puritans' foundational conception of law. The Puritan founders of Massachusetts never understood law to be a product of sovereign human will but rather believed that all the essential truths of law were revealed in the Bible. The job of human communities charged with administering law was to decipher those biblical truths and adapt them, using communitarian methodologies, to existing societal conditions. Thus, the lawfinding process always depended on maintaining a delicate balance between Puritan communitarianism and Puritan biblicism.

During the century and a half that Massachusetts was part of the British empire, the central task of maintaining the balance between text and communitarian interpretation of text never changed. What did change slowly and gradually was the relevant text and the community of interpreters charged with understanding it.

In the 1630s, the main source of Massachusetts law was the Bible. This biblicism made Massachusetts radically different from other English colonies outside New England. By the 1760s, in contrast, the common law was the foundation of the Bay Colony's law, just as it was of every other colony's law. But change was gradual and at any one point in time probably imperceptible. In the 1630s, the common law had not been absent from the Massachusetts legal system; it had served as a set of background norms to which lawmakers sometimes turned in contexts where the Bible provided inadequate guidance. And in the 1760s, Puritanical norms, such as those requiring Sunday worship and prohibiting sexual activity outside the confines of marriage, remained, as shall be seen, a significant element in Massachusetts culture. Nonetheless, sometime between the 1630s and 1760s, the relative importance of biblical norms and common law values shifted, although it is impossible to identify precisely when that shift occurred.

The other change happening between the 1630s and 1760s was in the community of interpreters. In the 1630s, clergymen and Puritan political leaders were in control of the biblical interpretive community. Their control, however, slowly declined. With the 1672 legislation empowering juries to find the law definitively in the cases before them, ordinary laypeople took on a greater interpretive role. The 1691 Massachusetts charter, which made top officials subject to appointment by the Crown, may have increased the coercive power of those officials, but it reduced their significance as interpreters of biblical law—a subject on which royal officials usually lacked expertise. Meanwhile, during the eighteenth century a legal profession slowly emerged. Lawyers brought to the fore the common law and their expertise as its interpreters. By the 1760s the lawyers and the jurors whom they addressed, representative as they were of local communities, often proved able to overrule the legal interpretations of royally appointed judges.

In short, by the time Massachusetts entered into the decade of constitutional controversy with Britain that culminated in the War of Independence, profound changes had occurred in its legal system. What once had presented itself as a Puritan utopia whose leaders aimed to provide a model of religious and political rectitude for England and the rest of Christianity no longer could serve that religious end. In the language of John Murrin, Massachusetts had become anglicized. The concept of anglicization, however, captures only part of the change. Of course, the Bay Colony's gradual, halting adoption of the common law between 1690 and 1760 made its governance structure more English than it had been in the seventeenth century. But, contrary to Murrin's characterization, the Massachusetts bench and bar had not eagerly transformed itself and the province's legal system into copies of England's. At the same time that courts adopted common law procedure, puritanical norms remained at the foundation of much substantive law, and a communitarian societal structure derived from the Puritan past remained in place to apply those norms through juries to individual cases. In this dual emphasis on common law procedure and local lawmaking on the basis of customary norms, Massachusetts had become more like Britain's other North American colonies than like the mother country itself; it had been Americanized, not anglicized. It was this Americanization that enabled the people of Massachusetts to join with the people of twelve other colonies to oppose the claimed power of a sovereign British legislature to alter law by statute.

It would be foolhardy, of course, to proclaim that the common law caused the American Revolution. But it does seem plausible to assert that reception of the common law was a precondition for a revolution in Massachusetts that other colonies could join—that reception, together with the common law's incorporation into a structure of local self-rule, made a contribution.

Connecticut, New Hampshire, and Rhode Island

Reception of the common law in the smaller New England colonies occurred mostly at the same pace and in the same fashion as in Massachusetts. New Hampshire, which had begun to copy Massachusetts law when it was first split off from the Bay Colony in 1679, continued to do so thereafter, with the result that its rules of pleading and procedure closely resembled those of the larger colony.

Connecticut likewise adopted the common law of pleading, although it continued to abide by some local peculiarities, such as one permitting plaintiffs to bring actions of debt on book accounts. Rhode Island was the third colony to receive common law pleading and practice rules. In short, by the mid-eighteenth century, the common law had firmly planted at least its procedural roots throughout New England.

Ready Acceptance of the Common Law: Pennsylvania, New Jersey, and the South

In New England and New York, English authorities had to demand that established legal systems be replaced by the common law. That demand encountered considerable resistance, although ultimately the struggle against it collapsed and the common law took hold. Similar resistance occurred in East Jersey. In West Jersey and farther south, in contrast, the common law was readily received with little or no pressure from the Crown.

Virginia and Maryland

Although Virginia was initially governed under military law, by 1620 it had begun to turn to the common law. No pressure from Crown officials forced it to do so; Virginians accepted the common law willingly in an effort to induce people from England to immigrate and invest. The Virginia legal order departed from the common law's institutional design, however, in three significant respects. One was the assumption of ecclesiastical jurisdiction by secular courts. Another was the blending of chancery jurisdiction with that of the common law in a single hierarchy of courts. A third was in the design of local courts and their relationship to the highest court, the General Court.

The basic pattern of jurisdiction throughout the colonial era was for Virginia to have one central court and a series of county courts, each, unlike most courts in England, with jurisdiction over both civil and criminal matters. Local courts also would have "liberty to make laws for themselves . . . to be binding upon them as fully as any other law" and to nominate the men whom the governor would then appoint to the bench.[1] Note how the grant of power to make laws and to choose the men who made and administered them turned the county courts into powerful constitutional entities with substantial independence from provincial authorities.

The county courts were directed to function "the same as in England."[2] Although statutes at times directed local institutions to depart from English rules, English legal practice remained the baseline, and for three reasons that baseline proved enormously valuable to those who were crafting Virginia's law. First, English law was what Virginians remembered. They did not need to study alternatives about which they knew nothing to get their legal system off the ground. Second, English law—in particular, the common law—provided a rich body of rules and doctrines that could serve definitional functions without anyone's having to sit down and write a legal dictionary. Third, the common law offered a cheap means of governing peripheral localities distant from the center. The common law enabled the Crown to govern through unpaid, high-status volunteers who, in turn, worked closely with other subjects in the locality to ensure that crime was punished, disputes resolved, and the peace kept. By conferring power and honor on local leaders, the Crown coopted them, and they, in turn, coopted the people around them by doing justice and preserving order.

Maryland also adopted the common law of its own accord, perhaps as early as 1635—a mere year after the colony's initial settlement—and certainly no later than a 1639 statute. But whatever the reason for Maryland's quick adoption of the common law, like Virginia it did not adopt it without modifications. When Maryland law and English law were in conflict, courts were "bound to proceed according to the laws of this Province."[3] Later courts agreed that Maryland need not follow the law of England if "there be some law or precedent to the contrary in this Province."[4]

What mattered was not whether English jurisdictional, procedural, or substantive rules were followed in every detail. What mattered was judicial adherence to the rule of law—to the idea that fixed, certain rules applied by professional lawyers and impartial judges would govern economic and political relationships. For without fixed law "no man [would] ever have either security for his debt or certainty of his cause whatsoever."[5] The rule of law, in the form of adherence to the common law, enabled entrepreneurs to make plans.

Thus, when the advisors who surrounded Charles II on his restoration to the throne in 1660 adopted the approach of using the common law to govern England's colonial empire, that law already was in place in Virginia and Maryland. Both colonies continued to follow it. Virginia courts in the final four decades of the seventeenth century often proclaimed their adherence to English law. They also turned continually to the procedures and vocabulary of the common law. Finally, although there were limits to the willingness of courts to rely on common law technicalities, judges and the lawyers appearing before them routinely cited both English statutes adopted before the settlement of Virginia and other English authorities as bases for decision. As a result, late seventeenth-century Virginians considered themselves entitled to "the benefit of the laws of England."[6]

Maryland likewise aspired to a rule of law based on the common law. To achieve this end, Maryland lawyers and judges quickly developed the habit of raising and ruling on questions of law, recording their rulings for the future, and thereby creating a body of precedent following the common law, as modified by indigenous law. As a result, even when control of Maryland oscillated during the seventeenth and early eighteenth centuries between the initially Catholic heads of the Calvert family, who held Maryland as a proprietary colony, and the Protestant English Crown, which for a quarter century governed it as a royal colony, the common law remained throughout the foundation of the province's legal system. In short, by the beginning of the eighteenth century the legal systems of both Virginia and Maryland were firmly rooted in the common law as that law had been adapted to meet local needs and conditions.

Pennsylvania, Delaware, and New Jersey

Like Maryland and Plymouth before it, Pennsylvania was founded as a refuge for a sect, in this instance the Quakers, that had been persecuted in England. Historians have, to some extent, disagreed about Quaker attitudes toward law. One view is that William Penn, the colony's founder, who had studied at the Inns of Court, discovered the faults of English law, especially the common law, and therefore turned against it. Another view, however, is that although Penn and others were aware of the faults of the common law, their awareness led them not to reject it but to bring it to Pennsylvania in a modified, reformed fashion. Penn and the other founders of Pennsylvania understood that preserving Quaker hegemony was necessary to preserve liberty of conscience, and they saw courts and the rule of law as the means for doing so.

This latter view seems correct. We know that William Penn accepted the ideal of the rule of law as a restraint both on the governed and on the governors. As he wrote in a 1679 broadside in support of Algernon Sydney's campaign for a seat in the House of Commons, the only legitimate "power" of "government" is "a *legal* power . . . : that which is not legal, is a *tyranny*, and not properly a *government*." On a later occasion, he observed that "any government [was] free" only "where the laws rule[d]." Aspects of the common law such as its protection of property and the right to trial by jury were central to Penn's legal and constitutional beliefs.[7]

In any event, Penn and the other founders of Pennsylvania had little choice but to turn to the common law, however much they modified it. Pursuant to its policy of governance through the common law, the Crown granted Penn a charter that required Pennsylvania to adhere to the common law unless and until legislation modified that law, and all legislation had to be submitted to the Privy Council for its approval. The Privy Council, in fact, disallowed a good deal of legislation, much of it because it deviated from the common law; of 114 laws passed in 1700–01, for example, only 105 acts were submitted to the Council and only 50 survived review.

Pennsylvania, in fact, adopted the common law with amazing rapidity. Even before the founding of Philadelphia, the court that had been sitting in the former Swedish settlement of Upland was discharged and a new court constituted in the renamed town of Chester. The new court immediately changed the mode of transacting business by adopting common law forms and procedures. Comparable common law formalism likewise emerged in the mid-1680s in another rural county, Bucks.

Legalism and reception of the common law took a significant step forward with the 1682 founding of Philadelphia, which quickly became a center of commerce and commercial litigation. As early as the mid-1680s, only three years after Philadelphia had been founded, litigants were using common law pleadings, although they did make some errors, and a decade later, under the guidance of trained attorneys, common law pleading had become quite sophisticated.

Pleading practices in Philadelphia quickly spread to the two adjacent rural counties of Bucks and Chester. Of course, lawyers and judges occasionally made mistakes, but on the whole, Pennsylvania lawyers knew by the 1690s how to plead and were expected to plead their cases under the common law's rules. If they did not, they might find their cases thrown out of court. Cases also were dismissed for other procedural defects.

Statutes contributed to Pennsylvania's commitment to common law formalism and the rule of law when in the colony's early years its legislature adopted and published forms for writs of arrest and summons. These forms were important not only because they constituted commands that courts meeting in Philadelphia were required to follow but also because they served as written and readily available mechanisms for transmitting legal knowledge from the capital to the outlying counties. In the absence of legislated forms, the courts in Bucks and Chester might not have known what courts and lawyers in the capital were doing. The published forms made transmission of legal knowledge easy and readily ensured legal uniformity throughout the province. Judges also contributed legislatively to the formalization of law by adopting and publishing rules for the courts' own procedures.

How can we account for this rapid spread of the common law throughout Pennsylvania within a few short years of its settlement? As we have seen, at least part of the explanation was the commitment of William Penn and his followers to adhering to the common law as well as the charter's insistence that the colony do so. The founders of Pennsylvania appear to have understood that legalizing government guaranteed social stability—that is, that the rule of law protects those with wealth, power, and the ability to employ lawyers, at least when the law on which government is based protects property rights, as seventeenth- and eighteenth-century common law in fact did. The rule of law thereby ensures that the families and groups who emerge at the top of a social order at one point in time are likely to remain at or near the top in future times. While the rule of law may not by itself create a hierarchical society, it surely does nothing, at least when grounded in early modern common law, to further egalitarian redistribution.

Like Pennsylvania, both Delaware and much of New Jersey quickly accepted the common law, although resistance to its reception occurred in part of the latter colony. Although an early influx of English settlers in Delaware had resulted in the haphazard introduction of some common law, albeit in an unlearned or, one might say, bastardized form, full-scale adoption occurred only with William Penn's 1682 assumption of jurisdiction. That made the three Delaware counties part of a centralized common law regime dominated by high-court judges and highly trained lawyers operating out of Philadephia. Little change occurred even after Delaware separated from Pennsylvania in 1704.

Reception of the common law in New Jersey was more complicated. Quakers brought common law with them to West Jersey as soon as they settled it in the 1670s. As was seen above, Quakers tended to support the rule of law. They also found the pursuit of worldly goods and property, at least within proper bounds, commendable, and they appreciated the significance of law in protecting property rights. They understood, in turn, that holders of wealth and property enjoyed pivotal influence over the law and that law and wealth, working in conjunction, offered the best guarantee that religious minorities, like themselves, could obtain to protect their religious freedom.

These ideas were reflected in West Jersey's founding document, the Concessions and Agreements of 1677. The Concessions and Agreements provided for the distribution, recordation, and protection of property rights and sought to safeguard law and property by declaring the "fundamental rights and privileges of West New Jersey . . . to be the foundation of the government," which because they had been "individually agreed upon by the proprietors and freeholders thereof" were beyond alteration by legislative authority. The legislature was empowered only "to make such laws as agree with and maintain the said fundamentals" and could "make no laws that in the least contradict, differ or vary from the said fundamentals." In particular, it was "agreed and ordained that no person" should be "in the least punished or hurt, either in person, estate, or privilege, for the sake of his opinion, judgment, faith or worship towards God in matters of religion" and that everyone would be free to enjoy "the exercises of their consciences in matters of religious worship throughout all the said province."[8]

The Concessions and Agreements also required that the law of the new colony "be, as near as may be conveniently, agreeable to the primitive, ancient, and fundamental laws of the nation of England." As a practical matter, this requirement meant little more than that West Jersey would adopt the common law, albeit a modified version written in English rather than Latin and Law French and somewhat simplified to eliminate excessive formalism.[9] Quaker influence also emerged in rules regulating the power of juries. Again, the Concessions and Agreements constitute the starting point. Chapter 17 provided that no one should "be deprived or condemned of life, limb, estate, property or any ways hurt in his . . . privileges . . . without a . . . judgment by twelve good and lawful men of his neighborhood," while chapter 19 declared that judges should "pronounce such judgment as they shall receive from and be directed by the said twelve men, in whom only the judgment resides, and not otherwise." Any contrary judgment would be "held null and void," and anyone giving a contrary judgment would be fined and declared incapable of holding office in the province.[10] Juries in fact were unusually powerful in West Jersey. Some sorts of cases had to be tried by juries, even if both parties agreed otherwise, and other juries exercised equity powers, directing one litigant, for example, to make a conveyance of land.

East Jersey, in contrast, resisted adoption of the common law. When England in 1664 assumed control over what soon became East Jersey, scattered Dutch settlements existed along the west bank of the Hudson River in what had been incorporated in 1661 as the township of Bergen. And, when thirty-two citizens of Bergen took an oath of loyalty to the new English regime, they were permitted to retain their own court, nominate their own magistrates, and most likely govern themselves under some form of Dutch law.

Anxious to attract English settlers, Richard Nicolls, the first governor of New York, who briefly exercised jurisdiction over New Jersey, granted land to Long Island and New England Puritans, who immediately established towns at the sites of modern Elizabeth, Newark, Woodbridge, and other places. A new proprietary governor of East Jersey, Philip Carteret, then authorized these towns to create their own town courts to administer justice among their inhabitants, with the colonial legislature authorizing additional county Courts of Sessions and a colonywide Court of Assizes that functioned from 1675 to 1680.

The oldest records, those of the town of Newark, date back to 1666. These records leave no doubt that Newark's settlers were committed to the establishment of a Puritan regime governed by Puritan law. Only members of the Congregational Church could vote or hold office. The church was supported by taxation, and anyone who did not accept its establishment had to leave the colony. Like the early settlers of Massachusetts Bay, the settlers of Newark required men to come with their families; to receive land, they had to occupy it with their families for two years before they could sell it, and even then, they had to offer it first to the town and then sell it only to buyers of whom the town approved. Like the inhabitants of Southampton on Long Island, the Puritans of Newark agreed to govern themselves through a town court, which tried cases with the assistance of six-man juries and also legislated.

The mechanism for imposing the common law on East Jersey was a new court created by a colonywide legislature in 1683, the Court of Common Right, which, in turn, was assisted by practitioners from New York City. With as broad a jurisdiction as any court in an American colony, the Court of Common Right could adjudicate any criminal case or civil suit, including proceedings in equity, of £5 value or greater, as well as any appeal from lower courts. It was the highest appellate court in East Jersey; no appeal lay to the governor and council, although appeals to the Privy Council in England were allowed. County courts had concurrent original jurisdiction in most cases, although in later years legislation deprived them of jurisdiction over criminal cases involving possible penalties of life or limb.

Use of the common law forms of action was routine in the Court of Common Right. Common law technicalities raised by pleas in abatement and demurrers surfaced, as did special pleading and the occasional return of special verdicts. Counsel also were adept in citing English precedent. At times, however, the court was prepared to excuse technical failings either because of the infancy of the country or because of the want of lawyers.

The new Court of Common Right did not succeed, however, in eliminating fully the vestiges of New England law with which East Jersey had begun its legal existence. One such vestige was the power of juries to determine law as well as fact. The criminal law also retained vestiges of East Jersey's early Puritanism. Perjury committed in a capital case, for example, was itself a capital crime, as it was in Deuteronomy. Buggery and sodomy also were capital offenses, although after 1683 the penalty for sodomy was reduced. Adultery, fornication, bastardy, cursing, and Sabbath breaking were all punished out of a belief that sin "provoke[d] the indignation of God" and thus had to be eradicated.[11]

Although the Court of Common Right administered justice successfully in routine litigation, even in property and commercial cases of considerable complexity, it failed to effectuate proprietary and Crown policies in politically salient cases. The primary issue on which the proprietors sought to enforce their policies was the collection of quit rents on lands they had granted. A key question was how to proceed when rents were not paid. First, the proprietors tried to use writs of scire facias. But they met determined resistance. Major John Berry, who was both a member of the council and a judge of the Court of Common Right, responded to a writ against him with a plea to the court's jurisdiction.

He noted "that the act of the General Assembly which constituted the Court of Common Right was not confirmed by the Lords Proprietors" and that the court therefore had no legal existence.[12] Although Berry's jurisdictional argument had substantial merit, he was promptly fined and required to give a bond for good behavior.

But that did not end the quit rent controversy. Another defendant, Richard Hartshorne, responded that scire facias was not an available remedy because it lay only after a judgment had been obtained or a debt had been acknowledged in a court of record, which was not true in the quit rent cases. Hartshorne's plea was upheld and put an end to the attempt to use scire facias.

Next the proprietors turned to the remedy of distress to collect the rents. *Noews v. Ball*[13] was a replevin suit against a bailiff who pleaded that on behalf of the proprietors, he had distrained ten head of cattle; when the plaintiff replied that he held the land not by virtue of a grant from the proprietors for which quit rents were due but from the Crown directly, the jury returned a verdict in his favor. The bailiff moved to set aside the verdict on the ground that the jury had improperly failed to award damages, but the motion was never decided because the proprietors escalated the controversy by resorting to other remedies.

As *Noews v. Ball* demonstrated, issues of title underlay the quit rent controversy. *Fullerton v. Jones*,[14] decided the day after *Noews*, addressed that issue. Fullerton, who claimed under a grant from the proprietors, brought an ejectment action against Jones, who claimed under a grant from Governor Nicolls, which Nicolls had made prior to the Duke of York's grant of the Jersey proprietorship. It appears that the jury returned a verdict in favor of Jones but that the court set the verdict aside and gave judgment for Fullerton. Jones then appealed to the Privy Council, which reversed and granted judgment to Jones.

The proprietors had one other approach, and here they were initially more successful. In *Hallewood v. Smith*,[15] decided on the same day as *Fullerton*, a jury found that because of a technical defect in the habendum clause of his 1676 deed from the proprietors, the landowner held only a life estate rather than a fee simple. In simplest form, the issue was whether a grant to "A or his heirs" rather than to "A and his heirs" conferred a fee, with the jury ruling that it conferred only a life estate. The proprietors were willing to convert such life estates into fees simple upon payment of quit rents, but the legislature was not. Pursuing a political agenda in opposition to quit rents, the legislature enacted a statute declaring that grants to "A or his heirs" created a fee simple, but the governor vetoed the act as contrary to the laws of England. Nonetheless, the legal battle persisted and the legislature continued to reenact its law until a subsequent governor, near the end of the proprietary period, approved it.

The beginning of the end for both the Court of Common Right and the proprietary government occurred in 1698, when a new governor, Jeremiah Basse, declined to appoint Lewis Morris, a former member of the court and of the council, to either. Morris then questioned the authority of the court, for which he was held in contempt, fined £50, and imprisoned. But with the aid of friends he escaped. Morris thereupon politicized his challenge and called the legitimacy of the entire proprietary regime into question. He argued that because Basse's appointment as governor had never been confirmed by the Crown, neither Basse nor his judicial appointees possessed any authority; in view of the controversies over quit rents and land titles, Morris also declared that proprietary judges were unfit to administer justice since "they are both judge and party." When Morris and others were imprisoned in May 1699 for stirring up opposition, a group of friends again released them, and, when the General Assembly met two days later after an electoral victory by the Morrisites, Morris appeared as a newly elected member in effective control of the assembly's proceedings. Two months later the proprietors offered terms to the Crown on which they would surrender their authority.

In 1702, the two proprietary colonies of East and West Jersey came to an end, to be replaced by a royal colony of New Jersey. In that new colony, the common law quickly became the foundation of legal authority.

The mechanism for imposing the common law was a new Supreme Court, which limited the power of local courts and centralized power in its own hands. As early as 1706, the records of the Supreme Court contain entries of writs of habeas corpus and error as instruments for reviewing lower court judgments. Seven years later the justices of Essex County were arrested for failing to return a writ of certiorari, and cases of removal on certiorari continued thereafter. The Supreme Court and the lower courts, in fact, developed a close interrelationship, as the Supreme Court remanded appealed cases to the lower courts for trial and even sent down cases commenced before it. The judiciary, at least to some degree, also cut back the lawfinding power of juries.

One last gasp of localism in 1716 illustrated the growing power of the central court. In that year, the chief justice of the Supreme Court was indicted in a county court for a judgment he had rendered. The case was immediately brought to the Supreme Court on certiorari, where, on motion of the attorney general, the court, with the chief justice recused, quashed the indictment on the ground that it was the chief justice's duty to issue judgments. The attorney who had been instrumental in procuring the indictment in the lower court was then prosecuted for sowing discord and sedition, and central power was totally vindicated.

The consequence of these assertions of power by judges was that the common law, already fully in place in West Jersey and significantly so in East Jersey in 1702, quickly became the uniform rule throughout the province. Lawyers deployed all the standard writs, and there were pleas in abatement and demurrers both to declarations and to pleas in bar. At least rudimentary special pleading began. The standardized, common law nature of early eighteenth-century practice emerges most clearly perhaps in the use as early as 1718 of prewritten forms with blanks to be filled in by attorneys using them and in 1728, of printed forms with blanks.

Standard criminal and regulatory practices also emerged. On one subject, however, New Jersey did not follow strict common law norms. Perhaps because of the religious origins of West Jersey and many towns in East Jersey, both the legislature and the royal courts of New Jersey often were more solicitous of religious interests and values than comparable institutions in other middle and southern colonies. This solicitude was especially clear as courts addressed issues arising out of the refusal of Quakers to take oaths—a matter on which the legislature intervened by providing that an affirmation by a reputed Quaker would have the same force and effect for all purposes as an oath.

The New Jersey act, however, did not fully resolve the question of Quaker affirmations because Parliament soon thereafter passed an act that allowed Quakers to affirm rather than swear an oath, but it further provided that although such an affirmation would exempt Quakers from criminal liability, it would not permit them to serve on juries. When the Quaker foreman of a 1715 grand jury sought to take an affirmation instead of an oath, the claim was made that the act of Parliament repealed New Jersey legislation and practice. But in an act of great wisdom the Supreme Court held otherwise. It was "of the opinion" that because the "patented copy" of Parliament's act had "not com[e] over from the Secretary of State or any public officer," the court was not bound to take judicial notice of the act so "as to set aside the usages and privileges" of the province. The clerk of the court nonetheless refused to qualify the jury, declaring "that he made as much conscience of keeping the laws of England as they [the Quakers] did of taking an oath." The court thereupon declared him in contempt and directed him to appoint another to act in his stead.[16]

This case makes two central points about New Jersey's legal system in the early eighteenth century. First, the law of England—in particular, the common law—was in force. The justices of the Supreme Court simply were smarter lawyers than the clerk: they never refused to apply English law but did demand that they have properly authenticated notice of it before applying it. Second, they remained free as a result of their intelligent wriggling to continue applying the customary norms of the religiously oriented society they were governing. In short, like many able judges throughout the common law's history, they found a path by which to navigate between the strict requirements of the law, on one hand, and the political and cultural realities of their society, on the other.

New Jersey's courts did the same in regard to Puritanical moral norms. During the early decades of the eighteenth century, New Jersey continued to enforce those norms strictly, as prosecutions were brought for adultery, attempted buggery, profanity, and working on the Sabbath. Above all, there were many prosecutions throughout the colony for fornication, described by one court as "the abhorred and detestable sin of fornication ... committ[ed] to the great displeasure of Almighty God."[17] As a result, at least in connection with the enforcement of morality, New Jersey, which had been settled in part by New Englanders, continued to look somewhat more like New England than did the other middle or southern colonies.

The Carolinas and Georgia

Like New York and Pennsylvania, South Carolina owed its founding as an English colony to changing concepts of empire on the part of Charles II's regime. By the 1660s Virginia and its tobacco had come to possess substantial value to England and to the Crown, and it seemed prudent to establish some sort of outpost between the southern flank of Virginia and the still dangerous Spanish empire in Florida. In March 1663, Charles II accordingly granted a charter making a group of eight highly placed confidants proprietors of a new colony encompassing what is now most of North Carolina, South Carolina, and Georgia. Virginians had already begun settling the northeast corner of the new colony along the Albemarle Sound, and the proprietors immediately directed one of their number, Sir William Berkeley, who was also governor of Virginia, to establish a government for them.

But two efforts to establish settlements farther to the south stalled. Following the two failures, Sir Anthony Ashley Cooper, who as Earl of Shaftesbury subsequently became Charles II's lord high chancellor, assumed management of the proprietorship. With assistance from his personal secretary, John Locke, Lord Ashley made plans for the settlement and government of South Carolina.

As the expedition that ultimately founded Charleston was preparing to set sail from London in 1669, Ashley and Locke were drafting an instrument for South Carolina's permanent governance, the Fundamental Constitutions. Some parts of the instrument had lasting impact, most notably the sections insisting that all subjects worship God publicly but also promising that all dissenters, even slaves, would be tolerated and in no way disturbed in their worship.

But many sections amounted to no more than innovative curiosities. Among them were the provisions creating a neo-feudal polity that balanced the power of an aristocracy that would own 40 percent of the colony's land against the power of the freemen, common people, each of whom would own at least 50 acres of land, by providing that the colony's aristocrats together with elected representatives of the freemen would meet in a unicameral parliament. In it designated agents of the eight proprietors would hold the balance of power between the two groups. Aristocrats also would preside over the colony's judiciary, while the power of the people would be preserved by adherence to the right of trial by jury. The Fundamental Constitutions also introduced a number of other innovations into South Carolina's law, though most of them—like Ashley's neo-feudal plans for a unicameral legislature, which was replaced by a bicameral one in 1691—were inconsistent with economic and political realities and did not long endure. One innovation sought to avoid multiplicity of laws by providing that all legislation would automatically expire one hundred years after its enactment. A second prohibited "all manner of comments and expositions" on the Fundamental Constitutions or any common or statute laws of the colony since such "Comments . . . serve[d] only to obscure and perplex." A third declared that no one could receive any fee or compensation for rendering legal services.[18]

The common law had more lasting significance. It provided a wealth of precedent for regulating South Carolinians' internal relationships and their trade with outsiders, and South Carolinians quickly turned to it. Early judges almost invariably followed English law in their determination of cases; part of the oath taken by members of the council was to "observe . . . the Laws of England,"[19] and an order of the council in 1692 declared that "the measure and rule of Government . . . shall be the Laws of England," where "they can be adapted to the use of this country as it hath been practiced from the beginning of the settlement."[20]

Recourse to English law continued. As South Carolina's chief justice announced from the bench in 1703, "the main body of the English laws, as [the] Common Law, & those statutes that are declarative of [the] Common Law," was "of force in this Province," as were "particular statutes of England . . . made of force, by a particular act of Assembly," which together with "particular acts of this Province make [the] laws thereof."[21] A statute of 1712 was even clearer: it contained a long list of English statutes declared to be of force in South Carolina and further provided that "all and every part of the common law of England, where the same is not . . . inconsistent with the particular Constitutions, Customs and Laws of this Province," was "declared to be in as full force and virtue within this Province" as in England.[22]

Within a few years of South Carolina's settlement, common law courts hearing criminal cases and common law cases under the writ system—a Court of Sessions of the Peace and a Court of Common Pleas—were sitting in Charleston, and in 1712 a separate Court of Chancery was created with power to follow the same rules as the lord chancellor of England.

The arrival of royal government in 1719 did nothing to change South Carolina's internal legal system. On the contrary, the new governors let it develop of its own accord, which was mainly in directions satisfactory to an emerging alliance of royal officials, lawyers, and the wealthy merchants and planters who were their clients. On occasion, though, each of these groups gave developing law a special push, albeit in ways typically consistent with the interests of the others.

Lawyers, for example, pushed pleading in increasingly technical directions. Special pleading, in particular, became a very precise art. Another matter on which change occurred from the 1720s onward was debt collection, a subject of particular interest to wealthy merchants and planters. A huge amount of legal energy was devoted to debt collection, and, as a result, a great deal of highly specialized law emerged. The Crown's main interest in the law was to keep control of the judicial system. Judges accordingly monitored jury fact-finding and began to control the potential power of juries to find law.

The legal system also became a completely centralized one, which, of course, facilitated royal control. All courts sat only in Charleston, where they were subject to oversight by a Court of Chancery, which was put on an explicit statutory footing in 1721 with the governor of the colony himself sitting as the presiding officer. The courts had no power, however, beyond Charleston and its environs.

Founded in the mid-eighteenth century, Georgia, like South Carolina, had principal courts only in Savannah, its capital. There a General Court and a Land Court adjudicated civil cases; a Court of Oyer and Terminer, criminal cases. The governor also presided over a Court of Chancery and a Court of Appeals. Little is known about the procedure of these courts, although there was a requirement that the "rules and practice of the Courts of Westminster Hall . . . be as strictly followed and adhered to as the circumstances will admit."[23] Nonetheless, the courts appear to have had difficulty exercising jurisdiction in distant parts of the colony. Like South Carolina, Georgia did not attempt in mid-century to extend the jurisdiction of its principal courts over any significant geographic area.

North Carolina was quite different from its neighbors to the south. Settled as an offshoot of Virginia, it also differed dramatically from that colony. Unlike South Carolina and Virginia, North Carolina never became one of the jewels of the British empire's North American crown. A major reason is that from the 1720s until the end of the colonial period some courts at various times in much of North Carolina were dysfunctional, in that suitors could not get them to meet and pass judgment, while, at other times and places, suitors could not enforce the judgments they had obtained. Unlike the legal system of South Carolina, which went through the transition from proprietary to royal government without any sharp break and emerged totally intact, the legal system of North Carolina imploded in the 1720s. And it never fully recovered.

Initially North Carolina was a tiny colony centered around the Albemarle Sound. Its colonywide court with common law jurisdiction, the General Court, developed late. Although a 1685 statute provided for separate justices for the General Court, the governor or a deputy acting in his stead continued to preside over it until the early eighteenth century. Only in 1694 were one or two assistants, presumably trained lawyers, added to the court to assist it on technical points; only in 1702 did justices who were separate from the council and lower house of the legislature hold court by themselves. Finally, in 1713 the office of chief justice was created and conferred on Christopher Gale, an able lawyer who held it for nearly two decades. Appeals from the General Court were heard by the governor and council, sitting as the Court of Chancery.

Like South Carolina, North Carolina in 1712 enacted "that the common law is and shall be in force in this Government, except such part . . . [as] cannot be put in execution."[24] This statute merely codified preexisting practice, as the common law already had become the foundation of North Carolina law. As early as the mid-1690s, for example, litigants before the General Court were using common law writs, often correctly. Attorneys for defendants similarly followed common law practice. Many defendants pleaded the general issue properly, and occasional defendants, rather than interposing a general denial, also began to use special pleading to raise specific defenses.

English common law did not, however, always apply; sometimes, the laws and customs of North Carolina governed. Moreover, there were many inexplicable lapses from English practice in the generally sophisticated approach of North Carolina lawyers. The lapses make it plain that North Carolina's legal system differed from its counterpart in South Carolina in its level of professionalization and adherence to English forms. At least on occasion, the North Carolina General Court was willing, whereas the South Carolina Court of Common Pleas was not, to ignore the formal requirements of the common law. Perhaps the judges were not even aware that they were at times violating formal rules; it may be that North Carolina's judges often were left at sea because the North Carolina bar never attained the same professional sophistication that South Carolina's did and thus never possessed the capacity to inform the judiciary of all the law's formal requirements.

An even more important difference between North and South Carolina law occurred in the structure of the judiciary. Until the 1770s, South Carolina had a single court for civil cases that sat only in Charleston and possessed the totality of common law jurisdiction over civil actions other than petty disputes. In North Carolina, in contrast, a series of local courts, known as Precinct Courts, existed beneath the General Court. In addition, the Court of Chancery heard appeals from the General Court without any showing that legal remedies were inadequate or that a matter was otherwise within its jurisdiction.

The broad appellate jurisdiction of the Court of Chancery, without any of the limitations on chancery power usually associated with English law, had two consequences. First, it gave North Carolina a three-level system of courts of general jurisdiction that probably was unique in the British American colonies; no other colony had more than two levels of courts beyond justice of the peace courts with petty jurisdiction. Second, together with the informality tolerated in the General Court and the Precinct Courts, it gave North Carolina a perspective on law totally different from that of South Carolina.

Learned, sophisticated application of English law by a well-educated bench and bar quickly became the norm in South Carolina. It was not the norm in North Carolina. Although North Carolina had adopted the common law, in a sense it had no law; all it possessed was a series of institutions striving to work out governance problems and to hear disputes brought to their attention. The first such institution, not yet discussed, was the jury. Both the General Court and the Precinct Courts sat with juries and relied on them heavily. Judges, even in Chancery, always relied on juries to assess damages, and juries passed on legal issues, such as the validity of service of process, that were more appropriately raised with a court prior to trial.

We must stress, however, that the lawfinding power of North Carolina juries and the freedom from judicial supervision that they enjoyed did not make the colony into a jurisdiction like Massachusetts, where juries applied broadly shared societal norms in adjudicating cases. It is not clear whether such norms existed, even in the tiny colony in the decades around 1700 on the banks of the Albemarle. In any event, North Carolina juries did not have the type of final power that Massachusetts juries routinely wielded; appeals to Chancery, sitting without a jury, were possible and frequent and could result in reconsideration of all aspects of a case. Thus, North Carolina did not offer litigants in its courts a coherent body of law grounded in broadly shared community norms. Rather, it offered a set of dispute-resolving institutions and a hope that as litigants tried different forums they ultimately would find an acceptable one or alternatively exhaust themselves in the process of search.

The availability of appeals to a Court of Chancery which, unlike South Carolina's court, was not bound by the limitations of English equity meant, in short, that North Carolina, as already suggested, had no law beyond the governor's arbitrary will and power. English common law was present in the background, and the General Court, in particular, frequently applied it. Community institutions, perhaps, also applied local norms as a form of popular law. But ultimate authority lay not with juries and local community norms nor with the General Court and the common law, but with the governor and council, who sitting in Chancery could resolve disputes or solve problems however its members thought best. North Carolina law thus had little reach greater than the length of the chancellor's— that is, the governor's—foot, and much depended on the governor's commitment to doing justice rather than promoting idiosyncratic goals or advancing his own self-interest.

Despite the potential for arbitrary gubernatorial lawmaking, North Carolina's three levels of courts functioned effectively into the 1720s, perhaps because the people viewed them as committed to doing justice. Under the leadership of competent and fair-minded governors from 1691 to 1705 and 1712 to 1725, the colony's legal system generally followed the common law and gained some traction, at least within the confines of the small Albemarle region. But then, in the face of political divisions in the late 1720s, North Carolina's judicial system, as will appear in chapter 12, fell apart.

7

The Emergence of the Legal Profession

The legal profession emerged and grew in tandem with the reception of the common law. Development of the common law and of the legal profession were reciprocal. The arrival of lawyers in the American colonies generated support for adoption of the common law, and reception of the common law created a demand for lawyers. The common law and the lawyers who practiced it emerged hand in hand.

By the middle of the eighteenth century, competent practitioners were working in all the colonies, with the possible exception of Georgia. The most distinguished bars functioned in the urban centers of Boston, Charleston, New York, and Philadelphia, although prominent attorneys also practiced in the Chesapeake colonies of Maryland and Virginia.

One of the oldest colonial bars was that of New York. As seen in chapter 4, three lawyers trained at the Inns of Court had arrived in Manhattan along with the English soldiers who landed there in the fall of 1664; the Duke of York appointed them to high office while expecting them to be paid by private clients whom they would influence to obey English law. Also shown in chapter 4, the underlying idea was that government jobs would secure the loyalty of the three attorneys and give them leverage to convince private clients to support government policies; the private clients, in turn, would pay fees to the lawyers and provide them with most of their income. For the regime of Charles II, which had no money to hire either soldiers or bureaucrats, the appointment of lawyers to fill the small number of government posts that in any event had to be filled and the use of those lawyers to inform subjects of the requirements of the law and to obtain their obedience to it was the cheapest way to rule.

At least a few other professionally trained practitioners continued to come to the colony over the next two decades. These lawyers quickly began to practice in New York City, and as early as 1667, the judiciary began policing the bar when the Court of Assizes found one Francis Hall unfit and unqualified to be an attorney. Lawyers who appeared before the court soon possessed considerable sophistication about the rules and procedures of the common law, and representation by counsel with English surnames quickly became the norm in civil cases before the Court of Assizes and the courts of New York City.

In the early eighteenth century the profession in New York continued to move forward. In 1709 the city's lawyers organized North America's first bar association. Next, with judicial sanction, the lawyers developed an apprenticeship system ensuring that students could learn the law in New York rather than at the Inns of Court and hence that the bar could replicate itself domestically. In 1730, eight leading lawyers obtained a monopoly over practice in the Mayor's Court of the City of New York, where most commercial litigation took place. In 1758, the profession attained another milestone, when the Supreme Court came to be composed only of professional lawyers, nearly all of whom had enjoyed long careers in New York. Through the course of these developments, the bar slowly developed a professional solidarity and commitment to the rule of law that enabled its members, at least at times, to transcend the colony's political battles.

In addition, New York's legal profession was learned in what academics today would call political theory as well as legal doctrine. They also were political publicists. James Alexander, for example, publicized the *Zenger* case, while William Smith Jr. wrote a *History of the Province of New York* and, with two colleagues, William Livingston and John Morin Scott, published the *Independent Reflector*, a collection of thoughtful essays. Collectively these lawyers developed and put into print a coherent conception of the place of New York and its lawyers in the British imperial system. More important, the profession's political theory, grounded in a faith that the common law was essential to the preservation of liberty, kept members of the profession who ascended the bench loyal to the local legal community's constitutional values, even when they were politically in disagreement. The New York bench, as a result, was tied intellectually to the New York bar in a fashion familiar to judges and lawyers in England, but unusual in the American colonies, and New York judges often did what the profession understood the law required rather than what the Crown desired. Lawyers of distinction in the immediate Revolutionary era included John Jay, the first chief justice of the United States, and Alexander Hamilton, the first secretary of the treasury.

An equally distinguished bar that dated its origins to the founding of the colony existed in Pennsylvania. The first English-trained lawyer, David Lloyd, settled in Philadelphia in 1686 and began to practice there permanently. Other distinguished lawyers, among them James Logan, soon followed. At least six lawyers practiced in Pennsylvania at one time or another before 1700, and by the first decade of the eighteenth century four attorneys were practicing at the same time.

A key element in the success of Pennsylvania's legal profession was its per-ipatetic nature. The province did not have a series of local bars on a county-by-county basis. Nearly all lawyers were based in Philadelphia and traveled to outlying counties when the courts there were in session. For example, every lawyer who appeared in Chester County courts during the first half century of the county's existence also was a member of the Philadelphia bar. Eight of eleven men appearing in the first six years of litigation in Lancaster were members of the Philadelphia bar and six of those eight, of the Chester bar as well.

Philadelphia's lawyers drew in their professional work on significant collections of lawbooks. For instance, when Ralph Assheton, one of the colony's leading lawyers, died in 1746, he left a library containing some 200 English lawbooks. Moreover, a number of the works in lawyers' libraries were local productions. Philadelphia printer Andrew Bradford, for one, published pamphlets in the early 1720s describing the duties of sheriffs and of justices of the peace, and both pamphlets circulated widely. Lawyers in Pennsylvania also were aided by the ready availability of forms. In 1752, for instance, during the first session of the Court of Common Pleas in Northampton County, located in the upper Delaware Valley, an attorney filed a technically perfect action of debt; twenty-one years later, at the first session of the same court in Bedford County, located in an Appalachian Valley some 200 miles due west of Philadelphia, a young lawyer and future jus-tice of the United States Supreme Court, James Wilson, filed a proper action of assumpsit. They were helped by the legislature's having prescribed the forms of writs by statute; those forms were easily accessible to the bar. The 1752 lawyer in Northampton, for example, arrived in town with a prewritten form for an action of debt, with blanks to be filled in with names, dates, and amounts. The heading on the form read, "Philadelphia County Court June Term 1752." The lawyer simply crossed out "Philadelphia" and "June" and substituted "Northampton" and "September" and filled in the blanks. Two decades later in Bedford, Wilson had a preprinted form and simply filled in the blanks. No wonder they both got it right.

The existence of prewritten forms was not novel, moreover, in the mid-eighteenth century. Such forms already were in use when Lancaster, Pennsylvania's first new county, was established in 1729. Thus, the Chester Court of Common Pleas in 1730 ordered a plaintiff's lawyer to "fill up the blanks in the declaration" by a stated date,[1] and there is a printed form for a power of attorney in the papers of a mid-eighteenth-century lawyer, John Ross. Similarly, in Lancaster itself, the court ordered an attorney in the winter of 1730–31 to "fill up the blanks in his narrative,"[2] while a year earlier a plaintiff creditor had obtained a judgment using a pre-prepared warrant of attorney, in which a borrower at the time he or she took a loan executed a document authorizing an attorney at a later date to con-fess judgment on his or her behalf.

Thus, Pennsylvania's peripatetic bar had all that it needed to develop excellence. It had an urban, commercial base in Philadelphia that produced lucrative litigation for its attorneys. Its lawyers had ready access to printed English books, and its printers provided additional books and highly useful forms. Most important, perhaps, the colony was geographically small; as late as the 1730s it contained only four counties—the original three (Bucks, Chester, and Philadelphia) plus Lancaster. The attorneys could easily travel from one county seat to another. Travel became a habit. Among the great Philadelphia lawyers, Andrew Hamilton came from Maryland, where he had drafted that colony's judicial code, and traveled to New York, where he represented John Peter Zenger; James Wilson traveled in his early practice some 200 miles to the frontier, and John Dickinson, the Philadelphia lawyer who wrote important pre-Revolutionary pamphlets, served as chief executive of both Pennsylvania and Delaware under their first state constitutions, and represented Delaware in the 1787 constitutional convention.

A third urban profession developed around Boston. Unlike the bars of New York and Philadelphia, the Boston bar did not begin to develop until the eighteenth century. During the seventeenth century, Massachusetts had been hostile to lawyers and the legal profession; the 1641 Body of Liberties, for example, had allowed litigants to employ anyone they wished to represent them in court but had prohibited them from giving that representative any fee or other reward. The legal profession was, of course, the victim of this provision; without fees, it could not exist. As a result, the first truly professional lawyer did not develop a practice in the Bay Colony until the eighteenth century, when an immigrant from Connecticut, John Read, who had begun practice in that colony in 1708, later moved to Massachusetts.

Even then, the legal profession in Massachusetts was slow to mature. At least in comparison with such colonies as New York, Pennsylvania, and South Carolina, where technically sophisticated bars developed in the late seventeenth and early eighteenth centuries, the Massachusetts bar lagged. As late as 1740, there were only fifteen trained attorneys in the entire province, located almost entirely in Suffolk, Essex, and Middlesex counties. The first bar association was not founded until 1758 in Suffolk, and as late as the 1760s and 1770s untrained practitioners continued to appear in court.

By the 1740s, however, the Massachusetts bar had developed sufficiently for the courts of New Hampshire to seek its advice. By the middle of the century, Edmund Trowbridge, the greatest colonial lawyer in the province, was working as a litigator to rationalize Massachusetts pleading, and in the pre-Revolutionary decades such astute figures as John Adams, James Otis Jr., and Robert Treat Paine would emerge.

At least three factors contributed to the evolving proficiency of the Massachusetts bar. One was the tradition of learned professionalism centered in the Puritan ministry and cultivated at Harvard College. John Read, for one, began his professional life as a clergyman and then switched to the law, and John Adams, as a young Harvard College graduate, contemplated becoming a minister before turning to law. A second factor was circuit riding: lawyers in Massachusetts traveled around the colony with the judges of the Superior Court and thus spent several months out of every year together in a professional community. Finally, there was the commercial prosperity of Boston, which provided enough litigation to support an elite bar.

The final urban bar, that of Charleston, South Carolina, also emerged late, although not as late as the Massachusetts bar. A lawyer, Stephen Bull, who had practiced in England, was a member of the colony's council in its early years, but the scope of his practice in Charleston is unclear. Only with the arrival of Nicholas Trott in 1699 did a strong legal profession emerge. Over the next two decades, at least seven lawyers practiced in Charleston, and thereafter the number continued to grow. Unlike Boston, New York, and Philadelphia, however, Charleston did not develop its own systematic program of legal education; instead, along with Virginia, it was one of the two colonies that sent the largest number of young men for education to the Inns of Court. As a result, perhaps, of their English training, lawyers in South Carolina had a level of sophistication and technical skill as advanced as any in mainland British North America.

Lawyers trained at the Inns of Court appeared earlier in Virginia than in any other colony. Indeed, Virginia sent more of its sons to study law in the Inns of Court than did any other North American colony—over sixty in all. Edmund Scarborough was one man trained in the Inns of Court who came back to Virginia from London in the mid-seventeenth century. Another English-educated lawyer who came to America a few decades later was Francis Mackemie. But men like Scarborough and Mackemie did not come back to practice law. Scarborough was a gentleman landowner who used his legal education mainly in his service as a county court judge, whereas Mackemie was a Presbyterian minister who used law to promote religious liberty for Protestant dissenters.

In general, the men from Virginia who went to England to study law came home to manage their estates and fortunes, with the result that the structure of legal authority in Virginia was very different from what it was elsewhere. In Massachusetts and Pennsylvania, for example, trained lawyers aware of the work product of their colony's highest court brought their legal knowledge to bear on local judges who were not trained in the law; in Virginia, on the other hand, county benches contained men who had independent knowledge of what the law required. Thus, in Massachusetts and Pennsylvania, lawyers taught law to local courts, whereas in Virginia county courts had sufficient confidence to determine the law by themselves.

The early Virginia bar, in short, was weak compared to local courts. In a colony like Pennsylvania, the bar served as the glue holding the legal system together. In Virginia, in contrast, lawyers who practiced in the General Court were not permitted to practice in county courts, and vice versa, and county court lawyers tended to practice only in their own county and immediately adjacent ones. County courts determined who could practice law before them, and efforts by governors to take control even of initial admissions to local bars failed. Moreover, especially in the early eighteenth century, many Virginia attorneys were comparatively insignificant men: one of them, a man called Jacob Laton, for example, kept a tavern in addition to engaging in some practice of law.

County courts also disciplined lawyers and thereby determined how they could practice. In one case, for example, a court imprisoned a lawyer named Prosser, who had refused to ask leave of the court whether the questions he proposed to ask witnesses might be asked of them, declaring "he would ask what questions he pleased."[3] Local courts also determined such issues as the liability of lawyers for clerks' fees and whether, on the basis of the court's view of the strength of the evidence, attorneys' fees should be awarded in cases won by plaintiffs.

George Eskridge was an early eighteenth-century Virginia lawyer who did devote himself principally to practice. His practice was a lucrative one because as a wealthy gentleman planter he sat on the county bench while at the same time representing litigants appearing before that bench. Eskridge, indeed, provides a perfect example of how the Crown in the early eighteenth century used lawyers in lieu of salaried bureaucrats to govern localities cheaply: his power and prestige as a judge brought him fee-paying clients for whom he negotiated a relationship with law and government. In 1708, however, a litigant did object, claiming that because Eskridge was a justice of the peace and a member of the County Court he ought not be permitted to plead as an attorney before the court. And, eight years later, when Eskridge's commission as a justice was renewed, he declined to serve, alleging that he was a practitioner before the court in cases involving most of the business of the court and was unprepared to give up the income he derived from his practice.

Nonetheless, there were limits to the practice Eskridge could build. He represented only clients in his home county and in immediately adjacent counties, and in view of the prohibition against local attorneys practicing in the General Court, he most likely never appeared before that court in Williamsburg. In short, Virginia's immense size compared to most other colonies, the fact that its General Court did not ride circuit but sat only in Williamsburg and only for a few weeks every year, and the further fact that Williamsburg, unlike Boston,

Charleston, New York, and Philadelphia, was not an important commercial center able to support a thriving legal practice meant that Virginia did not at an early date develop an elite bar based in its capital city as did Massachusetts, New York, Pennsylvania, and South Carolina.

That began to change in the 1760s, when George Wythe, an exceptionally able lawyer who held colonial office and therefore lived in Williamsburg, took on young men and trained them for the profession; Thomas Jefferson and later John Marshall were among his students. The Revolution gave men like Jefferson, Marshall, Patrick Henry, and Edmund Randolph, who might otherwise have remained ordinary, largely unknown gentlemen planters who dabbled in law, a pathway to fame and created what was perhaps an illusion that a brilliant young legal profession existed in Virginia in the 1760s.

Colonial Maryland and Virginia paralleled one another's development in many ways, and the development of their legal professions was no exception. Lawyers had been welcomed in Maryland as soon as the colony had been founded, and the legal profession was quickly established. As early as the 1650s, a man could not act as an attorney unless he could demonstrate his qualifications if they were challenged, and by the 1660s the Provincial Court was formally regulating the admission of attorneys to practice. By 1673, that court had admitted at least fourteen lawyers, two of whom had studied at the Inns of Court. Then in 1674, control over admission was delegated to the county courts, which after 1697 were required to examine applicants to determine the adequacy of their legal knowledge. Along with this growth in the profession came an increase in the number of lawbooks that were available in the colony.

Maryland's legal profession continued to develop in the eighteenth century. At least eleven lawyers who practiced in Maryland before 1730 had studied at the Inns of Court, and for the entire colonial period some thirty-five men associated with Maryland were Inns of Court members. Although it was a small colony, Maryland ranked in the top three, along with South Carolina and Virginia, in the number of practitioners who had obtained legal training in London. It produced some outstanding lawyers, among them Charles Carroll Sr., Charles Carroll Jr., and Daniel Dulany. And, as early as the 1720s, the profession was sufficiently organized so that when the legislature adopted a fee act unacceptable to practitioners, they refused to appear in court to try their cases and eventually secured Lord Baltimore's nullification of the legislation.

Less is known about the development of the profession in the remaining seven colonies. Public prosecutors were appointed as early as the 1660s in Rhode Island and the 1680s in New Hampshire, in the form of an attorney general for the entire colony. With the emergence of public prosecutors, courts also began to appoint counsel to assist defendants being tried for felonies, although in seventeenth-century New Hampshire defense counsel could address only matters of law. Law books also appeared. For example, William Harris, an early Rhode Island attorney, left a library of thirteen law books on his death in 1681. Later, when Newport became the center of practice in the colony, a group of attorneys founded the Redwood Library; its prized possession was Charles Viner's multi-volume *A General Abridgment of Law and Equity*, published in England between 1742 and 1748 and acquired at the substantial cost of £420.

Connecticut similarly developed a competent, skillful profession by the mid-eighteenth century. But Connecticut lacked a dominant political-commercial center in which an elite profession could grow. New Haven and New London were significant port cities but not major centers of transatlantic trade, and the capital was located elsewhere, at Hartford. The profession in the final New England colony, New Hampshire, probably mirrored that of Connecticut. In the absence of a major city, no elite profession arose, although it appears that mid-century lawyers had learned to do their work competently and skillfully.

As we turn farther south, the magnetic character of New York and Philadelphia emerges. Within a few years of the 1682 incorporation of Delaware into Pennsylvania, men denominated as attorneys began to be identified in the court records. Although these attorneys probably lacked formal legal training, they appeared in court with sufficient frequency to learn their art. Moveover, they seem to have enjoyed connections with the professionally astute Pennsylvania bar; at least one of the Delaware attorneys, Griffith Jones, also was identified as a merchant of Philadelphia, and two early Chester County, Pennsylvania, attorneys, Alexander Keith and John Robinson, were also lawyers in New Castle. Even after Delaware's separation from Pennsylvania in 1704, lawyers from Pennsylvania dominated practice in Delaware.

Philadelphia lawyers played a similar role in southern New Jersey. From its early years, the West Jersey colony always had at least one local lawyer, but the work of local lawyers was supplemented by the appearance of Philadelphia attorneys such as David Lloyd. Similarly, in northern New Jersey, New York lawyers seem to have grabbed most of the best cases.

In the Deep South, the picture of professional development is mixed. South Carolina, as already seen, had a distinguished bar. Almost nothing is known about the legal profession of colonial Georgia, and it appears that except for a chief justice who had come from England, no learned lawyers existed in the colony, which had been founded only four decades before the Revolution.

North Carolina likewise does not appear to have had colonial lawyers of the quality, for example, of George Eskridge in Virginia, Edmund Trowbridge in Massachusetts, or Andrew Hamilton in Pennsylvania. Nonetheless, in the second and third decades of the eighteenth century, a competent bar was beginning to develop under the leadership of Chief Justice Christopher Gale. In later years Edward Moseley was an able lawyer who ultimately ascended the bench.

Thus, outside of Georgia, a competent legal profession had emerged in Britain's North American colonies by the mid-eighteenth century, with pockets of distinction in Virginia and Maryland and in major port cities. Development of the legal profession mattered for at least two reasons. First, development of the profession solidified the reception of the common law. The common law was no longer in force simply because a few proprietary magnates like Lord Baltimore and William Penn had decided to adopt it in their colonies or because Crown officials insisted that it be followed. The common law now had an additional and important constituency—lawyers. Lawyers, who had devoted time and energy to learning how to resolve disputes through common law litigation, had a substantial investment that they did not want to jettison. Nor did they wish to turn to some new, perhaps less complicated and less sophisticated dispute-resolution system that others might learn to operate, thereby increasing the competition that lawyers faced in attracting clients.

Second, mid-eighteenth-century lawyers trained in the common law shared a common education, a common vocabulary, a common conceptual apparatus, and in some respects common understandings about how people interact with and relate to each other. The profession thereby became a glue that could hold together the diverse people of all thirteen colonies. It is difficult to imagine how a Puritan minister in the mold of Increase Mather could have cooperated in continental conclaves with the likes of Thomas Jefferson, a deist, or Benjamin Franklin, who had rejected classical Puritan thinking and left the Bay Colony, to develop a common strategy to oppose the Stamp Act and afterward to attain American independence. It mattered that men such as John Adams, John Jay, and Thomas Jefferson had enough in common to work both with each other and with other lawyers in their own colonies—that they all were common lawyers, who shared the language, the conceptual apparatus, and the professional experience of local self-government that the practice of law had taught them. They could strategize with each other about what needed to be done and then explain to others back home why those others should join them in doing it. In the process, lawyers became societal leaders ready to step in and replace British officials when those officials were forced out of the colonies. Lawyers became the closest equivalent in America to a nobility that would never exist.

By the mid-eighteenth century, in short, the common law and the lawyers who practiced it had attained a significant level of societal power that would thrust them into positions of leadership in the new nation that was about to materialize.

Property, Commercial Law, Labor Law, and Slavery

With reception of common law pleading and the emergence of a common law legal profession, substantive common law rules also appeared in Britain's North American colonies. Especially in connection with property and contract law, all of the colonies tended to adopt common law rules. The same was true in regard to the law regulating the employment of servants, although one specially degraded category of servitude—slavery—developed in America despite its lack of precedent in England.

The Law of Property

By the mid-eighteenth century, nearly complete uniformity existed among the colonies in regard to the law of real property. The law everywhere recognized the principle of private ownership of land. But things did not start out that way. As was shown in chapter 1, all land in the earliest colony, Virginia, was owned by the governing entity, the Virginia Company. At the time of its initial settlement in 1620, the Plymouth Colony also practiced communal ownership of land. Both colonies struggled, however, with communal, monopolistic ownership, and in both private property ultimately emerged.

In other colonies, private ownership occurred without much thought. In one colony, Pennsylvania, and perhaps a second, Maryland, private ownership of land was an important element in the founding proprietor's constitutive plans. William Penn, the founder of Pennsylvania, was a strong believer in property rights, and within the first year of the colony's existence he conferred vast property holdings—some 875,000 acres—on his mostly Quaker followers. These holdings quickly became valuable. Even though the Quakers became a minority as people of other religions and of non-English ethnicity settled in Pennsylvania, the Quakers' land and wealth guaranteed that they would constitute much of the leadership of Pennsylvania and would therefore retain significant power in the province as long as their land and wealth were secure. Their power, in turn, would protect their religious freedom.

Lord Baltimore, the proprietor of Maryland, likewise may have understood the connection between land ownership and religious freedom when he founded Maryland as a refuge for Roman Catholics half a century earlier. Like Penn, Baltimore conferred large tracts of land on early Catholic settlers. And, over time, Catholics' resulting power over Maryland's economy protected them from the whims of what quickly emerged as a Protestant majority.

In any event, long before the eighteenth century, private property was the norm everywhere in British North America. Everyone agreed that government necessarily had to "depend . . . upon its natural bottom of property" because a man could have the independence required to participate in the politics of a free state only when his economic well-being was firmly protected by law.[1] But, at the same time, an equally fundamental countervailing principle, still central to American law today, provided that private ownership was subject to regulation in the public interest as well as to a variety of public practices, stimuli, and procedures that aimed at promoting community development. As chapter 10 will suggest, this countervailing principle was grounded in communitarian concepts of Christian brotherhood that lay at the root of colonial Protestant religiosity.

Thus, property owners were not permitted to use land in a fashion that threatened harm to the public or reduction of the public's rights. Urban landowners, for example, were required to obey restrictions designed to prevent fires, such as having their chimneys periodically inspected and swept. They also were required to maintain their buildings so that they would not become dilapidated or in danger of collapse. Rural landowners had to maintain fences, and owners of dams had to maintain sluiceways so that fish could pass upstream. A landowner in North Carolina had to obtain permission before he could construct a drain, and Maryland witnessed a unique case that today would be labeled an environmental protection suit involving a criminal prosecution for dumping ballast into a river.

Private rights of other sorts were similarly regulated to protect the public interest. In Massachusetts, for example, courts regulated ferry rates, safety, and service, even to the extent of requiring a ferryman to be polite to his passengers and to obtain judicial approval before discontinuing service for lack of passengers. They also required holders of liquor licenses to maintain their premises in such a fashion as not to impair public morals. Other colonies had similar rules. Other practices, however, were more unusual. County courts in Virginia, for instance, had jurisdiction to approve the amount of rent charged for leases, while magistrates in New York City had the unusual duty of regulating use of public wells.

Colonial judges, as will be seen in chapter 11, also assumed vast powers to promote development of local economies. Private enterprise was thus at the core of the colonial American economy, but entrepreneurs everywhere were regulated and also granted economic assistance by government to ensure that their property was used for the public good.

By the mid-eighteenth century other elements of the common law of property likewise were in place. Every colony, for example, followed the common law doctrine of estates, including the common law fee tail and the use of common recoveries as the means for docking fees tail. There was only one important matter on which there was divergence—the law of intestate succession. Most colonies south of New England adopted the common law rule of primogeniture, under which the eldest son of a landowner who died without a will inherited all of that owner's land. Connecticut, Massachusetts, New Hampshire, and Pennsylvania, in contrast, adopted the biblical rule that divided land equally among all children, except that an eldest son received a double portion. Rhode Island followed the biblical rule until 1730, when, under a concern that the Privy Council might nullify the rule, the colony repealed its legislation and thereby left town probate judges without any statutory direction as to what rule they should follow.

At first, the Crown sought to impose primogeniture everywhere. In the 1727/ 28 case of *Winthrop v. Lechmere*,[2] which arose out of Connecticut, the Privy Council adhered to the policies of the earlier Stuart era and attempted to impose the common law in its entirety. Like Massachusetts, Connecticut had adopted the Old Testament inheritance scheme under a 1699 statute that copied a 1692 statute of Massachusetts. When Wait Winthrop, the grandson of John Winthrop, died intestate in 1717, the Connecticut statute was called into question. Winthrop left two children, a son named John and a daughter married to one Thomas Lechmere. At common law, John inherited all of his father's land, but under Connecticut law his sister inherited a third. Lechmere brought suit against Winthrop on his wife's behalf. Court proceedings continued in Connecticut for nearly a decade, with Lechmere the ultimate victor and Winthrop taking an appeal to the Privy Council.

In *Winthrop v. Lechmere*, the Privy Council reversed the Connecticut judgment and declared the 1699 act null and void as repugnant to the laws of England. Connecticut thereupon commenced a lengthy campaign to obtain either an act of Parliament or a Privy Council declaration recognizing titles that had already passed under the 1699 act and authorizing Connecticut, except in the case of *Winthrop v. Lechmere* itself, to continue enforcing the 1699 act. Connecticut's campaign made little progress, but the colony nonetheless continued to administer estates under the 1699 act.

Meanwhile a somewhat analogous case, *Sabere v. Sabere*, was being heard in Rhode Island, which had rejected the common law rule that joint tenants take from each other by right of survivorship and instead granted partition of joint tenancies at the request of one of the heirs. Because partition had been the "custom" of Rhode Island "from time out of mind," partition, in the words of the Rhode Island Superior Court, had "become equal to a common law and . . . the only safeguard against an inexpressable confusion threatened by putting in force" the common law right of survivorship. The Privy Council, however, rejected the concept that a local custom could be equal to the common law, reversed the Rhode Island decision, and imposed the common law rule.

The next event in the saga was the case of *Philips v. Savage*, which challenged the validity of the 1692 Massachusetts intestacy act from which Connecticut's 1699 act had been copied. The lawyers for Massachusetts argued the *Philips* case before the Privy Council more effectively than Lechmere's lawyers had argued *Winthrop v. Lechmere*; they emphasized that innumerable titles that stemmed from intestate distributions under the 1692 statute would be cast into doubt if the statute were invalidated and that younger sons who received no land from their parents had far fewer economic options in America than did younger sons in England. In addition, there was a key distinction between the *Philips* and *Winthrop* cases, in that the 1692 Massachusetts statute had received confirmation from the Privy Council following its enactment, whereas the 1699 Connecticut statute had not. Without clearly specifying its reasoning, the Privy Council apparently accepted the arguments of the Massachusetts lawyers and in 1737/38 upheld the 1692 Massachusetts act.

While *Philips* was pending, the Connecticut Superior Court in March 1732/33 decided another case, *Clark v. Tousey*, in which it also upheld the 1699 act. The loser in that case appealed to the Privy Council, but he did not prosecute his appeal diligently, with the result that the Privy Council did not render judgment until 1745—a judgment that affirmed the 1732/33 Connecticut Superior Court decision. Again, the Privy Council did not specify its reasoning, and thus it was not clear whether the council had affirmed the Connecticut judgment on the merits or dismissed the appeal for want of prosecution. Connecticut treated the decision as one on the merits, especially after the Board of Trade decided in March, 1747/48 not to challenge New Hampshire legislation departing from common law rules of inheritance. Puritan law, as a result, remained in place not only in Massachusetts pursuant to *Philips v. Savage*, but in the rest of New England as well.

Divergence in regard to the law of intestate succession was far less significant, however, than a rule of English law that every colony accepted—namely, that a landowner could dispose of his or her property at death by making a will directing the desired disposition, subject only to appropriate provision for a surviving spouse. Spousal relations in regard to property also were uniform throughout the colonies. The law of coverture was in effect in every colony, as were the rules of dower for widows and curtesy for widowers.

The Law of Contract and of Debtor-Creditor

The same policies of a regulated free market, of subsidization of economic activity, and of protection of society's most disadvantaged were in place by the mid-eighteenth century in connection with contract law and debtor-creditor law. Liberty of contract was the foundational principle. Entrepreneurs were free to make whatever bargains they wanted to make and were not bound by obligations that they had not freely and willingly made. But the law did intervene to prevent fraud and overreaching, to uphold the moral norms of the community, and to protect those left destitute through no fault of their own. Consider, for example, the common law rule making infancy a defense in contract litigation. On the presumption that youths were unable to make rational business judgments and thus were in danger of being defrauded and overreached, the law permitted anyone to disclaim a contract that he or she had made before attaining the age of twenty-one. Servants and slaves likewise could not be bound by contracts unless their masters had explicitly authorized them to enter the marketplace; the concern here was that they might sell their masters' property or otherwise bind their masters to liability.

The law of coverture similarly disabled married women from entering into contracts. Perhaps, the law of coverture rested on a presumption that women, like minors, were unable to make rational business judgments. But that seems unlikely. Single women and widows were deemed sufficiently competent to bind themselves by contract, and, as Cornelia Dayton has demonstrated, mid-eighteenth-century wives engaged in extensive and profitable economic activity. Rather, as Dayton suggests, coverture may have received continuing legitimation from an emerging sexist ethic of gentility, respectability, and refinement that steered women into restricted roles—as moral educators, consumers of luxury goods, and mistresses of what Dayton calls the rituals of the table and the garden—rather than unleash them into the bustling world of competitive enterprise.

Like the law of property, the law of contract also recognized the importance of government subvention and stimulation of economic activity. Money is the lifeblood of commerce, and Parliament, recognizing that fact, enacted legislation in 1704 making promissory notes negotiable throughout the empire. The 1704 legislation transformed those notes into a colonial money supply. The capacity to borrow money and thereby import capital from England was equally important to colonial economies.

But borrowed money had to be repaid. Everyone understood that if creditors faced undue difficulty in collecting their debts, "prudent m[e]n" would become "very averse from giving credit," which would "prove very inconvenient to trade."[3] Thus, eighteenth-century courts specialized in debt collection proceedings. In one Connecticut county, for instance, debt collection suits constituted some 80 percent of all litigation during the decade of the 1740s and involved the vast majority of men, who appeared either as plaintiffs or as defendants. Percentages such as these were typical of mid-eighteenth-century litigation in other colonies as well.

Another way in which judges promoted trade and commerce was by exercising jurisdiction to establish and maintain facilities for processing local products, such as tobacco, and by engaging in inspection of those products to assure buyers in distant markets that the products were of acceptable quality. As it promoted trade and commerce and helped to secure the repayment of debts, the legal system also tried to ensure that debtors who suffered insolvency through no fault of their own would remain able to earn a living and thereby avoid becoming burdensome to their local economy. Every colony accordingly enacted debt-relief legislation, including insolvency legislation under which debtors who delivered up all their property could obtain release from debtors' prison. Much debt-relief legislation, however, was disallowed by the Privy Council.

The Law of Labor and Slavery

Labor law and the law of slavery were yet other matters on which the thirteen colonies had much in common. Much harshness occurred everywhere in the treatment of indentured servants and slaves. Servants who ran away, for example, were required upon recapture to serve extra time to compensate their masters for the loss of their labor—often a considerable amount of time, say six months, for only a brief absence, say eleven days. Extra time was also required of female servants who gave birth to illegitimate children.

The treatment of slaves was even worse. Slaves guilty of crimes against whites received especially severe treatment. In South Carolina, for example, any homicide by an enslaved person, except by accident or in defense of his or her owner, was punished by death, as was the burning not only of houses but even of naval stores, stacks of grain, or any other commodity or produce of the colony. Runaways were especially brutalized: one runaway slave who ostensibly could not be deterred by lesser methods of punishment was castrated. In addition, slaves lacked the protection of the law, in that whites charged with murdering them invariably avoided the death penalty when juries, rather than sentence the whites to death, found them not guilty.

Despite the harshness of slavery and other forms of servitude, all the colonies nonetheless strove to make the two practices as fair as possible. Blacks held in slavery brought many suits for freedom in the mid-eighteenth century and often won those suits. Indeed, in one North Carolina case, the court even appointed an attorney to represent a slave suing for freedom, although in that particular case the court ultimately denied the enslaved plaintiff relief on the merits. Servants also brought suits for freedom, often with success. Yet another path to freedom for slaves was manumission. Other rules throughout the colonies sought to prevent masters from mistreating or excessively exploiting servants and slaves. As early as 1719, the Philadelphia Yearly Meeting urged Quakers to treat enslaved people "with humanity and in a Christian manner."[4] There were prosecutions of masters, with some resulting in convictions, for what one Connecticut court called "an immoderate and extravagant degree of correction"[5] and what the South Carolina legislature called "too great rigor and cruelty."[6] In Virginia, anyone wishing to punish slaves with more than a whipping was required to obtain judicial approval, and even in the Carolinas enslaved people were entitled to a day of rest on the Sabbath. Masters were also required to provide their servants and slaves with suitable meat, drink, lodging, and apparel.

Despite some similarities, however, the law of slavery differed profoundly from colony to colony. According to Daniel Dulany, who wrote in 1767, "the condition of slaves in the different colonies [was] considered on various principles, established either by peculiar local laws, or dictated by the diverse genius and situation of the people."[7]

The law of slavery in South Carolina, one of the two major centers of southern slavery, was related to the colony's two eighteenth-century exports. Few Africans were enslaved in South Carolina's early years. The original plan for South Carolina was to have family farms produce foodstuffs that could be traded to West Indian planters to feed their slaves. By 1674, only four years after Charleston was founded, South Carolina had a good harvest and export of food began. Meanwhile, a treaty with the Westo Indians led to the development of two additional exports, captured Native Americans and deerskins, which Charleston merchants could sell abroad at large profits.

The Westoes were a large Native American tribe at war with many smaller tribes allied with Spain, and they often captured their enemies. Charleston merchants willingly bought the Westoes' captives in exchange for cloth, rum, and especially guns, which would facilitate the capture of even more enemies. The merchants also negotiated trade alliances with other tribes, resulting in the acquisition of even more captives. Although South Carolinians enslaved some of these captives, most were sent overseas, mainly to West Indian sugar plantations. Trade in Native American captives quickly reached commercial proportions, becoming the first profitable branch of the southern Indian trade.

The other profitable branch, which took slightly longer to develop, was trade in deerskins. Vast herds of deer populated what is now the southeast United States and by the end of the seventeenth century Charleston was exporting an average of over 50,000 deerskins annually. In the early decades of its settlement, South Carolina owed its subsistence to the Indian trade, which was the first big business in the South. But South Carolinians did not employ African slaves in their businesses.

Only after 1700, when South Carolina developed a plantation economy based on rice and indigo, did African slaves become necessary. White Europeans never provided the exhausting, often deadly physical labor needed on South Carolina's plantations. As a result, these eighteenth-century plantations were unlike the family farms of New England and the Middle Colonies or the tobacco plantations of the Chesapeake. They were not homes to leading colonial families or even to leading families of localities. Instead, they were factories of sorts, populated almost entirely by black slaves and a handful of white overseer-managers, engaged in highly specialized production of goods for the Atlantic market. Often, the plantations were parts of tightly integrated commercial enterprises, owned and controlled by entrepreneurs who lived in Charleston, its immediate suburbs, or, at times, even London. Like many other absentee owners, the owners of South Carolina's plantations, who had little if any contact with their enslaved laborers, viciously exploited and repressed them.

In Virginia, the first mainland colony in which slavery developed, slavery grew out of the colony's pattern of land ownership. Tobacco, which was Virginia's main export, is a crop that quickly exhausts the soil, and thus, if planters wanted to enjoy long-term success, they needed power in government to secure periodic land grants. Planters who possessed such power used it, however, not merely to maintain their existing plantations but to obtain ever-increasing grants, with the result that by the second half of the seventeenth century a small number of planters held title to most of the best land in the colony.

This unequal distribution of land, in turn, produced a weak, unstable legal order. Rapid immigration by whites lay at the root of the instability; Virginia's planters needed laborers, mainly in the form of young, mostly male, indentured servants, for the economy to grow and prosper. But because the great planters tended to monopolize ownership of land, the colony proved unable to absorb those newcomers as landowners after their period of servitude was completed. Instead, the freed laborers grew into a landless, sullen, and unruly lot that in 1676 turned to open rebellion under the leadership of Nathaniel Bacon. When their rebellion failed, Virginia's existing pattern of land distribution was solidified.

The result was that colonies other than Virginia, where land was available to indentured servants who had completed their term of servitude, became more attractive destinations than Virginia for young people emigrating from England to America. The pace of white immigration to Virginia slowed.

Virginia's planters nonetheless needed workers, and they began to import black slaves to replace the white immigrants they could no longer obtain. Before the late seventeenth century, slavery was economically and culturally unimportant in Virginia; in 1660, Africans and descendants of Africans constituted only some 3 percent of the population—fewer than 1,000 blacks out of a total population of roughly 25,000. During that decade, however, slavery developed in Virginia as a clear legal category. The key to its development was a series of statutes that first differentiated slaves from non-slaves along racial lines. The first, in March 1660/61, recognized that runaway "Negroes" who already were condemned to serve for life were "incapable of making satisfaction by addition of time" and accordingly required white servants who ran away with them to serve their time.[8] The recognition also led several years later to another act allowing masters to inflict corporal punishment on runaways. A year earlier, when doubts had arisen whether baptism made free a person now described as a slave, the legislature responded by declaring that it did not alter the condition of a person as to his bondage or freedom. The decline into slavery continued in 1669 when a statute provided that a master would not be guilty of murder if an enslaved person who was resisting punishment from his master died as a result of the extremity of the punishment, for it was presumed that no one would destroy his own property. The next year a statute barred free blacks from purchasing Christian servants, and a decade later the first act for preventing slave insurrections prohibited blacks from carrying guns or other weapons and from meeting together under pretense of feasts or burials.

Even by the 1680s, however, slavery had not replaced indentured servitude as the principal form of plantation labor; planters continued to rely mainly on indentured servants. Only after 1690 did Africans and their descendants become the primary providers of plantation labor, although even then it was not clear that all black servants were slaves. Indeed, as late as the 1740s, a runaway black was dealt with as a servant when he was required to serve extra time for running away—a penalty that made no sense if he was a slave already required to serve for life.

Once slavery was established, the status of slaves in the South sank markedly. It was easier for masters to exploit slaves than it had been to exploit indentured servants, who could send reports of mistreatment back to England. White fears of slave rebellion produced added patterns of repression. Below the Mason-Dixon line, enslaved people were treated as less than human—simply as chattels "on the same footing," according to Daniel Dulany, "with a mare or a cow."

The law was especially harsh in connection with sexuality. Although, as Dulany recognized, the "propensions" of slaves in regard to sex were "as ardent and irresistible as those of others," slaves throughout the South as a general rule could not marry. Thus, an enslaved person could not "maintain[] an action against the violator of his bed." Slaves, like horses and cattle, also could not be "admonished for incontinence, or punished for fornication or adultery."[9]

In New England, in contrast, slaves typically were treated as people who possessed legal rights, although they also suffered under unique legal disabilities. Except in Rhode Island, slaves were not numerous, and hence there was little fear of rebellion. Meanwhile, the Puritan tradition kept them from being excessively exploited. Thus, in Massachusetts the law recognized that people of African descent were human beings and entitled to be regarded as people, whether as saints or sinners. For instance, when two black slaves not married to each other and owned by different masters had intercourse with each other, they each received fifteen lashes for fornication—the "heinous crime against the light of nature [and] the law of God & man . . . which too much abounds among us."[10] Blacks, that is, were treated in the same fashion as whites, except that, because they had no wealth, they could not be fined or made liable to support their child. Instead, their two masters were charged with support of the child resulting from the relationship, and, in return, each owner received a one-half interest in the child's future labor.

Punishing slaves for fornication raised a question, however, about the circumstances under which they could engage in their normal "propensions" for sexual activity. In particular, could enslaved people marry? In a key Massachusetts case, two black slaves owned by two different masters who wished to marry each other were permitted to do so; in the court's understanding, they were people who should "be not denied marriage provided [they] attended the directions of the law."[11] Similarly, when a white man in Massachusetts attempted to rape a black woman, the woman's humanity was recognized: he received a significant fine and was required to post a good behavior bond, just as if he had attempted to rape a white woman.

In New England, in short, slaves had some right to family life; in the South, they did not. Another important difference between North and South was in the law of debt. The structure of Virginia's economy and of the law undergirding that economy made slavery in Virginia particularly unjust and inhumane. Virginia law stood directly in the path of anyone treating slaves as human; they were merely assets that, in addition to performing labor, served as collateral for the payment of debts. Slaves were the principal assets against which Virginia planters borrowed, and judges, as shown above, were clear that debts had to be paid.

Hughlett v. Schreever,[12] a suit by an administratrix against a defendant claiming under a decedent's will, illustrates the inhumanity that the law of slavery made inevitable in Virginia. The decedent had owned four slaves whom his will gave to his subsequently deceased daughter, through whom the defendant Schreever, in turn, claimed. Perhaps the goal of the bequest was to keep the slaves together within the daughter's family and thereby preserve ongoing human relationships. In any event, when the daughter died, Schreever took possession of the slaves and kept them together. The court, however, was concerned, as it had to be if Virginians were to continue borrowing money, about the "just rights and dues" of creditors and "that the debts" of the decedent "ought to be satisfied before any legacies." Accordingly, it ordered that the administratrix be given possession of "the whole personal estate" of the decedent "as well Negroes as other his said estate of what nature or condition soever." The administratrix could then sell the slaves and thereby convert them and other property of the decedent into cash that creditors could accept to satisfy debts. And, if she failed to do so, the slaves could be attached and sold by the sheriff to pay off the debts.

The same preference for the rights and dues of creditors and the satisfaction of debts applied even while debtors were alive. Masters might try during their lifetimes to treat enslaved people decently and kindly, but it was more important that the masters earn enough money to repay whatever debts they had accumulated and to keep from borrowing more. If meeting their obligations meant that they had to work slaves harder, they had little choice. If it meant selling a few slaves and breaking up slave families and communities, they also had little choice. Perhaps slaveowners who had good relationships with their creditors could make promises for the future and thereby postpone the day of reckoning. But ultimately, if planters failed to use their slave property to satisfy the claims of creditors, their slaves could be attached by the sheriff and sold at auction to pay off debts even while the original borrower remained alive.

Even in the administration of solvent estates, slave relationships were likely to be broken up after a slaveowner's death to satisfy the claims of various heirs. Law in the South, in short, rendered all slave relationships precarious. Whatever masters may have done, the law and the underlying economy did not treat enslaved people as humans but as fungible property convertible into cash. The law said they were property—"considered no otherwise than horses or cattle"[13] —and the British merchants who lent money to Virginia planters thought of slaves, who were people the merchants never met, as cash equivalents for securing their debt. In the perspective of merchants, enslaved people were mere capital in an impersonal marketplace established to satisfy Europe's demand for tobacco.

New England again was different. A Connecticut court, for example, recognized the humanity of people of African descent by holding that, unlike chattels, they were not proper security for informal book debts. Even more to the point was a verdict of a Massachusetts jury refusing to permit a creditor to attach a "Negro man" for his master's debt.[14] Perhaps this verdict reflected a general rule in seventeenth-century New England that slaves could not be seized and sold by creditors to assure repayment of debts. If so, the rule was reversed by Parliament's act of 1732 allowing creditors to sell enslaved people in payment of judgments obtained against their debtors, and at least one subsequent Connecticut case did uphold a creditor's taking and sale "by virtue of [a writ of] ... execution ... of [a] ... Negro girl in common form of law."[15] But it is impossible to be certain how thoroughly New England juries enforced Parliament's statute and thus whether the process of seizure and sale of slaves for debt became as routine and automatic in New England after 1732 as it was in the South.

A third important difference between North and South was in criminal procedure. Slaves accused of crime in the South did not receive a jury trial but were tried before local magistrates who sat without the presence of a petit jury and did not require the indictment of a grand jury to proceed to trial. Slaves were also prosecuted and punished for offenses of which only they could be guilty, such as verbal abuse of a white man. In the South, enslaved people could not testify against whites but only against other slaves.

In the North, by contrast, enslaved people accused of crime received the same sort of trial as did white defendants. Thus, when an African American named James was charged with murder for running down a three-year-old with a cart, he was tried by a Massachusetts jury and acquitted. Another example of fairness and equality occurred in a case charging a master with cruelty to "his Negro woman" in which another Massachusetts jury found the master guilty. Even major cases involving large groups of African American defendants in the North received jury trials: thus a series of prosecutions arising out of an alleged slave conspiracy in New York City in 1741 was commenced by grand jury indictments and tried by petit juries. Although thirty-four of the accused conspirators were found guilty and executed and another eighty-six were exiled, thirty-four others were acquitted.

Colony v. Barney[16] is yet another example of the more humane, more egalitarian nature of northern slavery in comparison with southern slavery. Barney, a teenage slave, was prosecuted for castrating Thomas Allyn, the six-year-old son of Barney's master. Although Barney pleaded guilty, the court had difficulty with the case and postponed sentencing Barney until the next court term. The difficulty was that "no special provision [existed] in any law of this Colony for the punishment of such crimes," and earlier cases left doubt whether a defendant could be punished in the absence of an explicit statute. The Superior Court accordingly sought the guidance of the General Assembly, which ordered that Barney spend one hour on the gallows with a rope around his neck, be severely whipped, and then be castrated.

What is striking about Barney's case is that the law dealt with him as it would have dealt with a white man. He was not executed or castrated through any form of vigilante justice, as a slave might have been in a colony farther to the south. Indeed, although his crime posed a serious, or at least symbolic, threat to white male supremacy, he was not executed. To the contrary, the court applied the same forms of law to an African American slave that it would have applied to a free white Englishman.

The most striking difference between North and South was the effort on the part of Pennsylvania's Quakers to abolish first the slave trade and ultimately slavery itself. The effort went back to the Philadelphia Yearly Meeting of 1719, which urged Quakers not to participate in the slave trade. The movement to ameliorate the condition of slaves then progressed toward abolition, with the result that Pennsylvania Quakers manumitted a significant number of slaves before the War of Independence. But just as benevolence toward servants was balanced with strict discipline, freedom for slaves was balanced with protection for the community. Anyone who manumitted an enslaved person was required to give a bond to the town or county of the slave's residence protecting the locality against any expenses caused by the freed slave's sickness or otherwise. If the bond proved inadequate to support freed slaves and they proved unable to support themselves, their former master or his heirs became liable to provide support and then could seek judicial authorization to re-enslave them.

Moreover, even after they were freed, blacks were not equal citizens. One "free Negro," for example, who "unfortunately [had] married a bad woman," went to jail for "express[ing] some harsh words against her" and was freed only on the undertaking of a white man that the black man would not be "further troublesome" to the community.[17] White men who beat their wives, by contrast, would be required only to give peace bonds and guarantees of support for their wives; no one ever required them not to be troublesome to the community because they *were* the community.

Blacks were not. It is essential at this point to be clear. The cases just discussed do not establish that northern blacks were, in general, treated as the equals of whites. Blacks and whites were not equal anywhere in Britain's North American colonies in the mid-eighteenth century. My claim is not about equality but about something different. The claim is that slavery in the colonial South was so entrenched in the South's economy and society that it could not be abolished after American independence had been achieved without a radical transformation of southern society. In the North, on the other hand, colonial slavery was not vastly different from the unequal, racist legal system of the pre–Civil War era that replaced it. The economy of the North, the structures of capital formation and debt in the North, and the policing of the northern social order did not require the maintenance of slavery in a legal form, although it did demand the continuance of racial discrimination.

In short, the colonial law of slavery created a foundation on which later generations would construct competing legal superstructures for race relations, one in the North and a different one in the South, that ultimately would lead to civil war.

PART III

ALTERING EMPIRE TO DEFEAT FRANCE 1689–1750

The Local Structure of Power

When the Glorious Revolution placed William III and his wife Mary on the throne of England in 1688, changes occurred in English colonial policy. However, full appreciation of the nature of those changes requires that the accession of William and Mary be understood not simply in the context of colonial law and policy but in a larger context of European diplomacy and English domestic politics.

Charles II and James II, as was discussed in chapter 4, both strove to strengthen the power of monarchy and wipe out the vestiges of republicanism remaining in England and its colonies in the aftermath of the English Civil War. James, in particular, set out to transform England and its empire into an absolutist, rational Catholic state with power centralized in the king—a state modeled on the French regime of Louis XIV. To achieve this end, he and Charles endeavored to impose the common law throughout the empire and to use lawyers to govern its colonies. In the years before 1689 the Crown directed the imposition of the same royal policies everywhere, especially in New England, as it tried to obtain centralized control. Under Charles II and James II, the Crown demanded the replacement of Puritan law by common law in New England, sent a royal official to enforce the Navigation Acts, and even sent a small number of regular troops as an occupation army to New York and to help suppress Bacon's Rebellion in Virginia.

Meanwhile, in the Dutch republic, politics was taking a different course. The republic had named William of Orange its stadtholder in 1672, when it was under attack on all sides by Catholics, especially by Louis XIV, who threatened the very existence of the republic and its Protestant religion. For the next two decades in the Netherlands, William, unlike Charles II and James II, did not work to enhance his own quasi-monarchical power. On the contrary, he used the stadtholder's office to inspire the people of the Netherlands, the people of other Protestant states, and the leaders of Catholic states bordering on France to join a coalition to contain Louis XIV's territorial ambitions. By the time William III died in 1702, his accession to the English throne and the emergence of England as the leading member of the coalition seeking containment of France—a pattern of British leadership that remained in place after William's death—had put an end to French expansionism and had laid the foundations for British world hegemony that first appeared in the War of Spanish Succession and fully emerged in the Seven Years' War. By harnessing British power, William III thus accomplished the goals to which he had aimed in 1672—the defeat of Louis XIV's bid for what William called "universal monarchy,"[1] the preservation of Dutch and more generally European independence, and the safety of Protestantism. Upon assuming the English throne, William III reversed important domestic and colonial practices of Charles II and James II in a fashion consistent with and in some cases necessary to building the grand anti-French coalition that he was working to establish.

First, William ended what had been nearly a century of conflict between the king and Parliament. Intent on uniting the nation behind his war policies, William abandoned the efforts of Charles II and James II to strengthen the monarchy's authority and to wipe out alternative sources of power in English society. William, Queen Anne, and the early Georges instead allied themselves with powerful pro-Protestant forces in English society, as they were mirrored in Parliament, and pursued policies for which they and their allies in Parliament could generate widespread political support. The monarchy began to work with rather than against the legislature. William and his successors thereby solidified the monarchy, but in a constitutional, almost republican form. Within decades, ultimate power in England lay not with the king but in Parliament.

In the colonies, William III similarly abandoned the efforts of Charles II and James II to strengthen the monarchy's central authority and to wipe out alternative sources of power. A key element in the strategy of William III and the parliamentary forces supporting his anti-French policies was to bind together the disparate entities that still existed in the British Isles and in England's overseas colonies. The seventy-five years of intermittent war between Britain and France that began in 1688 had that effect. The years of war produced a maturation of British nationalism, resulting in an ideology that united most people in the British empire in a belief that they enjoyed a liberty and well-being unique to them among all the peoples of the European world.

The British, as they saw it, enjoyed liberty and self-government whereas the French lived under arbitrary, hierarchical rule. For decades to come, British writers elaborated how a prosperous, tolerant, Protestant, and therefore free Britain differed from autocratic, Catholic France. As Linda Colley has written, "A powerful and persistently threatening France became the haunting embodiment of that Catholic Other which Britons had been taught to fear since the Reformation in the sixteenth century."[2] Of course, high taxes were required to support continual war with France. But they were necessary to prevent the French kings from "accomplish[ing] their scheme of bringing in the *Pretender*," the Stuart son of James II who, if he came to the throne, would become James III and, it was feared, reimpose tyranny and Catholicism on England. In any event, England's subjects were not "more burdened to maintain the publick *Liberty*, than the *French* Kings's [were] to confirm their own *Slavery*."[3] As a result, while France was bent "beneath the tyrant's lust" and its people "crawl[ed], and lick[ed] the dust," the "manly genius" of Britain and its colonies "disdain[ed] all tinsel slavery, [and] golden chains."[4]

Eighteenth-century Americans enjoyed the benefits of membership in a British empire that was experiencing economic growth and that they understood to be uniquely free. Americans read widely in the literature expressing the British nationalist ideology of prosperity, liberty, and Protestantism. They absorbed much of it. Authors connected with the American colonies even participated in writing some of it. Indeed, a number of North American colonials were such full participants with writers and readers back home that when Parliament in the 1760s sought to tax them and legislate for them, they began to complain that they were being "reduced from free men to a level with the subjects of France and Spain."[5]

In short, a fundamental transformation occurred in British domestic and imperial beliefs and practices as a result of the Glorious Revolution. The attempt of Charles II and James II to build a modern, monarchical state with a robust regulatory capacity modeled on the French regime of Louis XIV was rejected. In its place, William III, his ministers, and their successors promoted a policy of defeating French territorial expansionism. In America as at home, the primary goal of British policy after 1689 was no longer, as it had been under Charles II and James II, the enhancement of royal power and the elimination of remnants of republicanism. Instead, the new goal was the defeat of France and the maintenance of Protestant hegemony, ideally that of the Church of England but alternatively that of other reformed sects as well. Crown officials were delighted to have nationalist writing emphasizing British liberty and prosperity transmitted to and read in America.

The liberty-loving nationalism of decades of war against France assumed a somewhat different meaning in America, however, from the meaning that it took in Britain. At home, anti-French ideology was consistent with state-building: the liberalism spawned in 1688 was activist and interventionist rather than passive and anti-statist. The decades after 1688 witnessed the founding of the Bank of England, immense growth and professionalization of the royal navy, the development and regularization of a standing army, and the genesis of a proficient civil service capable of collecting taxes. Above all, parliamentary government and the institutions surrounding it, such as the cabinet, matured.

In the eighteenth-century British North American colonies, in contrast, institution-building was more difficult. In the colonies, liberty came to mean immunity from centralized institutional control. Although some efforts were made to create colonywide legal institutions, especially courts of chancery, few of those efforts succeeded. On the contrary, the main institutions that continued to develop and mature in America during the eighteenth century were those of local government, such as towns, parishes, and especially county courts, which had jurisdiction over all entities and officials within their geographic bounds.

William III and his successors did little to halt this devolution of power to local institutions, especially local courts. The Crown continued to demand that the colonies receive the common law, but as long as local courts followed common law procedures, royal officials were willing to leave most policy choices in local hands. Arguably, the Crown's deference made sense both for it and for its colonial subjects. In the context of continuing wars against France, Britain could obtain the support it needed from most colonials, and, although the people of some localities might oppose British policies, the localization of power prevented opponents from organizing on a scale wide enough to obstruct meaningfully whatever policies the king and Parliament wished to follow. For colonials, localization meant that although they had little capacity to influence British policy, neither did they have to effectuate decisions with which they disagreed.

Localization of power and policy choice assumed different forms, however, in different colonies. The remainder of this chapter analyzes the development of three different models by which local people either controlled the work of local courts, the main institutions of colonial government, or at least resisted control by central authorities, as well as a fourth model that allowed for greater central control.

Government by Jury

In the four New England colonies and also in Maryland and New Jersey, the power of localities rested on juries drawn from and responsive to local communities. These juries determined law as well as fact in both county courts and colonywide appellate courts. Massachusetts, which had the most powerful juries, provides the paradigm for how local communities, through juries, controlled the substance of the law.

Unless both parties waived it, litigants in Massachusetts had a right to trial by jury in nearly all cases before the Superior and Common Pleas courts and in criminal and many other cases before the Courts of Sessions. Jury panels were selected by the clerk of court sending to each town in the county a writ of venire facias directing the town to select by lot a specified number of inhabitants for jury duty. The vital fact about Massachusetts juries, however, was not that they tried nearly every case but that they had vast power to find both the law and the facts in those cases. Jurors reflecting the values of the communities from which they were randomly drawn thereby controlled the substance of the Bay Colony's law.

Although the common law had several devices for controlling jury findings of law, few of them were used in Massachusetts. One device was special pleading, which sought to define a single, narrow issue of fact for a jury to decide and to restrict the litigants to presenting only evidence relevant to that issue of fact. Legal issues were resolved by the court as the parties interposed their pleas and the court determined whether the pleas were dispositive as a matter of law. All that remained for the jury to decide was the single, narrow factual issue.

Special pleading beyond the initial plea by the defendant and replication by the plaintiff was rarely used, however, in Massachusetts. Instead, most cases went to trial under a general issue. Under the general issue, litigants were permitted to introduce a wide range of evidence in support of their claims, and the jury, which gave a simple verdict announcing only which litigant won the case, determined not only whether the evidence was credible but also whether it was sufficient as a matter of law to support the parties' claims. Under the general issue, Massachusetts juries decided not only the facts but also the legal consequences of facts; that is, in the absence of other restrictions they possessed the power to decide the law as well as the facts.

A second technique for controlling juries is for courts to instruct them on the law and on how to sift and weigh the evidence. In colonial Massachusetts, however, instructions were ineffective. In many civil cases no instructions were given at all, and, even in cases where the jury was charged, the charges often were brief. A further reason for the ineffectiveness of instructions was that they often were contradictory. One potential source of contradiction was counsel, who on summation could argue the law as well as the facts, at least as long as he did not clearly misinform the jury. Most confusing of all was the court's seriatim charge: each judge sitting on the court that tried a case gave his own interpretation of the law—an interpretation that could and sometimes did differ from those of his brethren. Since all cases were tried before at least three judges in addition to counsel, jurors often were left with final power to determine whose interpretation of the law was correct.

Even if instructions had provided a useful mode of communicating rules of law, Massachusetts juries could not have been compelled to adhere to them. For once juries had received evidence on several factual issues in a case, the only way to compel them to decide in accordance with the court's view of the law would have been for the court to grant a new trial when a verdict was contrary to the court's instructions on the law or contrary to the evidence. But that was never done in eighteenth-century Massachusetts; it was clear that a court would not grant a motion for a new trial on the ground that a verdict was against law because the jury had disregarded the court's instructions or against evidence because the jury had seen the facts differently from the court or misapplied the law to the facts. Only the legislature could grant a new trial and then only through a special act that was expensive to procure. In a few cases in which large sums of money were at stake, an appeal to the Privy Council also was possible.

With some exceptions, eighteenth-century Connecticut, New Hampshire, and Rhode Island followed Massachusetts practice. Judges in Connecticut, for example, were permitted to urge a jury twice to reconsider its verdict, but if the jury remained adamant, judgment had to be rendered in accordance with that verdict. Ultimate legal power throughout New England thus rested mainly in the hands of juries, whose verdicts generally were dispositive, although litigants could try to avoid the jury by engaging in special pleading or by interposing a procedural plea, either a demurrer or a plea in abatement, to a plaintiff's action; they may have done so more frequently in colonies other than Massachusetts. They also could seek legislative approval for a new trial or could appeal to the Privy Council, but both processes were cumbersome and expensive. On the whole in New England, power to resolve disputes and affirm societal policy through litigation remained in the hands of representatives of local communities assembled on juries.

Maryland was a fifth colony in which judges lacked power to set aside jury verdicts inconsistent with their view of the law or the evidence. Maryland's reliance on juries went back to the seventeenth century, and preserving the power of juries to find law may have been a compromise that allowed Protestants in 1689 to take control of the colony government while leaving Catholics, who continued to serve on juries, secure in possession of their property, their religious freedom, and other rights, and thus willing to accept Protestant power. But, unlike New England, Maryland did not give juries completely free rein to find law: Maryland judges strove to control jurors by keeping legally irrelevant evidence away from them and by routinely instructing them on the law they were to follow. But judges could not set aside a verdict simply because they disagreed with whatever result the jurors reached once a case had been placed in their hands.

New Jersey was the final colony in which juries had broad lawfinding power. But New Jersey law was parallel to Maryland's in that judges could strive to control juries by limiting the evidence they could hear and by giving them instructions on the law, but not otherwise by setting jury verdicts aside.

Government by Local Judges

Virginia exhibited a second, totally different model of local control. In Virginia, juries were largely under judicial control. Local Virginia judges, for example, routinely controlled the evidence they permitted juries to hear. They also frequently set aside verdicts and granted new trials when in their view juries returned verdicts contrary to the evidence. On occasion they also penetrated beyond the rubric that a verdict was contrary to evidence, which implicitly meant that a jury had disobeyed the law, and explicitly set aside verdicts as contrary to law. And on at least one occasion, a court dispensed with a jury entirely and concluded that particular evidence constituted a bar to a plaintiff's suit; it accordingly rendered the equivalent of summary judgment for the defendant. An even more effective form of jury control than the motion for a new trial that courts used throughout the eighteenth century was a chancery decree enjoining execution of judgment on a jury verdict. It is noteworthy that a litigant could turn for injunctive relief to a county court sitting in chancery even after denial of a post-verdict motion by the same court sitting at law.

The power of judges over juries did not, however, give Virginia a centralized legal system. The reason was that the judges who exercised control over juries were local, county court judges. Those judges, in turn, were independent of central political authorities and felt free to ignore, and sometimes did ignore, the judgments and orders of higher courts.

County courts were largely self-perpetuating bodies that recommended to governors whom they should appoint to the bench, and governors typically did appoint those who were nominated. On the few occasions when governors failed to appoint the men recommended by the sitting judges or appointed men who were not recommended, judges typically resigned en masse and left their locality bereft of a court and hence of a government. Governors then had little choice but to cave in and appoint the men whom local leaders desired.

Appeals from county courts to the General Court remained the norm. But at times, county courts denied appeals, and at other times appellate courts refused to consider appeals from general verdicts when evidence had not been taken down in writing and submitted on appeal under proper seal. County courts also refused at times to obey orders from the governor and the General Court. A case of direct disobedience occurred, for example, when a county court declined to obey a mandamus from the General Court requiring the county to build a specified bridge, which the county court declared would be useless and require a needless tax.

Thus, ultimate control of the substance of Virginia law, like the substance of New England, Maryland, and New Jersey law, lay with local, country courts.

Virginia differed from the other colonies only in regard to who in a locality possessed control. In Virginia, self-perpetuating local elites consisting of wealthy
planters controlled the law; in the other colonies, a larger group of middle-class
male property holders who were eligible for jury duty was in control.

New York's system was a hybrid of New England's and Virginia's. New York
trial practice was quite similar to that of Virginia. New York trial courts, like
those of Virginia, granted many post-verdict motions for new trials and in arrest of judgment, although court records typically failed to state the precise legal
grounds of the motions. At the other end of litigation, defendants could interpose a demurrer to a plaintiff's action, thereby seeking its dismissal for lack of
legal merit even before it reached a jury. Plaintiffs similarly could obtain rulings
on the legal sufficiency of defendants' defenses. The most important jury-control
device, however, was the demurrer to the evidence, by which one litigant at the
close of the other litigant's evidence moved for judgment on the ground that the
other side's evidence was insufficient as a matter of law to warrant submission
of the case to the jury. Trial judges thus possessed ample power with which to
control juries.

But there was real doubt whether officials of the provincial government in
New York City could control the outcome of cases in local trial courts. The
simplest form of control would have been the governor's appointment and removal power. By the middle of the eighteenth century, however, some judges
explicitly had been granted tenure during good behavior, and others had such
tenure by implication. Moreover, the governor did not possess a free hand in
the appointment process. By the mid-eighteenth century, he appointed judges
at the county level following nomination by the assembly, which almost certainly meant nomination by local assemblymen, and to the Supreme Court
only from members of the bar, nearly all of whom had enjoyed long careers in
New York practice. The assembly had even further influence over judges, in that
it controlled their remuneration.

Appellate courts also enjoyed substantially less freedom to review jury
verdicts than did trial judges. Cases came before them only on writs of certiorari
and error, which brought before the appellate court only the record of the proceedings below. Matters outside the record, such as the grounds of jury verdicts
and the evidence admitted in support of them, were not within the scope of the
writs. Thus, the appellate process did not enable central authorities to control either juries or more generally the outcome of proceedings below. In this respect,
New York practice resembled that of New England.

In New York, as in New England and Virginia, the substance of the law accordingly remained largely under the control either of local juries or of local county
judges responsible to the communities that chose them. That, in turn, meant
that law did not mirror the will of a political sovereign in London or New York

City. Law instead reflected common values inherent in the common law and acceptable to the communities from which local judges and jurors were drawn.

Government Only of Localities

The legal systems of the Deep South exhibited a third, more centralized model of local control than those to the north, with South Carolina providing the paradigmatic example of centralization. Judges in South Carolina not only circumscribed the power of juries to find law but also monitored jury fact-finding. Often, juries cooperated by returning special verdicts that resolved only issues of fact and left the court free to determine the legal significance of those facts. When juries tried to exercise greater freedom, judges kept them under tight control. Judges strictly limited the evidence that a jury could hear and routinely granted motions for new trials when verdicts were in their view against the evidence or contrary to law. In one case, the court even set aside a verdict and granted judgment on the law for a defendant.

The result was a legal order totally under the control of the bench. It was, moreover, a completely centralized system. Until the 1770s, the Court of Common Pleas in Charleston was the only court in the colony with jurisdiction over civil common law adjudication. Individual justices of the peace heard misdemeanors not requiring jury trial as well as petty debt cases, but the justices never met together as county Courts of Sessions. Outlying regions did not even have their own sheriffs: one provost marshal for the entire colony served all writs and executed all judgments, and local constables were appointed by the chief justice of the colony and his associate judges sitting in the colonywide Court of Sessions in Charleston.

The centralized Court of Common Pleas sitting in Charleston was subject, in turn, to firm supervision by the Court of Chancery, which was put on an explicit statutory footing in 1721 with the governor of the colony himself sitting as presiding officer. Chancery, which sat without a jury, continued its old practices of overseeing the administration of estates, supervising guardians, enforcing the equity of redemption to mortgages, implementing trusts, and enjoining actions at law. Over time it became increasingly intrusive, with the result, as one lawyer argued, that "the Court of Chancery . . . had a Concurrent Jurisdiction in many cases with the Court of Law."[6]

Enforcement of regulatory law and criminal law through the Court of Sessions, which like Common Pleas and Chancery sat only in Charleston and was presided over by the chief justice of the colony, was nearly as centralized. Except in prosecutions against slaves, where local justices of the peace could impose even a penalty of death, local justices had almost no power; until 1772, they did not even routinely examine prisoners arrested for crime. Juries in the Court of Sessions, however, had somewhat greater power than juries did in Common Pleas, in that grand juries had power to refuse to return indictments and petit juries could return general verdicts of not guilty or guilty only of a lesser offense. Juries also could recommend mercy. Otherwise, the judiciary was in charge.

In short, civil litigation and most criminal law enforcement in colonial South Carolina were under the total control of a small group of men in Charleston—the governor of the colony sitting as chancellor, an English placeman appointed as chief justice of the colony, and a small number of others, mainly lawyers, sitting as associate justices. A well-trained professional bar, many of whose members had studied in England and had close ties to the planter-merchant elite, acted hand in hand with the bench. Jurors—that is, the representatives of outlying localities and lower-class Charlestonians—had no power over the law and limited power even to find facts in Common Pleas. Common Pleas itself was subject to routine interference by Chancery, which sat without a jury. The criminal jury played a lesser role in South Carolina than in most colonies.

But this centralized legal system, unlike those of colonies to the north, did not reach into a hinterland of settled communities extending as far as 200 miles from the capital; in essence, the writ of South Carolina's courts ran only in a small area centered around Charleston. Every court sat in the capital, all lawyers resided there, all legal business was transacted there, and all suits were filed, heard, and decided there. Before the 1770s, South Carolina had no circuit courts and no local courts organized in a hierarchical structure with appeals to a central court in the capital; in short, it had no legal mechanisms, such as those developing in the Chesapeake and the North, for extending the reach of law across the continent.

This limited reach was possible because of the pattern of residence in the colony. South Carolina was small. As late as 1750, it had only 25,000 white inhabitants, and nearly everyone possessing significant political or economic power resided in Charleston or its immediate environs. That pattern of residence was the same for royal officials as well as South Carolina's lawyers and merchants. It also was the same for the colony's planters, who lived only part of the year on their plantations and also maintained homes in Charleston, where they resided much of the time. Families often intermarried, and everyone who mattered knew everyone else. Charleston and its surrounding area, according to one Carolinian, constituted "our little world."[7] As a result of this pattern of residence, there was little demand for breaking up the highly centralized judiciary that conducted all legal business in Charleston. There was no need for powerful juries to represent local interests because all the people who mattered were able to influence the judiciary and central officials by virtue of their personal contacts with them.

Thus, despite all the differences between South Carolina and the colonies to the north, its legal system resembled theirs. The South Carolina courts were local courts, in that first, they were subject to local influence, and second, they did not impose law beyond the locality where they could rely on that influence to enforce their judgments. Moreover, they were local courts whose power would collapse when the interests of British officials and the local community diverged.

As a royal colony in the mid-eighteenth century, Georgia, like South Carolina, had principal courts only in Savannah, its capital. There a General Court and a Land Court adjudicated civil cases; a Court of Oyer and Terminer, criminal cases. The governor also presided over a Court of Chancery and a Court of Appeals. Georgia, like South Carolina, did not attempt in mid-century to extend the jurisdiction of its principal courts over any significant geographic area. To the extent those courts were able to function under tight central control (and it is unclear how tight that control was), they could do so only by limiting their jurisdiction to the locale where they sat.

North Carolina, unlike South Carolina and Georgia, was a geographically large colony, but it failed to extend the power of its courts beyond short distances from where they sat. Part of its difficulty stemmed from a history of politicization of its courts beginning in the mid-1720s. But the underlying cause was that the legal system's roots in North Carolina had not penetrated as deeply as they had in some other colonies. The educated members of the bar were few, and they all resided in the small northeast corner of the colony along the Albemarle Sound and practiced almost entirely before the General Court and Chancery. North Carolina had no urban center like Philadelphia, nor did it possess the foundational cultural structure that Puritanism had given to a colony such as Massachusetts. As a result, when North Carolina began to expand in the eighteenth century, the legal profession could not keep pace with the expansion, and, when a period of political chaos occurred in the late 1720s, the legal system broke down.

Political conflict began with the arrival of the last proprietary governor, Richard Everard, who served from 1725 to 1731. His predecessor as penultimate proprietary governor and later his successor as first royal governor, George Burrington, expressed his opposition publicly to the appointment of Everard. Everard, in turn, had Burrington indicted on charges of sedition and assault, as well as for breaking into a house where the collector of customs was a lodger, apparently while Burrington had still been governor.

Burrington left for England before proceedings on the indictments could go forward. The indictments remained on the calendar until 1728, and, as a result, political conflict and the judiciary's involvement therein persisted.

Other Burrington supporters who had remained in North Carolina also caused a great deal of trouble. Several months after Burrington's indictment, one

Edmond Porter complained to the General Court that he had been assaulted in a public street by Governor Everard and several others. Concluding that Porter was the aggressor, the Court rejected his complaint. Later Porter was indicted for that assault and for beginning an affray in the presence of the governor. The grand jury also indicted Porter for slandering Chief Justice Christopher Gale.

In dealing with former Governor Burrington and his supporters, the North Carolina power structure—that is, the governor, the attorney general, and the judiciary—initially presented a united front. But soon that front disintegrated as Porter persevered in his efforts to disrupt North Carolina's government.

The matter on which Porter's efforts finally divided the power structure occurred in the colony's Court of Admiralty, of which Porter was the judge. The issue arose out of two suits that had been brought in admiralty against a ship captain named Samuel Northey—the first by one James Trotter for victuals furnished to the vessel while it was in port in Edenton and the second by a Dr. George Allen for damage to medicines shipped under Northey's command from Virginia to Edenton. Northey's defense was that Allen and Trotter both failed to allege that their causes of action arose on the high seas and that they had, in fact, arisen on land. Northey therefore sought writs of prohibition from common law against admiralty on the ground that the two cases were not within the jurisdiction of admiralty. In the two most extensive opinions delivered up to that time in the General Court, Chief Justice Gale granted the writs of prohibition, and when Edmond Porter, the admiralty judge, ignored the writs and ordered Northey's arrest, Gale, with the approval of Governor Everard, issued a writ of habeas corpus and commanded Northey's release.

This conflict between common law and admiralty might have amounted to nothing more than one of the many periodic jurisdictional conflicts in the history of Anglo-American law, except that Governor Everard switched sides, probably because of direction received from England that he rein in the jurisdictional claims of the common law courts. Everard procured an assignment of a claim against Chief Justice Gale held by the master of a vessel sailing out of New York and, as assignee, personally brought a libel in admiralty against Gale. In April 1729, Gale informed his colleagues of the libel and proposed that, despite the Board of Trade's denial of their power to do so, they issue a writ of prohibition and an order to arrest Judge Porter and to hold him in custody until he obeyed the prohibition. The other judges took Gale's request under advisement.

Meanwhile, Porter had engaged in an affray in the view of the court. For this, the General Court judges held Porter in contempt, issued an order for his arrest, and sent John Parke, who had been serving as provost marshal, to seize him. Parke found Porter in the company of Governor Everard, who announced that he would protect everybody in his company. Parke returned to court without arresting Porter.

A major rupture between the governor and the General Court had clearly opened as each side refused to recognize the legitimate authority of the other's agents and took coercive steps against them. Once opened, the rupture only grew, others became involved, and new alliances were formed. In 1727, Dr. George Allen, who practiced both law and medicine in Edenton and who had sued in admiralty, it will be recalled, for breach of contract, apparently had been a supporter of George Burrington. But something occurred thereafter to cause Allen to change sides. At the April 1729 term of the General Court, Dr. Allen found himself in custody under an admiralty libel for contempt because while acting as advocate in that court on behalf of Chief Justice Gale, he had filed an allegedly scandalous answer to a citation. Allen accordingly sought habeas corpus in the General Court, which promptly granted him his release. Next William Little, the colony's attorney general, was arrested on a charge of contempt of admiralty. He too was released.

This narrative of the two-year conflict between the General Court and the Court of Admiralty and the supporters of the two sides does not even begin, however, to capture the chaos that enveloped the North Carolina bench and bar in the late 1720s or the central role of Governor Everard in that chaos.

Governor Everard further contributed to the ongoing confusion by intervening in the judicial process. First, he personally came to court to order a halt to a criminal prosecution of one James Bremen for opening a window in one Robert Pearce's house and assaulting Pearce; Everard, it turned out, had assisted Bremen in the assault.

On an earlier occasion, Everard had come into court and accused John Lovick, the secretary of the province and also one of the judges, of tampering with the grand jury by conversing with its foreman during its proceedings. After requesting leave to clear themselves, the members of the grand jury testified that no person had ever tampered with them, although on further examination one of their members acknowledged that he had received a paper from Governor Everard. That paper was received into evidence. Everard then had Lovick arrested, allegedly for assaulting him. But a unanimous court held the arrest unlawful, although it did permit Everard to testify before the grand jury in support of an indictment against Lovick. The grand jury did inform the Court that Lovick on a specific date had "give[n] ill language & blows" to Everard, but the jurors refused to return an indictment. When the court directed them that "they must return it either Billa vera or ignoramus they said they could find it no[t] otherwise." The court concluded that the grand jury "return [was] invalid & insufficient . . . to proceed upon it" and accordingly ordered that proceedings against Lovick be quashed.[8]

Everard also tried to use the law against Attorney General Little. Again, Everard met resistance. He moved the General Court to issue a warrant against

Little directing him to turn over possession of the colony's statutes at large. The court denied Everard's demand but did send the provost marshal to Little to request return of the statutes.

Everard's actions against both Lovick and Little probably occurred in connection with an indictment returned against him in August 1728 for striking George Allen with his cane. It was during the grand jury proceedings resulting in that indictment that Everard had presented his paper to the jurors and that, he alleged, Lovick had spoken with a juror. And he probably needed the statutes that were in Little's hands to prepare his defense.

These various events and proceedings must have taught observant North Carolinians something painfully difficult, if not impossible, to unlearn—that the law in force in their colony was not a neutral and objective body of rules employed by the judiciary and the legal profession to achieve impartial resolution of disputes and just governance of the province. Rather, the law was a weapon that political actors, both on and off the bench, used in efforts to further their political agendas, promote their interests, protect their friends, and punish their enemies. Such misuse of law made the law "contemptible and odious to almost every person in the government" and made it difficult for anyone to respect the legal system.[9]

The ultimate problem was that the law became politicized not only in cases involving political issues or political actors, but also in run-of-the-mill cases that should have been completely apolitical. The key case was *King v. Smith*, where a jury had convicted Solomon Smith of premeditated murder and the court had sentenced him to death; Governor Everard, however, refused to execute the death sentence and sent the following message to the Court:

> As the life of a man is a thing of a very tender nature, . . . I must tell you gentlemen as the man was tried & condemned. . . [by a] Court . . . compounded of officers not duly qualified to open such court that all proceedings therein are extrajudicial and erroneous[.] [I] therefore cannot without injury to my conscience sign such a death warrant for the execution of the unhappy prisoner till a trial de novo and the court compounded of officers duly qualified and those of my appointment [is in place].[10]

This 1729 memorandum, declaring that the General Court was not properly constituted and that all its proceedings were therefore extrajudicial and erroneous, cast into doubt the validity of every judgment rendered by the General Court as far back, perhaps, as 1725, when Governor Everard had assumed office. Doubts persisted, moreover, for more than two years; in a 1731 prosecution for contempt for ignoring a writ of habeas corpus, for example, the defendant pleaded not guilty on the ground that "Christopher Gale, who is said to have signed the writ, was not then as he apprehends a legal judge to grant such writs."[11]

With the publication of Governor Everard's 1729 memo and the chaos in its aftermath, there was no colonywide legal system left in North Carolina. Only raw power remained, and no one possessed very much of that. The government was "in the greatest confusion," and the colony had "sunk so low that neither peace or order subsisted, the General Court suppressed, the Council set aside . . . some of the precinct courts fallen, . . . [and] a general discontent and ferment among people."[12] The result was such "frequent tumults and riots . . . that men" did not have "security even in their own houses."[13] With the legal system of North Carolina at its nadir, the proprietors in 1729 surrendered their control over the colony's government to the king.

Pennsylvania and Delaware

A fourth model of control existed in the proprietary colonies of Pennsylvania and Delaware, where there was more success than elsewhere in extending central power to localities.

Despite the commitment of most Quakers to allowing juries to decide law as well as to find facts, the courts of Pennsylvania ruled in the colony's early years that judges should determine the law while juries should be restricted to finding the facts. As a result, common law trial courts set aside jury verdicts and granted new trials. In the colony's early years, local judges sitting in equity also enjoined enforcement of jury verdicts.

However, there was a persistent undercurrent of opposition to this disempowerment of juries and to the colony's equity courts. This opposition led as early as 1693 to legislative restriction of the equity powers of local courts and in 1735 to abolition of the central court of equity. To preserve their power over juries, judges then needed to develop new procedures of jury control, but persistent opposition allowed them to do so only gradually.

The first device to come into use was the demurrer to the evidence, which was used with some frequency. At the same time as the demurrer to the evidence grew in use, other lawyers, perhaps with less sophistication, were striving to develop alternative mechanisms. By the mid-1770s demurrers were being replaced by these alternatives. One was the motion in arrest of judgment. Another was the procedure of a bill of exceptions, followed in Pennsylvania practice by a writ of error (rather than an appeal) to bring discrete legal issues rather than an entire case before a higher court. Accordingly Chief Justice Benjamin Chew announced less than two years before Americans declared their independence that "the law [was] not uncertain": it was "a settled rule, that courts of law determine law; a jury facts. Upon which maxim," he added, "every security depends in an English country."[14] As long as counsel took the necessary steps to make it so, "the opinion of the court" on points of law was "conclusive to the jury."[15]

Still opposition remained. As judges were making "encroachments . . . upon the *rights* of juries" through such devices as the bill of exceptions and the demurrer to the evidence, their opponents urged friends of liberty to stand fast. One essay, for example, flatly rejected the argument that juries should "only judge of naked *matter of fact,* and are not at all to take upon them to *meddle with . . . matter of law,* but leave it wholly to the court." It declared that "*if a jury will take upon them the knowledge of the law . . . , they may.*" In this essayist's view, juries had "*ever been vested with such power,*" and to "disseise *them of the same were utterly to* defeat the end of their institution," which was to serve as "*guardian* of our legal liberties against arbitrary injustice" and to protect against "judges," who were "more likely to be under an influence which is injurious to the rights of the people." The judiciary's efforts to deny the jury its rightful power to find law, in the words of this article, were turning the institution into "a *snare,* or engine of oppression."[16]

Thus, as the American Revolution approached, central control of the institutions of the law remained at issue. The judges of the Pennsylvania Supreme Court believed their control of the law and their disempowerment of juries to be a settled rule. Opponents, however, disagreed.

And, as chapter 15 will show, the ability of Pennsylvania's eastern Quaker establishment to enforce law in the west was a growing issue as the American Revolution approached and the west broke into near open rebellion.

Delaware, which initially had been part of Pennsylvania but had split off into a separate colony, followed Pennsylvania's practices of jury control. In the years before the two colonies split, there were many instances both of appeals to the Pennsylvania Provincial Court in Equity and of reference to local county courts in equity to overturn jury verdicts, and appeals to equity courts from jury verdicts continued in Delaware long after it had been separated from Pennsylvania. As a result, law in Delaware was firmly under judicial and perhaps even central control. Delaware, however, was a tiny colony and hence its law, like the law of nearly every other colony, remained an essentially local phenomenon.

Summary

Because the small size of some colonies rendered them intrinsically local, because local elites controlled the courts, or because juries determined the law, coercive power in Britain's thirteen North American colonies was effective when it was local in nature and, except perhaps in Pennsylvania, problematic when it was not. Colonial Americans had a strong preference for local self-government.

Colonial reactions to two mid-eighteenth-century developments confirm that preference. The first was the reaction to the 1754 Albany Plan of Union. The Albany Plan began with a provision that "each Colony . . . [would] retain it[s] present constitution," localist as it might be, except in regard to three delegations of power to the union—(1) the power to make war against and regulate trade with Native Americans, (2) the power to raise military forces although not through impressment, and (3) the power to regulate and govern new western settlements. Nonetheless, the colonies almost unanimously opposed the plan out of concern that it would endanger local liberty; in the words of the lower houses of Massachusetts and New Jersey, it would "be destructive of our happy constitution" and "affect our Constitution in its very vitals."[17]

A curious decision of the Rhode Island legislature provides the second confirmation of the colonial preference for local control. Like the rest of New England, Rhode Island rejected common law primogeniture as the rule for inheritance of land in the absence of a will; if a landowner died intestate, each child received an equal portion of land that had been held by the deceased, except that the eldest son received a double portion. At the beginning of 1730, this Rhode Island rule was recorded in a colonywide statute. But with the 1728 decision of *Winthrop v. Lechmere*,[18] in which the Privy Council held Connecticut's identical rule void as repugnant to the common law, Rhode Island legislators worried that their statute might be held void as well. Accordingly, when they printed a new edition of their statutes in 1730, they repealed their intestacy law and left it out of the code. A note in the printed edition declared that distributions already made under prior law remained valid, but said nothing about the rule for intestate inheritance in the future. Town probate courts thus were given the authority to distribute intestate estates as they wished. Those courts could be trusted to do what was right, and the legislature could trust that it would be near to impossible for officials in Britain to police them. The absence of written law was better than bad law made in London. Like the lawfinding jury, the disappearance of law from the 1730 code gave local people freedom of self-government.

Rhode Island's repeal of its biblical rule for intestate distribution demonstrates a main argument of this chapter. British officials made policy choices, and when an entire colony, such as Connecticut in the *Winthrop* case, refused to follow their choices, officials felt bound to take action. But when power was devolved to localities, the Crown could ignore the devolution. Local people remained free to behave as they wished, while the empire endured.

10

The Law of Religion

As was true of much other law in Britain's North American colonies, the law regulating religion often differed from colony to colony. But when William III came to the throne in 1688, he pushed the colonies toward greater uniformity. He put an end to Catholic control of Maryland. His first Parliament extended toleration to all Protestant denominations as part of his program of building the grand anti-French coalition that he was working to establish. Although differences remained thereafter in the law of the various colonies, William's anti-Catholicism and policy of toleration for all Protestants pointed everywhere over time in the same direction—toward the disestablishment of specific Protestant denominations along with the maintenance of a pluralist, generic Protestant religiosity.

Massachusetts

As was seen in chapter 2, church and state were intimately conjoined in the Massachusetts Bay Colony, with the word of God constituting a foundation of secular law. The restoration of Charles II, however, had posed a threat to the existence of Massachusetts as a distinct Puritan entity. Recall from chapter 4 the efforts of the royal governor of New Hampshire, Edward Cranfield, to force Puritan ministers to administer the holy sacrament pursuant to the rites of the Church of England—efforts that raised the question of whether, with the revocation of Massachusetts's charter in 1684, the Crown would try, as Cranfield had, to wipe out Puritanism. However, as was shown in chapter 5, traditional patterns of government support of Puritanism persisted. Legislation enacted in 1692–93 and 1695–96, which received explicit confirmation from the Crown, retained Puritanism as the Bay Colony's established religion, albeit with a compromise requiring toleration of dissenting Protestant denominations.

Law and religion thus remained deeply intertwined. Eighteenth-century courts, like those of the seventeenth century, engaged in considerable efforts to support the Puritan establishment. There were prosecutions for blasphemy, for example, as when one defendant "den[ied] the existence . . . of God" and declared "the Bible [was] not the word of God . . . and that men now a days can write as good works as . . . the Bible."[1] Other prosecutions occurred for failing to hire a minister, for defaming the churches of the province, for disturbing public worship by saying during services that the pastor "had no right to speak,"[2] for laughing at a minister while he was preaching, for publishing a "mock sermon in immitation & mimicking of preaching,"[3] for assaulting a minister and calling him a "murderer of souls" while he was coming out of church,[4] and for "reviling the minister and speaking slightly of the ordinance of baptism."[5]

The law also made efforts to protect the Sabbath. Those efforts included innumerable prosecutions of people who failed to attend church and other forms of Sabbath breaking—a "sin increasing & growing upon us to the great provoking of God,"[6] with one of the more extreme prosecutions being for unnecessarily walking in the streets on the evening preceding the Lord's Day.

The greatest difficulty for the Puritan legal order continued to arise out of the proliferation of churches. Much of this proliferation occurred as towns grew and additional Congregational churches were needed. The establishment of new churches, in turn, led to disputes about ownership of the original church's property. One such dispute arose in Dedham, where the Superior Court ruled that the second and third churches in that town were entitled to share in the landholdings of the first church.

Worse still was proliferation resulting from schism. A schism in Watertown, for instance, consumed the attention of the courts for some fifteen years. The Great Awakening produced even more schisms, and the judiciary inevitably became involved. At the outset of the Awakening in the 1730s, the court in Hampshire County witnessed a prosecution of a Connecticut Valley man for calling Jonathan Edwards "as great an instrument as the Devil had on this side [of] hell to bring souls to hell."[7] A case of even greater significance, *Pynchon v. First Parish in Springfield*,[8] occurred two months later.

The *Pynchon* case began when a dissenting minority in the first parish in Springfield objected to Robert Breck, the existing minister, because he had preached, among other things, that those who "lived up to the light of nature should be saved without faith in Christ." The dissenters regarded these views as unorthodox and brought suit to compel the first parish to obtain a minister who was orthodox. There is no doubt that if someone patently unorthodox had been the minister in Springfield, the court would have been obliged to order the parish to replace him. The first parish responded, however, that Breck was orthodox and that the complaint was "preposterous and absurd." The parish further pleaded that Breck had been "regularly ordained to th[e] office" of minister of the first parish and that the dissenters "do not allege that he is since dead or removed and therefore admit him to be the incumbent minister." Accordingly, the parish pleaded in bar that it was "not subject to the orders of this court by the plain provision and meaning of the law as a defective parish or church, but such ecclesiastical power under Christ as have ordained and placed the said Robert Breck there must first remove him before the king's justices can intermeddle with their orders."

The court, probably feeling compelled to resolve the conflict and thereby bring peace to the community, rejected this effort to remove it from the case and overruled the plea. It then turned to the merits, at which point the parish pleaded not guilty (common law rules, which had no procedures for dealing with schisms in Puritan parishes, provided no better plea) and "put themselves on the country." The judges thereupon expressed their "opinion that this case could not be tried by a jury" and undertook to decide the case by themselves. At the next term, they concluded that Breck was, in fact, "an orthodox minister of good conversation" who should remain in his post.[9]

Pynchon v. First Parish in Springfield illustrates that however much Puritan religiosity may have declined or otherwise changed by the 1730s, little change had come to Massachusetts religious law. The Hampshire County court behaved in many respects just as the seventeenth-century Puritan Court of Assistants had behaved in the 1630s when it confronted the likes of Anne Hutchinson, Roger Williams, and other dissenters. The Hampshire court, like its Puritan predecessor, understood that it had the duty to preserve unity and harmony within the religious establishment and that it could not rely on a jury to perform the task. Juries existed to protect Massachusetts from the Crown and lesser British officials, but they could not be counted on to preserve the unity of the church when the communities from which they were drawn were themselves divided. Only judges committed to preserving the religious establishment, albeit now in office by virtue of royal appointment rather than election by the faithful, could perform that task. The main legal difference between the *Pynchon* case and the 1630s prosecutions was that the Connecticut Valley court functioned under a veneer of common law pleading—but only a veneer because the common law had no procedures for enforcing Puritan religious unity. What had to suffice in the 1730s, as in the 1630s, were lay officeholders, acting perhaps in consultation with clergymen, striving to keep dissidence and schism in check.

Within a few years, the failure of the Puritan leaders of Hampshire County to preserve religious unity produced the Great Awakening, and the Connecticut Valley burst into a religious conflagration. The courts could not extricate themselves from the fire, and, in turn, ordinary people became entangled with the law. For instance, John Moor was prosecuted in 1741 for libeling Thomas Little by writing that Little "had gone on the way to hell so long that he believed ... that if he goes to hell the elders ... can pray him out."[10]

Partly as a result, perhaps, of the law's failure to control the Great Awakening, cracks in the establishment began to open in the mid-eighteenth century. The law began, for example, to protect dissenters' services by punishing rioters who disrupted them. At least at times, courts also recognized the legitimacy of non-Congregationalist ministers, such as Baptists, and thus the exemption of those ministers from taxes, and the Superior Court upheld the exemption of Quakers from military service. A final crack appeared when legislation allowed members of dissenting churches to pay religious taxes to their own congregations, although the courts made it difficult to claim exemptions by placing technical obstacles in the path of claimants.

In short, by the 1770s, Massachusetts, like the other American colonies, was no longer populated by members of a single denomination. There were Anglicans in and around Boston, Quakers in the old Plymouth colony, Baptists throughout the colony, and both New Light and Old Light Congregationalists. Courts still strove to support the Congregationalist establishment, but they grew increasingly ineffectual.

Connecticut and New Hampshire

As was shown in chapter 2, Connecticut and New Hampshire both were Puritan offshoots of Massachusetts. In their organizational structures and beliefs, their churches remained within the Puritan fold, with the word of God constituting a foundation for the legal systems of the two colonies.

Judicial support of religion continued into the eighteenth century. In March 1744–45, for example, the Superior Court of New Hampshire confronted a matter that it found unusually difficult. *Leavett v. Sinkler*[11] arose when Dudley Leavett announced during Sabbath services that he "could as well join with the devil as with Mr. Rust [the local minister of the established church] in prayer" and "could as well join with the Pope in saying mass as with the said Rust in prayer." On a subsequent Sunday, Leavett took "possession of the pulpit in . . . [the] meeting house" and "began to carry on . . . public worship." The local justice of the peace before whom a prosecution was commenced removed the case to the next General Sessions Court, which convicted Leavett of a breach of the Sabbath and fined him ten shillings. Leavett appealed to the Superior Court.

The court could not agree on whether Leavett's actions amounted to a Sabbath breach. It first adjourned the case so that the lawyers could consult other members of the local bar, but in the midst of the Great Awakening that adjournment produced no clear result. The court still remained divided. It accordingly adjourned the case again. This time the adjournment enabled the New Hampshire attorneys to "convers[e] with some of the principal lawyers" and judges of the Superior Court of Massachusetts, which was about to sit on circuit in York, Maine, immediately across the border from New Hampshire, and to "have their advice" on the "state of the case." Adhering to old Puritan ways still mattered.

Connecticut and New Hampshire also continued into the eighteenth century to adhere to old ways. Both colonies continued, for example, to punish religious offenses, such as blasphemy and breach of the Sabbath, as late as the 1760s. Nevertheless, Anglicans, Baptists, and Quakers, as well as the dominant Congregationalists, all were living and worshiping in Connecticut and New Hampshire by the mid-eighteenth century.

Rhode Island

Unlike the other New England colonies, Rhode Island sought to keep its churches entirely distinct from its government. Over time Rhode Island succeeded in maintaining the separation of church and civil government. Religious taxes were never imposed, and the judicial records of the colony contain none of the cases of enforced contribution, excommunication, schism, and subordination of the clergy that occurred in the other New England colonies. Without an established church, Rhode Island practiced religious toleration, even of a small Jewish congregation in Newport founded in the late seventeenth century. But Rhode Island did punish religious offenses, such as blasphemy, breach of the Sabbath, disturbing Sabbath worship, profanity, and swearing.

Rhode Island's lack of a religious establishment was challenged, however, both by the Church of England and by Massachusetts Congregationalists, and was not fully secured until the middle of the eighteenth century. The challenge arose in a case construing a 1668 grant, by which several of Rhode Island's founders had dedicated 300 acres of land in the colony's Narragansett region for the support of a minister whom they described as orthodox. But what did it mean for a minister to be orthodox in a polity without a religious establishment? The question remained dormant until 1722.

In that year a local Anglican parish, already in possession of 20 of the 300 acres by virtue of a grant from an assignee of one of the original 1668 owners, brought suit against the occupant of the remaining 280 acres. The Anglican parish claimed that its pastor was an orthodox minister and therefore entitled to the land. A local jury decided against the parish, and a second jury reached the same result on rehearing the case. The parish appealed to the Privy Council, but its agent in England failed to prosecute the appeal. In 1725, the Privy Council dismissed the case for non-prosecution, leaving in place both the then occupant and the Rhode Island ruling that the Church of England was not the orthodox church of the colony.

Next, in 1732, a Congregationalist minister sued for the 280 acres of land. After losing before a jury in the county court, he appealed to the Superior Court, where the jury returned a special verdict that if the court judged him to be an orthodox minister, the Congregationalist was entitled to the land but that otherwise the land should remain in the occupant's possession. By a 5–4 vote, the court ruled that the Congregationalist was not orthodox, implying thereby that no minister was orthodox under the law of Rhode Island. But the Congregationalists appealed to the Privy Council, which reversed the Rhode Island decision without, however, declaring Congregationalists to be orthodox.

Now the Congregationalists sued the Anglicans for the remaining twenty acres, on the theory that the assignee of the original grantors had no power to convey the land to someone, namely, an Anglican, who was not an orthodox minister. But a local jury rejected the Congregationalist claim, leaving the twenty acres in Anglican possession. The Congregationalists sought to appeal to the Privy Council, but the Rhode Island Superior Court denied the appeal on the ground that the value of the twenty acres was below the minimal jurisdictional amount required for an appeal.

This result prompted the Anglicans to sue the Congregationalists for the remaining 280 acres on the ground "that the English church was the truly and only orthodox [one] throughout his majesty's dominions." When the Rhode Island court barred the suit because that issue had already been decided, the Anglicans appealed to the Privy Council, which reversed and ordered the case to be tried on the merits. The case came to trial in Rhode Island in 1739, and the Anglicans lost. Again, they appealed to the Privy Council, where the case remained dormant for thirteen years. Finally, the Council heard the appeal in 1752 and affirmed the Rhode Island judgment.

In the line of cases growing out of the 1668 grant, in sum, the Privy Council twice rejected Anglican claims of orthodoxy and thereby scotched any effort of the Church of England to establish itself in Rhode Island. Although the Privy Council twice left the Congregationalists in possession of the bulk of the 300 acres, it never clearly declared them to be orthodox, and the Rhode Island courts twice rejected their claim of orthodoxy. The result was that neither Anglicans nor Congregationalists succeeded in establishing their claims of orthodoxy and religious preeminence. Arguably, the cases held collectively that there was no form of orthodoxy in Rhode Island; in any event, Rhode Island's brand of general Protestant toleration and disestablishment endured.

Delaware, New Jersey, and Pennsylvania

New Jersey was another eighteenth-century colony that had no established church. West Jersey, it will be recalled, had been founded as a refuge for Quakers. Two provisions in the Concessions and Agreements of 1677, West Jersey's founding document, were central to the colony's existence—first, "that no person" should be "in the least punished or hurt, either in person, estate, or privilege, for the sake of his opinion, judgment, faith or worship towards God in matters of religion" and second, that everyone would be free to enjoy "the exercises of their consciences in matters of religious worship throughout all the said province."[12]

When West Jersey was joined with East Jersey to form the royal colony of New Jersey, the Crown sought to use prerogative power to establish the Church of England. But the Crown's effort failed because too few Anglican believers resided in the colony. East Jersey had been settled mainly by Puritans, but neither Quakers nor the Crown would have supported a Puritan establishment, and the Society of Friends in West Jersey, by virtue of its lack of institutional structure, was not an entity capable of being established.

Pennsylvania, which was founded several years after West Jersey as another refuge for Quakers, remained under strong Quaker influence—arguably even dominance—down to the time of the American Revolution. But the Society of Friends was not an established church. Indeed, it was not a church at all; it was simply a group of friends who met together to worship God and to build community among themselves. The friends had no clergymen and hence no need of taxes to support them. Moreover, the Society of Friends, unlike Roman Catholics and New England Puritans, for example, did not administer public institutions such as schools and charities for the poor that members of the public were entitled to use. Again, there was no need for taxes. Accordingly, the government of colonial Pennsylvania withdrew all financial support from religion and provided little in the way of legal assistance.

In fact, management of most routine affairs of daily life were left to private ordering. Government withdrew from religious affairs and thereby embraced toleration of any and all religious belief. Indeed, the withdrawal extended far beyond mere toleration. Colonial Pennsylvanians understood that justice and the good were concepts, often religious in nature, about which individuals disagreed. As a result, the law allowed like-minded individuals who so desired to join together and practice their beliefs in segregated communities, such as those still inhabited by the Pennsylvania Dutch, or to live apart as individuals in whatever manner their values dictated. From the perspective of the law, it was almost as if religion did not exist.

Like Pennsylvania, Delaware, which was part of the larger colony for two decades, also had no established church.

Maryland, Virginia, the Carolinas, and Georgia

By the eighteenth century, the Church of England had been established in all five colonies south of Pennsylvania and Delaware. But its establishment had not always occurred without strife. It will be recalled, for example, that Maryland had been founded not under the aegis of the Church of England but as a haven for Roman Catholics. From the outset, its founder, Lord Baltimore, had understood that if he wanted what would become a Roman Catholic minority to be tolerated, he would have to create a colony where Catholics and Protestants could live together in peace. Nonetheless, religious conflict had been endemic in seventeenth-century Maryland. Indeed, the Calvert family had fostered conflict by appointing mostly Catholics to the bench and other high posts in government; for example, nineteen of the twenty-seven men who sat on the governor's council from 1666 to 1689 were Catholic, and fifteen of the nineteen were related by blood or marriage to Lord Baltimore's family.

In response, a group known as the Protestant Association formed, and when it learned in 1689 of the accession of William and Mary to the throne in England, it overthrew the Catholic government in Maryland. William and Mary, consistent with their pro-Protestant policies, sanctioned the overthrow, made Maryland a royal colony, and established Anglicanism as the colony's official religion. Thereafter officeholders were required by act of Parliament to take two oaths, the first declaring that no foreign prince or potentate "ought to have any jurisdiction . . . or authority ecclesiastical or spiritual" over any English dominions and the second proclaiming belief "that there is not any transubstantiation in the sacrament of the Lord's Supper."[13] The requirement of these oaths excluded Catholics from office and temporarily even from the right to practice law, thereby leaving Protestants in control. Catholics continued, however, to have possession of their lands, to serve on juries, and to enjoy freedom to practice their religious faith.

Anglicanism, in contrast, had always been the established religion of Virginia, but in the seventeenth century, Virginia's courts had proved themselves weak in dealing with most religious offenses. Although the courts succeeded in prosecuting such common offenses as not attending church or otherwise profaning the Sabbath, were able to prosecute some individuals who defamed clergymen and other church leaders, and did fine a father who failed to baptize his children, most challenges to religious authority received a weak response. Many Virginians in the seventeenth century simply were not churchgoing

Christians, in part, because the colony had only half the number of clergy it needed to fill its pulpits, and living conditions in many parishes were so bad that the ministers who served them were unsuitable.

Transforming Virginians into true Christians thus required both that church institutions be created for them and that once Virginians had been brought into churches, they be made to abide by the norms of those churches. A key figure in accomplishing those tasks was Reverend James Blair, who arrived in Virginia in 1685. Four years later, soon after the Glorious Revolution had placed William and Mary on the English throne, Blair was named the commissary or personal representative of the bishop of London. He immediately set about advancing the pro-Protestant policies of the new monarchs and thereby reforming the Virginia church. As early as 1690, Blair persuaded the Governor's Council to call for stricter enforcement of moral and other religious laws. He remained a significant force in Virginia government into the 1730s, when he was still a member of the council. By then, Blair's efforts had led to the formation of a close alliance between local courts and local churches, with the same gentry families who controlled the county bench also controlling local vestries that possessed substantial governmental responsibilities—to build and maintain churches, to discipline and pay the clergy, and to support the poor. These vestries typically levied the highest taxes that eighteenth-century Virginians paid.

Throughout the eighteenth century, church and state remained closely intertwined. The General Court asserted its jurisdiction over religion, when, for example, it disciplined a minister "of evil fame and profligate manners . . . much addicted to drunkenness" who "officiated in ridiculous apparel unbecoming a priest . . . , exposed his private parts to view in public companies, and solicited negroes and other women to fornication and adultery with him."[14] Likewise at the county level, the late seventeenth and early eighteenth centuries witnessed a revival of prosecutions for religious offenses, such as blasphemy, swearing, cursing, profanity, and Sabbath abusing, which had largely disappeared from court dockets in the post-1660 era. Indeed, by the early eighteenth century, grand juries had developed the habit of presenting and having prosecuted as criminal virtually any conduct on which members of local elites frowned.

In other ways as well, the justices of the county courts became dedicated in the late seventeenth century and thereafter to maintaining the hegemony of the established Church of England. As late as the 1740s, a main threat to that hegemony came from Roman Catholics rather than from dissenting Protestants, and thus the defense of Anglicanism began with the oath taken by the justices, who swore their belief "that there is not any transubstantiation in the Sacrament of the Lord's Supper or in the elements of bread and wine" and that "adoration of the Virgin Mary or any other saint and the sacrifice of the mass as . . . used in the Church of Rome are superstitious and idolatrous."[15]

Catholics faced other forms of discrimination as well. In one case, for example, the Stafford County Court ordered a Roman Catholic who was caring for several orphans to deliver them to specified Protestants to be bound as apprentices. Although the same court would not dismiss cases brought by a lawyer thought to be a Roman Catholic and thereby deny a litigant the right to be represented by a lawyer of his choice, the court over the dissent of three justices did order the lawyer to take oaths mandated by Parliament that were inconsistent with his Catholic beliefs, from which order he appealed to the General Court. And as late as 1756, legislation was enacted to disarm Catholics.

When it came to dissenting Protestants, England's 1689 Act of Toleration required the courts to dismiss charges of not attending church on Sunday if a defendant showed that he or she was a member of a dissenting Protestant communion. Courts were also under a duty to protect dissenting congregations from insult and abuse, although dissenters, in fact, frequently faced discrimination and even physical violence.

But the courts did not make it easy for Protestant dissenters to establish separate congregations. Dissenting congregations were not permitted to build places of worship without prior judicial authorization, which even at the end of the colonial period was not readily granted. In addition, dissenting preachers would be prosecuted for preaching without licenses, which were difficult to obtain. In fact, no dissenting clergymen were licensed until the 1730s.

At the same time that the courts created obstacles to dissenting congregations, they set up rules to further the effective functioning of Anglican parishes. County officials under judicial supervision paid the salaries of Anglican clergy. Judges specified the locations where Anglican clergy were required to preach and supervised vestry elections to ensure that the clergy would have adequate lay support. And in case such encouragement did not suffice, the courts prosecuted parishes that did not provide a minister or reader or failed to keep their church in repair.

Like Virginia, North and South Carolina established the Anglican church. As in Virginia, Protestant dissenters in North Carolina had to obtain judicial approval of the locations of buildings used to conduct their religious services. In South Carolina a political coalition of Anglicans and Huguenots gained a bare majority in the colonial legislature in 1706 and by a statute of that year established the Church of England. In addition to creating territorial parishes and authorizing the building of churches, the 1706 statute provided for the appointment of Anglican ministers and the construction of houses for them. The act, as later amended, also provided for funding churches out of the colony's treasury and for the creation of a powerful, colonywide religious commission. Finally, Anglican ministers received exclusive jurisdiction to perform marriages. The essentials of these laws remained on the books throughout the colonial period, although no evidence exists as to the extent of their enforcement or of the degree of discrimination against dissenters.

Dissenting Protestant sects, in fact, gained significant strength in southern colonies, especially in the decades after 1750. Virginia's Shenandoah Valley and the western parts of the Carolinas were settled not by Anglicans moving west from the eastern parts of the colonies but by Quakers, Baptists, Lutherans, Mennonites, Moravians, and Presbyterians moving southwest from Pennsylvania. Likewise, although the Church of England was officially established by statute in Georgia in 1758, the lack of parishioners had led to the founding of only two Anglican churches in that colony as of 1769.

Thus, at least the western sections of the southern colonies together with the middle colonies witnessed the emergence as early as the 1750s of the religious configuration of nineteenth-century America. It was a pattern of nondenominational Protestant hegemony grounded in communitarian concepts of Christian brotherhood, in which various Protestant sects worshiped separately but lived and worked together in peace and harmony with no one sect obtaining dominance over the others. It was the generic Protestantism that William III arguably had sought to create in 1688–89 with his demand for general toleration of Protestants. It was the direction in which all of Britain's continental North American colonies were moving as their independence approached.

New York

The final colony to be considered, New York, displayed a pluralist, generic Protestantism from its outset. That was because part of the colony, Long Island, was settled by Puritan migrants from New England whereas the Hudson Valley was settled mainly by the Dutch. Manhattan was governed until 1664 by the Dutch, but a substantial English minority and even a small number of Jews lived there. As a result of its diverse population, New York had a confusing conglomeration of religions and no clear pattern of religious domination.

As shown in chapter 3, Dutch courts like other colonial courts took steps in support of religion. When the English took power in 1664, they continued Dutch practices. Thus, the Albany court continued to take an oath "to help maintain here the Reformed religion,"[16] to obtain ministers for the established church from Holland, to pay their salary and expenses, to provide them with housing, and to maintain church edifices. The court also received requests from neighboring towns for Albany's clergymen to minister to their spiritual needs, and it tried to grant those requests without depriving the people of Albany of spiritual services.

These were the easy issues. More difficult problems arose when factions within the Reformed Church found themselves at odds and sought the magistrates' mediation, or when Lutherans complained, with some cause, that they were "looked at askance by the majority of the inhabitants of this place on account of their religion."[17] It was not until 1684 that religion began to gain some independence from government, when the Reformed Church was granted the right to choose its own church masters without judicial approval.

After the Glorious Revolution, the Church of England was established in four counties—New York, Kings, Queens, and Westchester—under 1693 legislation requiring all residents of those counties, except members of the Dutch Reformed Church, to pay religious taxes. Meanwhile Puritan Congregationalists dominated Suffolk County on eastern Long Island, and Dutch Reformed Calvinists were the dominant religion in the counties of the Hudson Valley north of Westchester.

Although no officials collected religious taxes outside the four counties adjacent to New York City, judges there continued to provide aid to religion. Only during the second decade of the eighteenth century did criminal prosecutions for religious offenses such as blasphemy largely cease, as did most efforts to regulate Protestant dissenters. The turning point occurred when in 1707 a jury acquitted a leading Presbyterian minister from Philadelphia in a prosecution for preaching without a license. The law continued, however, to require dissenting congregations to obtain judicial approval of the location of their religious meeting places.

All things considered, New York continued to maintain a partial religious establishment into the mid-eighteenth century. In the four counties of New York, Kings, Queens, and Westchester, most residents continued to pay taxes for support of the Church of England, and throughout the colony dissenting congregations were subject to trivial regulations from which Anglicans were exempt. But the general trend in New York, as elsewhere, was toward toleration of all Protestants and disestablishment even of denominations that enjoyed local religious preeminence.

11

Criminal and Regulatory Law

Criminal Law

The regulation of sexual behavior has long been an important element in the Christian tradition. It was especially important to nearly all of the Protestants who settled in British North America in the seventeenth and eighteenth centuries. As a result, colonial enforcement of the criminal law was closely tied to religious values that called for the prosecution and punishment of sexual offenses.

Of course, every colony at every point in its history also enforced standard prohibitions against violence and theft. Throughout the colonies there were prosecutions for murder, manslaughter, assault, grand and petit larceny, counterfeiting, receiving stolen goods, robbery, and burglary. Arson was another criminal offense in every colony, as was perjury. Political offenses such as treason, sedition, riot, and contempt of court or other authority also were prosecuted with some frequency. Whereas offenses of these sorts in England often were punished by death, few executions occurred in colonial America except in cases of homicide. In particular, almost no death sentences were meted out for convictions of theft.

Defamation was another, sometimes political, offense. But its history was complicated. Some defamation cases were criminal prosecutions brought against defendants who had made negative statements about public officials; the *Zenger* case was the most famous of these. Most cases, however, were merely civil suits typically brought against a defendant who had accused a plaintiff of some sexual or financial peccadillo. Especially in the seventeenth century, it was sometimes unclear whether a case was a criminal prosecution or merely a civil suit. And in the seventeenth century, defamation cases were far more frequent than in the eighteenth: in Connecticut, for example, roughly one-sixth of all civil cases filed between 1666 and 1675 were for defamation, whereas by the 1690s, defamation accounted for only 3 percent of all filings, and after 1700, only 1 percent. But defamation cases never disappeared entirely from court dockets in any of the thirteen North American colonies.

Every colony also punished at least some sex crimes, although significant variations existed from colony to colony. Rape, for example, was a crime in every colony, but it was defined differently. In Massachusetts, as shown in chapter 2, issues arose about whether intercourse with a female under the age of ten constituted rape. At first in 1641, when three servants of John Humfry had nonforcible intercourse with Humfry's three daughters, all under the age of ten, the General Court concluded that the servants were not guilty of rape, but some two decades later it ruled that Patrick Jeanison, who had intercourse with an eight-year-old girl, was guilty, and it sentenced him to death.

There were occasional prosecutions for heinous and apparently rare sex crimes such as incest and bestiality, as well as prosecutions in nearly every colony for sodomy and other forms of same-sex intimacy. Pennsylvania, however, was an exception. No prosecutions for homosexual behavior appear in the extant colonial Pennsylvania court records, and few people were disciplined by Quaker meetings for homosexual activities. The disciplinary advice of the Philadelphia Yearly Meetings offers a clue to the attitudes of Pennsylvania's Quaker leaders. The 1719 meeting, for example, did not specifically mention sodomy or other same-sex intimacies; it merely prohibited men and women from keeping unseemly company or engaging in indecent practices with each other resulting in public scandal. At the same time, discipline was recommended for those guilty of speaking evil or meddling where not concerned with the affairs of others. It appears that Pennsylvania's Quaker leaders worried about sexual misconduct that led to public scandal or had other public ramifications but did not wish to publicize sins in the closet, when publicity had a tendency to provoke discord or cause disesteem among neighbors.

Adultery was a crime in every colony, but it was treated quite differently in the different jurisdictions. In Massachusetts, the penalty for adultery was death and the crime was prosecuted with some frequency, although few adulterers were, in fact, executed; a frequent jury verdict found accused adulterers guilty of lying in bed together, but no more. In mid-eighteenth-century New York, in contrast, adultery was almost never prosecuted. Prosecutions were similarly rare in seventeenth-century Virginia but were more frequent in that colony in the eighteenth century.

Fornication was the most frequently prosecuted sex crime, but again there was significant variation in its treatment from colony to colony and in different time periods. In Massachusetts, fornication was punished because it was sinful, even if it did not lead to the birth of an illegitimate child. In one case, a woman was prosecuted, although acquitted by a jury, for "uncleanness with" a man, "being seen in the very act."[1] In another, two men and two women were prosecuted because they were together on a bed in a room for several hours with the men wearing nothing but their shirts and the women their shifts in what the court described as an unseemly posture. As late as the 1750s, married couples in Massachusetts were whipped or fined for having committed the sin of fornication before marriage if a wife gave birth less than seven months after marriage.

Pennsylvanians similarly regarded fornication as a serious crime and prosecuted it with frequency. In one of the earliest cases, the testimony was that the defendant, John Rambo, entered a room where three sisters, who were acquainted with him, were sleeping together in one bed. As they testified,

> He said he would lie in the bed. We said no. So he jumped in the bed. And so there was not room. So my sister and I went out of the bed and left Bridgett there, and I & sister lay on the floor a little way from the bed till daybreak. The deponent heard him ask Bridgett (about an hour after the deponent and sister left them) if she would have him. She answered no at first and then asking her again she said yes and the deponent heard him say the devil take him if he would not marry her.

A jury found Rambo guilty of getting Bridgett with child, and the court "enjoin[ed]" him to marry her "before she be delivered." If he failed to marry her in time, he was to be fined £10, as was Bridgett, and ordered to keep and support the child.[2]

Fornication was punished in Pennsylvania not only because it produced illegitimate children who might require public support but also because it had an impact on marriage—a process that Quakers regulated tightly. Quakers required couples contemplating marriage to obtain parental consent and the consent of two consecutive monthly meetings, at which the proponents' love for each other would be examined closely. Only after the community had been so assured that it was wise for a couple to marry could a modest wedding ceremony be scheduled. Of course, betrothed couples were directed to "not dwell together in the same house or family . . . until their marriage [was] consumated,"[3] lest they end up in a commitment before the community was satisfied that the commitment was appropriate.

Thus the court records also contain cases like one where Elizabeth Woodyard declared that Philip Yarnell, her betrothed,

> came to her house and asked whether she was a woman and she answered she was all one as other women she thought and he said he would feel and she said he should not and he said how should he know whether she was all one as other women if he did not feel, since she was she that was to be his wife. And then he took her hand being stronger than she and put it into his codpiece and would have her to feel his members how they went limber or stiffer. On another night, they lay

down in bed together and she fell asleep and thought she might sleep near an hour or thereabouts and as she was sleeping she thought she felt her clothes to go up and her feet to move and she awakening ... did happen with her arm to strike him and with her hand unawares she felt his members which did affright her very much.

Philip, in turn, confessed that "he had been foolish insomuch that something scattered from him which was his seed." Philip was not punished criminally for his weakness, but the outcome of the defamation suit he brought, probably for being accused of attempted rape, suggests that people looked at him askance. And Elizabeth announced that she "would never have anything [more] to do with him."[4] Another couple, in contrast, was prosecuted "for being too familiar with each other," although no child was born and they may not even have had intercourse.[5]

Unlike Massachusetts and Pennsylvania, South Carolina punished fornication only if it produced a child who might require public support. Legislation adopted in 1703 did not make sexual intercourse by an unmarried couple criminal unless pregnancy resulted, nor did it punish newlyweds if they had a child less than nine months after their marriage. Because the colony was not concerned with sin but only with protecting the public fisc, South Carolina was harsher on men than most other colonies and easier on women. Women would be prosecuted only for having a child out of wedlock, and even then they would be discharged if no prosecutor or witness against them appeared. In contrast, a man accused by a mother of being the father of her child would be so adjudged, notwithstanding his denial, unless the chief judge of the Sessions Court upon a bench trial found him innocent; the reputed father had no right to a jury trial, as he did in most other colonies. Moreover, if the mother were a servant, the father would have to compensate her master as well as pay support for the child.

In seventeenth-century Virginia, as in South Carolina, the law's concern with fornication was economic rather than moral: almost no prosecutions were brought for sexual activity unless it resulted in the birth of an illegitimate child with whose support the public might be charged. But in the early eighteenth century, following the religious reforms of the Reverend James Blair in the aftermath of William III's accession to the throne, couples were presented for "living in that notorious sin of fornication"[6] or "for being reputed to live in fornication,"[7] even when no evidence was brought forward of birth of an illegitimate child. Charges of fornication would be dismissed, however, if a couple married even after the charges had been presented—which suggests that the immorality of a couple's premarital sex still may not have been the law's primary concern. In New York, on the other hand, presentments for fornication and bastardy became very rare after the middle of the eighteenth century, as individual justices of the peace discharged accused fathers as long as they posted a bond to support their child.

Criminal law was applied more consistently throughout the colonies in countless cases dealing with petty crimes. Most common everywhere were prosecutions for liquor offenses, especially drunkenness and selling alcoholic beverages without a license. In Dutch New Netherland prior to 1664, many prosecutions also were brought for selling liquor after 9 P.M., the time at which establishments were required to close. Other petty offenses in some though not all colonies included gambling, trading unlawfully with Native Americans, failing to perform a public duty, unlawful fishing or hunting, obstructing highways, and dealing corruptly or otherwise improperly with public records.

A persistent issue through the colonial era was whether a defendant accused of some form of misbehavior could be prosecuted for a crime in the absence of a criminal statute or of some other form of fair warning. The issue first arose in Massachusetts in 1641 in the rape prosecution against the three servants of John Humfry discussed above. Although no express law made the acts of the servants criminal, they nonetheless received corporal punishment. Some two decades later, again in the absence of a statute, Patrick Jeanison was sentenced to death for a similar offense, and for several decades thereafter, Massachusetts courts seemed willing to entertain prosecutions for misbehavior even in the absence of explicit legislation, simply because a defendant had not conformed to "customary" norms.[8] But in the 1720s the courts began to show concern about criminalizing conduct not clearly prohibited by statute and started dismissing cases on the civil-criminal borderline for lack of jurisdiction.

Connecticut had a policy similar to the later policy of Massachusetts. In three seventeenth-century cases, its highest court reversed convictions for which no statutory bases existed. In one of the cases, in which the defendant had been prosecuted for reporting falsely that Charles II had died, the court refused to impose any punishment at all. In the two other cases (both prosecutions for murder), the court concluded that the relevant statute did not prohibit the conduct in which defendants had engaged; it therefore reversed their convictions, but it required one of the defendants to give a bond to keep the peace and the other to pay a fine.

Fifty years later the issue arose again in *Colony v. Barney*,[9] which was discussed in chapter 8. Barney, it will be recalled, was prosecuted for castrating his master's six-year-old son. Because "no special provision [existed] in any law of this Colony for the punishment of such crimes," the Superior Court had difficulty with the case and sought the guidance of the General Assembly, which authorized the court to punish Barney's crime harshly, but not by death.

In Rhode Island, a plea of ignorance of the law, apparently resulting from its inadequate publication, was similarly referred to the legislature. Likewise, in

New York, a jury refused to convict a defendant in a criminal prosecution based on a provision in the governor's instructions rather than on a statute. In Virginia, in contrast, grand juries by the early eighteenth century had developed the habit of presenting and initiating the criminal prosecution of virtually any conduct on which they frowned, whether or not statutory law authorized prosecution, and New Hampshire and South Carolina witnessed unusual prosecutions for which no explicit legislation existed, such as one in New Hampshire for breaking a horse on the town commons and one against a South Carolina magistrate for malpractice in acting with bias in a case filed before him.

An important development in nearly every colony in the late seventeenth and early eighteenth century was the reception of the procedures of the common law criminal process. Colonial New Yorkers, for example, became "aware that justice not dispatched by tested instruments was vulnerable" and "that proper forms were the sinews of the individual's protection."[10] The "grand bulwark of . . . freedom & safety, the trial by jury,"[11] along with motions to postpone trial, presentments put into indictment form, and motions in arrest of judgment based upon technical reasons, testify to the extent of common law procedural reception. Local prosecutors were appointed to represent the Crown in criminal proceedings at least from the outset of the 1700s; at the same time, the use of torture, placing people in irons, multiple prosecutions for the same offense, and unlimited powers of search and seizure disappeared. Judicial power in the criminal process, while still vast, became limited.

Similar development occurred elsewhere. In Massachusetts, prosecutions were quashed for lack of jurisdiction, and other cases were dismissed on technical grounds. In one case, for example, an indictment was dismissed because one of the defendants was misnamed. Another case, for abuse of a servant girl, was dismissed for irregularity in the proceedings, and a third was quashed because the indictment did not contain the king's entire royal style—the words Defender of the Faith were missing. Other indictments were quashed for uncertainty, such as failing to identify the time, place, or victim of the alleged criminal act. Courts were prepared to appoint counsel or allow a defendant to retain one when he or she so requested. They routinely honored the prohibition against double jeopardy and granted benefit of clergy in appropriate capital cases. They excused violence on grounds of self-defense and defense of property. The Essex Court of Sessions also released a man arrested on a general warrant, ruling that the law had not been properly followed, although the same court several years later issued the equivalent of such a warrant when it authorized its named agent "to repair to & enter into the housing & cellars or dependencies of such persons . . . convicted within this twelve month last of selling strong drink without license."[12] Seventeenth-century courts had not been scrupulous about adhering to the right of defendants to trial by jury, and in numerous prosecutions, mostly for minor offenses, convictions had been obtained by judgment of the court without either a guilty plea or a trial. But here too, the late 1720s saw pressure for change and adherence to proper procedural standards, especially in connection with the right to trial by jury.

The pattern elsewhere in New England was similar. In the seventeenth century, criminal prosecutions often were quite informal as courts often strove not to impose criminal punishments but to induce parties to make peace. An important result of informality was that defendants did not necessarily receive a jury trial or, indeed, any trial at all. Judicial informality did not, however, necessarily reflect a lack of concern on the part of ordinary people for their liberties. On one occasion, for example, when a constable appeared at a house with a warrant of debatable legality, the occupants stated that "they would not come out, but were resolved to knock down any man that should pry in upon them for their house was their castle."[13]

Libertarian values such as these caused criminal practice in New England to grow more formal toward the turn of the century, when prosecutions began to be dismissed with greater frequency when "due methods of law [were] not . . . attended."[14] Or perhaps it was simply the emergence of lawyers in criminal courtrooms that led to increased formalism. Public prosecutors began to appear in the smaller New England colonies as early as the 1660s in Rhode Island and the 1680s in New Hampshire, in the form of an attorney general for the entire colony. An important consequence of the emergence of public prosecutors was that they began to cut deals with defendants who cooperated with them: one defendant convicted of riot, for example, had his fine remitted when he assisted in the discovery and apprehension of other offenders. Courts also began to appoint counsel to assist defendants being tried for felony, although at least in New Hampshire counsel could address only matters of law.

Whatever the cause, formality sprouted. Greater attention was paid to doctrinal distinctions, such as that between murder and manslaughter. In 1686 the Dominion of New England adopted an important ordinance requiring prosecution witnesses to appear at trial, where they would need to face the accused and be subject to cross-examination, rather than testify by deposition. Courts also recognized a right for defendants to appear in court to answer to and review proceedings against them. And by the mid-eighteenth century, the finality of jury verdicts of acquittal was established, except in New Hampshire.

The same pattern was replicated in Virginia. In the seventeenth century, courts prosecuted crime with little regard for procedural niceties. In many cases, courts dispensed entirely with niceties, tried defendants summarily, and administered punishment. One servant, for example, who confessed to a theft but claimed it had been committed at the behest of his master was summarily given twenty lashes, whereas another man, who had fraudulently taken and sold a horse and was also found guilty by the court of previous thefts, was sentenced to jail until further court order. A third man "of a bad character and by pregnant circumstances . . . guilty" of a theft received thirty-nine lashes, even though "the evidence [would] not touch his life."[15] Similarly, a court refused to declare an indictment insufficient because it lacked an addition to the defendant's name stating his occupation or status. More significant, courts issued broad search warrants, such as one to search every such suspected place in response to complaints of crime, and another to seize twenty-nine hogsheads of tobacco, allegedly about to be shipped unlawfully from the colony.

Especially in the late seventeenth century, lines between the civil and criminal jurisdiction of the Virginia courts were not always clear. One plaintiff, for instance, brought a civil action for conversion of a horse, which a court in 1691 resolved by requiring the defendant to acknowledge his offense on his knees and give a peace bond. Another brought suit against a man who had stabbed him, which resulted both in damages and in the defendant's being jailed and required to give a peace bond. Yet another brought an ambiguous suit against a woman for sinful behavior toward him and others during Sunday services. The attorney general brought suit against a fourth defendant who had married the half-sister of his first wife; when the jury returned a verdict of not guilty, the attorney general appealed to the General Court, contrary to the principle that no appeal is available to the prosecution following an acquittal in a criminal case.

But by the mid-eighteenth century conformity with legal niceties increasingly came to matter in Virginia criminal practice. One presentment for profane swearing was dismissed, for example, because the defendant had never had the law delivered to him by the churchwardens and therefore was entirely ignorant of it; other presentments were thrown out because of uncertainty of the presentment or irregularity of the proceedings. For example, the case of a defendant charged in a county where his offense had not occurred was transferred to the proper county, and another presentment for swearing was dismissed because the particular oaths had not been inserted therein. Other presentments were dismissed for not including the names of the people who had instituted the prosecutions. Likewise, when a defendant following conviction moved in arrest of judgment because the information against him had not stated the date of the offense or the penalty provided by the legislature and had not prayed for the issuance of process against him, the prosecution dropped the proceeding. One defendant even moved in arrest of judgment on the ground that he should have been indicted at common law rather than under a statute.

Particular attention was paid to juries, which apparently had the power of nullification. One defendant, for example, obtained dismissal of a presentment because one member of the grand jury was not a freeholder, and another moved to set aside a verdict because some of the petit jurors who convicted him had served on the grand jury that had presented him. Except for trials before the General Court in Williamsburg, juries were drawn from the vicinage where the crime had been committed; even for trials before the General Court, six jurors were drawn from the county of the alleged crime. This reliance on jurors who often knew something about the defendant and the case, together with technical rules that limited prosecutorial freedom, inevitably reduced the freedom of judges, at least in some cases, to convict defendants whom they believed guilty.

North Carolina followed Virginia, as its courts appointed counsel to represent defendants who requested an attorney and became attentive to procedural issues by hearing motions to quash indictments for uncertainty and motions in arrest of judgment on similar grounds. One of the latter cases also contained interesting claims that a conspiracy could not be prosecuted if only one person was indicted and that a jury verdict was invalid because one of the jurors was not on the approved jury list.

Maryland was a notable exception to the trend occurring in most colonies during the eighteenth century toward greater protection of the procedural rights of criminal defendants. Criminal defendants in Maryland did receive the benefit of appointment of counsel throughout the century, and those convicted of all but a few felonies gained the life-sparing advantages of benefit of clergy. But as late as 1772, the Provincial Court declined to quash an information for forcible entry on the ground of an improper venire and the sheriff's return of jurors who were not freeholders, while in an earlier case a jury that could not by evidence find a defendant guilty nonetheless concluded that her flight made her guilty and justified a sentence of outlawry.

Regulatory Law

In addition to enforcing the criminal law, colonial judges assumed considerable regulatory powers, including power to promote development of local economies. Most important of all, perhaps, was the power to establish and maintain bridges and roads, including private roads appurtenant to a particular tract of land. In some colonies, such as Massachusetts, an owner whose land was taken for a road received just compensation, but in other colonies, such as Virginia, the owner received nothing, even for land taken for a neighbor's private road. Apparently it was enough that the private road enabled a landlocked plantation owner to bring his tobacco to a river and hence to market and thereby furthered the growth of the local economy.

Another task of colonial judges was to authorize the construction of mill dams and then to regulate their operation, including the fees charged by millers. One of the Virginia judiciary's most important powers, for example—a power explicitly authorized by statute—was to grant to owners on one side of a stream an acre of land on the opposite side, thereby enabling construction of a mill dam. In the process, the court would summon a jury to assess damages both to the individual whose acre was seized and to others along the stream whose land might be damaged by the mill pond created by the dam.

Judges also performed other regulatory functions not directly related to land but intended to promote local economies. They had power, for example, to impress men and goods into public service and to naturalize immigrants from foreign countries. Other duties performed by courts included supervision of the assessment and collection of taxes, administration of the poor law, oversight of the administration of estates, and appointment of guardians for minors or their placement in apprenticeships. Judges also regulated the practice of law, admitted men to the bar, and enacted rules for the administration of the courts. In many colonies, they assisted clergymen of the established church in the collection of their salaries.

Perhaps the most important regulatory power of courts was to watch over subordinate institutions, such as the militia and various local officials in the performance of their duties. It is noteworthy that, at least with the support of the bench, municipal officials had broad, almost dictatorial powers, to act in the interests of public health and safety. In one case, for example, in which a husband removed his wife who was ill with smallpox from a location where she had been quarantined and brought her into town, the New Hampshire Superior Court supported town officials and fined the husband 40s. In another case in which a wife alleged that her husband had "by the providence of God fallen into distraction" and was threatening to kill her and her children, the same court directed town selectmen "to take effectual care of" the husband "and prevent him from doing any injury or damage and to restrain . . . him . . . till his disorder shall be removed."[16]

A final duty, at least in some colonies, was the supervision of family life. From the earliest days of settlement in Massachusetts Bay, for example, settlers came as families and were promptly given sufficient land to support themselves as families. Once in Massachusetts, as was seen in chapter 2, the law required them to live as families. Magistrates worried even about an apparently homeless man who was living in Cambridge without any settled abode, and they found him guilty of disorderly living and of keeping company with students at Harvard, wasting their time and debauching their manners.

A persistent problem for all colonies was spousal abuse. Every colony sought to protect wives from abuse, although their approaches to doing so differed. Massachusetts courts, for example, sensing that women were equal human beings who could care for themselves in their husbands' absence, typically imposed criminal penalties on abusers that could result in their absence. In one case in which a defendant was found guilty of mayhem for boring out his wife's eyes and blinding her, he received twenty lashes with a cloth over his eyes, one hour on the gallows with a rope around his neck, nineteen additional lashes, and one year in jail. In other cases, courts fined men or ordered them whipped; occasionally, they required husbands to post good behavior bonds. Pennsylvania judges, in contrast, worried that women needed the help of men. Although some husbands were prosecuted for beating their wives, Pennsylvanians understood that criminal penalties are a blunt tool for remedying family violence and thus, in cases of family violence courts usually had recourse to bonds rather than corporal punishment. An even more effective remedy for most wives was to seek separation and support from a violent husband. Thus, when Hannah Pyle left her husband because he beat and abused her and was living with another woman in their marital home and threatening to squander the estate that Hannah had brought to the marriage, the court ordered him to pay her 3s. per week.

Courts also supervised how parents raised their children. Parents in seventeenth-century Massachusetts, for instance, had an obligation to raise and educate their children properly, not in a rude, irreligious, profane, and barbarous manner. A father who neglected his obligation could be prosecuted for neglect of family government, and children would be removed from a family by court order if a father failed to meet his obligation. In addition, individuals under family government were subject to correction by the head of the family at court order. Indeed, in one case a court ordered a father and mother to whip their son and daughter, respectively, in their own house in the presence of the constable, and children who persisted in disobeying their parents would be sent to the House of Correction.

Eighteenth-century Virginia courts similarly intruded into family governance. One father, for example, was prosecuted for failing to baptize his children, and other courts supervised parental upbringing of children to ensure that they received proper moral training and support. Thus, James and Elizabeth Lee were summoned to appear in court to respond to accusations that they brought up their children to pilfer and steal. Another court required Adam Hubbard to show why he did not keep his children as he ought or permit them to be christened and attend church; when Hubbard failed to appear, the court ordered the churchwardens to bind out his two eldest children. Other children were similarly bound out when courts found their parents too poor to support and educate them in a proper Christian manner.

Both the power of Virginia courts over families and the limits on that power emerged most clearly in a proceeding brought by a widow, Hanna Grey Jacob. When several of her slaves became infected with smallpox, she found it necessary to petition the county court to have her family inoculated against the disease. Her petition was granted, but the court refused to allow inoculation of the county at large—something it deemed too dangerous. Accordingly, the court exercised its power to prohibit other inoculations, although it did declare that other families that wanted inoculations could seek permission to receive them.

Regulation of family life, together with the general regulatory and criminal law jurisdiction of colonial courts thus shows that colonial America was not a laissez-faire society with weak government. The lives of ordinary people in colonial America were strictly controlled. Early America had little or nothing in the way of bureaucracy, and central governments were weak. But local officials, especially judges, and through them local communities were all-powerful. Dissident individuals were free to leave the locality where they lived, but those who remained had to obey community norms.

PART IV

THE COLLAPSE OF EMPIRE
1750–1776

12

The Well-Functioning Empire of the Mid-Eighteenth Century

Imagine a twenty-first century world power with its capital in London consisting of Britain, the United States, Australia, Canada, New Zealand, and perhaps other former British colonies in which the English language and democratic political culture have taken root, such as India and South Africa. Such would have been the most enthusiastic vision of the empire that William III started to build when he ascended the English throne in 1688. This enthusiastic vision, of course, looks absurd today. But it was very much the direction in which the British empire appeared to be moving during the middle decades of the eighteenth century, when common law institutions appeared to be enabling local societies in both Britain and her colonies to enforce England's law in whatever fashion best suited them, while leaving the king in Parliament free to establish imperial protocols and policies.

No government functions with perfect efficiency: people have disputes that may go unresolved, many fail to pay their debts, others do not pay their taxes, some commit crimes, and some criminals are never punished or even apprehended. Sometimes, civil strife becomes endemic. But, except in North Carolina and in parts of New York, government in mid-eighteenth-century British North America appears to have functioned efficiently.

Courts in the mid-eighteenth century routinely resolved disputes over ownership, inheritance, and boundaries of land. The vast bulk of litigation between 1720 and 1775, however, involved suits for debt collection. Courts processed these cases to judgment, mostly by default, quickly and efficiently, although collection of judgments was often difficult and time-consuming and it is unclear how successful the collection process proved to be for creditors. All that can be said with some certainty is that the collection process was sufficiently effective for the flow of lending and credit to continue.

Little is known about the administration of taxation in the first half of the eighteenth century. Smuggling did occur, with the result that some portion of the taxes imposed on commercial activity went uncollected. Most taxes, however, were imposed locally on real property or in the form of head taxes on people. In rural eighteenth-century America, it was impossible to hide land and extremely difficult to hide people for any significant period of time, with the result that in the absence of some sort of exemption, property taxes and head taxes had to be paid.

Except in a few places such as North Carolina and far upstate New York, the criminal law, on the whole, appears to have been effectively enforced. All the standard crimes of the common law—arson, assault, burglary, counterfeiting, forgery, homicide, jail break, perjury, rape, receiving stolen goods, riot, robbery, sedition, and theft, for example—were prosecuted. Moreover, no significant civil strife occurred in most colonies between 1692, by which time the confusion resulting from the Glorious Revolution had come to an end, and the 1760s. Of course, some crimes must have gone undetected, some criminals must never have been apprehended, and some defendants must have been erroneously acquitted. Such events occur in every polity and society.

South Carolina

Once it became a royal colony in 1719, South Carolina provided a notable example of effective governance. An experienced governor, Francis Nicholson, arrived in Charleston in 1721. One of his first endeavors was to work with the colonial legislature to reform the law regulating trade with Native Americans. Trade regulation had been a source of political conflict for decades, as Charleston merchants sought a competitive free trade system under which they could maximize their profits, often by cheating the natives. Local planters responded by seeking publicly regulated trade that would protect the natives and thereby minimize the threat that native tribes would turn to war.

The legislature responded with a 1723 act, which remained in effect for most of the colonial period, placing the Indian trade under the control of a single commissioner, nominated by the legislature after planters and merchants had agreed on a candidate, and then appointed by the governor. The commissioner had plenary power to enact regulations, to issue or deny licenses to anyone seeking to engage in the Indian trade, and to reside among the Native American nations, where he would resolve disputes among traders or between traders and Native Americans, fully and finally without any appeal.

The 1723 act is best understood as an effort to provide the entire colony of South Carolina with something it needed—a system of trade regulation under expert rather than interest group management. The office of trade commissioner became an important one, filled by knowledgeable South Carolinians rather than by placemen from England. Moreover, the office was filled through a process of compromise, between merchants and planters, on the one hand, and the legislature and the governor, on the other. Most significant, the British army stationed small garrisons at trading posts, which also served as frontier forts, to act as police at the trade commissioner's request to apprehend any disobedient trader. In short, public-regarding legislation reflective of political compromise and ultimately enforced by military power provided South Carolina with the law that it had long needed, bureaucratic in nature, for regulating its important Indian trade.

Meanwhile, royal governors permitted continuing development of the sophisticated, learned legal profession and legal system that already were in place to resolve disputes among South Carolinians and between South Carolina entrepreneurs and their commercial partners elsewhere in the Atlantic world. As was true in other colonies, a huge amount of legal energy in the mid-eighteenth century was devoted to debt collection. Another subject with which South Carolina courts dealt was criminal law. The Court of Sessions heard many cases involving standard sorts of criminal prosecutions as well as cases brought to police the conduct of minor officials, such as constables, road commissioners, and the Charleston market commissioners.

During the middle of the eighteenth century, the law developed increasing technicality and sophistication, especially in regard to special pleading in civil cases. Special pleading was especially important in ensuring that statutes were enforced. Thus, when Parliament in 1732 made land and slaves subject to execution in payment of decedents' debts, its statute was enforced in many cases in South Carolina. When executors or administrators of debtors pleaded specially that they had no assets in the form of personal property, creditors pleaded the 1732 act, the executors or administrators filed demurrers alleging the act was inapplicable, and the courts invariably overruled their demurrers. This process of special pleading thereby ensured, as Parliament wished, that creditors would receive their due.

Along with escalating technicality and sophistication came an increase in the power of the legal profession, one that judges on the whole facilitated. To monitor fact-finding and thereby retain control over the law in their own and the bar's professional hands, judges also subjected juries to tight control. Thus, if a jury failed to consider evidence, ruled on the basis of improper evidence, or acted contrary to instructions on the law that it received from the court, its verdict would be set aside and a new trial granted.

Grand juries in South Carolina did possess one unusual power that they did not enjoy in other colonies—a power to begin each term of court by presenting the grievances of the community. The justices appear to have taken these presentments seriously, disposing of nearly every one in every term. One grand jury, however, was not fully satisfied, and it presented "a very great grievance that the Presentment of the Grand Jury is so little taken notice of as to be looked on as a mere matter of form";[1] the court did not respond.

In the end, the legal system of colonial South Carolina was under the total control of a small group of men living in Charleston. Jurors had little power. Although grand jurors could present grievances, judges could dispose of those grievances as they wished. Meanwhile, South Carolina lawyers prided themselves more than most colonials on their Englishness—on their education at the Inns of Court, on the precision with which they copied English practices, and on their English legal learning. There was every reason for authorities in London, as well as leading subjects in Charleston, to be satisfied with the way in which the South Carolina legal system functioned in the mid-century.

Pennsylvania

Pennsylvania was a second colony in which law in the mid-eighteenth century functioned effectively, at least on the surface, in the interests of the Crown, the province's proprietor, and its dominant settlers—in this case, the Quakers. Having empowered themselves rather than juries, as was seen in chapter 9, to determine the substance of the law, Pennsylvania's judges used that law as they needed it—to control the province and maintain its stability. Possession of law-finding power meant that judges would make law; making law meant that judges would decide issues of social policy; and deciding questions of policy meant the assumption of broad political discretion, especially in an era when legislative and executive authorities were weak and there were no administrative bureaucracies.

In the absence of a strong executive and administration, judges had to act in what we would call an administrative and police as well as a judicial capacity. The practice of subjecting criminal suspects to examination before justices of the peace, which was common in eighteenth-century America, was one way that judges assumed policing roles. A more striking illustration of the judiciary's power occurred in connection with disputed election returns. In the ordinary course of events, one of the duties of judges was to certify election results. But sometimes they assumed far greater powers. When a sheriff reported, for example, that tumultuous behavior at an election had prevented him from making a proper return of the results, the court directed the incumbents to serve another term. Similarly, when an election official reported that ill health had prevented him from returning Jonathan Jones as duly chosen supervisor of public roads, the court appointed Jones; and when elected highway surveyors refused or appeared unable to assume their offices, the court appointed others in their stead.

The most extreme assertion of judicial power to ignore the electoral process occurred in Philadelphia. Charles Brockden was the duly elected recorder
of deeds for Philadelphia, but William Parr, who wanted his job, accused him
of being too old and infirm to perform the job properly. The court appointed
a committee to seek Brockden's response to Parr's charge and to inspect his
records. Brockden sent his deputy to answer, but the court apparently refused to
hear him because he had not taken any oath or given any security for his performance of Brockden's job. The court also inspected Brockden's records. It found
they were "kept in an irregular and disorderly manner" and that Brockden no
longer possessed "the capacity and ability . . . to execute the said office." It accordingly removed him and replaced him with William Parr.[2]

Pennsylvania judges sometimes acted forcefully in a variety of other settings.
In one case, for instance, the chief justice of the province was said to have
impeached a county court judgment not properly before him, and in another,
a county court ordered a justice of the peace whose judgment was on appeal
to state the reasons for his judgment. In a third case, judges acted without any
basis in law on a complaint from the neighbors of Owen McDaniels that he had
weapons of which they were afraid; the court confiscated the weapons and prohibited McDaniels from entertaining strangers or letting them abide in his house.

Pennsylvania's judges even challenged the authority of Great Britain. Thus,
they held that the Statute of Frauds, enacted by Parliament in 1677, did not extend to Pennsylvania. The basic rule about the overseas applicability of parliamentary legislation was that statutes enacted before the settlement of a colony
applied to that colony, whereas statutes adopted after settlement did not. The
Pennsylvania Supreme Court interpreted that rule to mean that although the
Statute of Frauds predated Charles II's 1681 charter to William Penn, it still
was not applicable because it was enacted after the Duke of York had assumed
jurisdiction over what later became Pennsylvania. This was a plausible but by
no means compelling interpretation of the basic rule, and one that might have
antagonized officials of the Crown if they had cared about reception of the
Statute of Frauds.

Crown officials probably did not care. In contrast, they had to be concerned
with whether overseas colonies complied with an act of Parliament prohibiting
the arrest of military personnel in civil actions—an act designed to leave soldiers
and sailors available for military duty. Although the Pennsylvania Supreme
Court held that the act did apply in Pennsylvania, it also held that the plaintiff's
"cause of action [was] just & [could] not be determined in th[e] summary way"
that would be required if the defendant could not be kept in jail while the plaintiff prepared his case. It therefore "ordered, that the defendant be committed to
the custody of the sheriff of the city & county of Philadelphia."[3]

The British military also had to be concerned about colonial interference with its efforts to enlist men into military service. One case from Philadelphia, for instance, kept the military from enlisting a man held prisoner in the city's jail for two key years during the French and Indian War, from 1757 to 1759. To the extent that officials in London paid attention to individual cases, they could not have been pleased. It was important, however, that Pennsylvania interfered with the royal military not as a matter of colonywide legislative policy but only in individual cases resting on narrow facts—cases that the Crown could overlook without sacrificing its fundamental policies.

The Pennsylvania Supreme Court also rejected the Crown's position on the issue of whether a general writ of assistance should be granted to customshouse officers. The court thereby made it signficantly more difficult to enforce the Navigation Acts and whatever tax laws Parliament might choose to enact.

Lessee of Albertson v. Robeson[4] raised an issue about the effect of the Privy Council's disallowance of an act of the Pennsylvania assembly. The province's Supreme Court held first that the colonial act was valid and of lawful effect until it was disallowed. But that ruling only raised the next question: What counted as the date of disallowance? Was the relevant date that of the Privy Council's action, or the date on which official news of that action reached Philadelphia? The court, applying Pennsylvania law expansively and minimizing the impact of the Privy Council's action, held that Pennsylvania's laws remained in effect until news of their disallowance reached Philadelphia. One suspects, again, that Crown officials may not have been pleased, although subsequent professional opinion in England accepted Pennsylvania's approach as legitimate.

Pennsylvania judges also were ready to reject English common law rules whenever those rules offended their sense of justice. Thus, when a defendant offered to prove want of consideration as a defense in a suit of debt on a bond, the plaintiff responded that at common law, a court could not inquire into lack of consideration for a bond. He cited four English cases in support of his position. But the court ruled that because there was no chancery court in Pennsylvania, it was necessary to allow defendants to prove mistake or want of consideration and that such had been the constant practice of the courts of justice in the province.

Crown authorities accepted the unfettered fashion in which the Pennsylvania Supreme Court dealt with the law of England, in part because the court dealt with the statutory output of its own legislature in a similar fashion. The authorities recognized that the colonial court was not taking a slap at Britain but rather was adopting a freewheeling approach to legislation similar to that of many modern courts. Thus, in one case the court rejected a claim advanced by a criminal defendant that it should adopt a plain meaning rule in interpreting statutes. Instead, it turned to the standard method of construing documents—authorial intention, reasoning that the colonial assembly "could never [have] intend[ed]" that "such a construction ought to be put on the act as that public justice may . . . be eluded" or that "offenders of the highest nature would escape being brought to justice."[5] On the other hand, when an attorney seven years later urged the court to construe an act on the basis of "the intention of the legislature, considering the whole of the act of Assembly together," the court refused because "the words of the act of Assembly were plain and express."[6] In yet another case, the judges avoided the plain meaning of an act, which did not provide for appeals in a certain category of case, because "review, though not taken notice of in the act of Assembly, had always been granted" and thus had "become a matter of right."[7] The legal realists were not the first to appreciate how the maxims of statutory construction can be manipulated to lead judges to whatever result they want; the Pennsylvania Supreme Court manipulated the rules nearly two centuries earlier.

Judges also were prepared to fill in gaps that the legislature either consciously or unconsciously had left open. Despite the absence of a statute, they fined a widow 10s. for harboring dogs that frightened and killed her neighbor's hogs; it did not help her cause that she had placed the dogs in the care of a young Native American who was her servant. Nor did it trouble the court that its treatment of the widow was unprecedented as long as the treatment led to a result the court wanted to reach.

The main point, with which British authorities had to be pleased, was that Pennsylvania judges used their vast powers to maintain political and social stability—that is, to maintain the status quo. Unlike New York, which had Leisler's Rebellion, and Virginia, which had Bacon's Rebellion, Pennsylvania into the middle of the eighteenth century suffered no major civil strife. Its legal system produced remarkable stability, typically by reaching results that advanced the interests of existing property holders.

One of the basic principles of Pennsylvania law was that "it would be very mischievous now to overturn" practices that had "generally prevailed in this province, from its first settlement, and undergone from time to time the notice of the courts of justice."[8] Courts held, for example, that a *feme covert's* joining in a conveyance without an acknowledgment or a private examination before a justice of the peace sufficed to convey her interest in land she brought to a marriage; they observed

> that it had been the constant usage of the province formerly for *femes covert* to convey their estates in this manner, without an acknowledgment or separate examination; and that there were a great number of valuable estates held under such titles, which it would be dangerous to impeach at this time of day.[9]

Similarly, the Pennsylvania courts held that an informal letter from the secretary of the land office sufficed to convey title to land; as the court noted, "a great part of the province had been settled" on the basis of grants arising out of such letters, and "the general conveniency" required that the letters continue to be given effect. In another case, the Supreme Court upheld a title based on twenty years of possession plus hearsay testimony that the land had been conveyed to the party in possession. Finally, they held that an ancient deed authenticated only by a witness who claimed to recognize the grantor's handwriting constituted sufficient evidence of title.[10]

The Supreme Court also adhered to established practice in commercial cases. An important issue was whether "the strict rules of law with regard to evidence ought . . . to be extended to mercantile transactions." The argument was "that this being a mercantile transaction, such evidence as merchants usually admit . . . should be received." The court agreed.[11]

The law not only confirmed the expectations of merchants about how they could do business; it also sought to establish rules of law that would bring added business to Pennsylvania. One way it achieved that end was to assist people in earning a living. In one case, for example, a minister was indicted for marrying a man to a woman who had another husband living. The attorney general demanded an immediate trial, but the defendant sought a postponement so that he could obtain a material witness. Although such delays normally were not permitted in criminal cases, a delay in this case was "granted by the court, the defendant being a clergyman, and his living depending on his acquittal." The court, however, carefully "declared" its decision "not to be a precedent."[12]

The most important step that courts took to promote Pennsylvania's economic development was to assist in the development of new procedures to facilitate collection of debts, such as garnishment of money and goods of a debtor in the hands of another. Other remedies were developed for dealing with insolvent debtors. One such remedy, for instance, permitted a group of creditors jointly to petition a court to appoint auditors to collect a debtor's assets and divide them proportionally. A creditor also could attempt to keep an insolvent debtor in jail. A debtor then had two options—either to be sold into servitude to the creditor or to some third party who would pay enough to square the debt or to assign all his or her property to creditors and, if no one objected, to seek to be discharged from prison. If a creditor objected, however, the debtor would not be discharged, at least for as long as the creditor was willing to support the debtor and the debtor's family.

William Penn and the leaders who followed him enjoyed remarkable success. Pennsylvania quickly became one of the most prosperous colonies in America and Philadelphia, the continent's leading city. Boston and New York were distant seconds to Philadelphia.

As Andrew Hamilton, perhaps the leading Pennsylvania lawyer of the colonial period, told the Pennsylvania Assembly, it was "not to the fertility of our soil and the commodiousness of our rivers" that the province "chiefly" owed its success. Rather, that success was "principally and almost wholly owing to the excellency of our constitution."[13] Pennsylvania's success, as another commentator noted, was a consequence of its "laws and institutions . . . whose pacific principles and commercial spirit . . . blessed it with tranquility and opulence."[14] Everyone— even officials of the Crown who could not always enforce their policies and had to accept compromise in the form of decisions by officials of the province that they may not always have liked—had to be pleased.

Virginia

The legal system of Virginia was in at least one important respect similar to that of Pennsylvania. Virginia judges like those of Pennsylvania possessed extensive power to control juries and used that power to determine the law and to set social policy. There was one significant difference, however, between Pennsylvania and Virginia. In Pennsylvania, the colony's Supreme Court and a colonywide legal profession based in Philadelphia was able to keep county judges under control and tied to the court's and to the profession's understanding of the law. In Virginia, on the other hand, county-court judges sometimes ignored the commands of the General Court and interpretations of the law advanced by local lawyers, who until the final decade of the colonial period did not, unlike lawyers in Pennsylvania, belong to a truly colonywide profession.

Crown officials accepted manifestations of independence on the part of local judges, who were the effective leaders of their communities. Until the 1760s, an implicit bargain governed the relationship between center and periphery in Virginia. Crown officials gave local judges the legal instrumentalities and economic power they needed to govern their communities, in the form of offices and land. The Crown respected most local judicial decisions about how to govern. In return, local judges protected critical British interests, such as the ability of creditors to collect debts and the requirement that merchants send tobacco to Britain for highly profitable resale to the world. As long as local judges continued to perform their part of the bargain, Crown officials retained them in office and kept granting them more land. The Crown did not need to insist on the symbols of sovereignty: it did not need to insist that local courts obey every mandate of the General Court. Its power to reward those who protected critical interests and to punish those who did not ensured that local judges would not get too far out of line.

In short, Britain governed Virginia as it governed Pennsylvania—through compromise rather than by demanding supremacy. As in South Carolina, Crown officials sought the products that colonials could produce as well as the markets for British goods that colonials sought to buy. They wanted colonial commerce. But they understood that they needed colonial assistance to obtain colonial commerce and that the best way to get that assistance was to compromise with the elites who could provide it. The Crown, that is, understood that a claim of supremacy (like the claim made in the 1766 Declaratory Act) would not obtain the assistance it needed. That assistance would come instead from a bargain with local elites, in which those elites agreed to govern in a fashion that promoted British interests in return for the Crown's enhancement of their power to govern and of the profits that came from that power.

This compromise bargain by which colonial Virginia was governed had emerged gradually during the seventy-five years following Bacon's Rebellion and reached its peak of efficiency around 1750. By the middle of the eighteenth century, Virginia's provincial elites together with Crown officials could look with some satisfaction on the legal order they had created. Although some fragility remained, the colony, on the whole, was governed effectively, with no outward signs of resistance to those in authority. Virginians were among the most docile and supportive subjects in Great Britain's colonial American empire. Beginning in the 1750s, however, as later chapters will show, the legal system governing colonial Virginia entered into decline and finally in the mid-1770s came apart.

New England

Even in New England, which had been a site of continual conflict between the Crown and its opponents in the seventeenth century, a policy of accommodation and compromise and the practice of mutual respect produced effective governance by the second quarter of the eighteenth century. Of course, some tensions persisted. But New Englanders adopted the common law, accepted the presence of a handful of Anglicans in urban centers such as Boston, and became proud members of the British empire at the same time that officials in London permitted residents of the towns in the rural interior to go on governing themselves and living in their accustomed Puritan ways.

Britain's policy of accommodation and compromise, and the willingness of New Englanders to respect it, appears most clearly in the fashion that the Privy Council exercised appellate jurisdiction. Consider, for example, Rhode Island litigation, discussed at length in chapter 10, construing a 1668 grant of land to a minister described as orthodox. The litigation gave the Privy Council two opportunities to declare the Church of England to be the orthodox and arguably the established church of Rhode Island, but on both occasions, in 1725 and again in 1752, the Privy Council accepted Rhode Island's policy of non-establishment and turned down the opportunities. Meanwhile, Rhode Island respected the Privy Council by recognizing the council's jurisdiction and participating intensively in argument of the two cases, as well as many others. Litigation over New England's rejection of the common law rule of primogeniture reveals the same pattern of deference and mutual understanding. *Winthrop v. Lechmere*[15] was the first case raising that issue to be decided by the Privy Council. As chapter 8 suggested, Lechmere's attorney did not argue effectively in support of the Connecticut rule of partible inheritance, and the Privy Council accordingly held it invalid as repugnant to the common law. Connecticut respected the result and enforced the judgment in the case, but it began a lobbying campaign to limit the *Winthrop* holding to the particular case, and in *Clark v. Tousey* the Connecticut court ruled that *Winthrop* was not binding in other cases. When the defeated litigant immediately appealed to the Privy Council, Connecticut respectfully awaited the council's judgment.

Meanwhile, in the Massachusetts case of *Philips v. Savage*, the council upheld a 1692 Massachusetts intestacy act rejecting primogeniture—the act from which Connecticut's rule of partible inheritance had been copied. Next the Privy Council dismissed the appeal in *Clark v. Tousey* without stating its reasoning and let stand the holding of the Connecticut Superior Court that primogeniture was not that colony's law.

We can interpret these cases as part of a sophisticated dance in which colonials conceded their obligation to submit their legislative acts and judicial judgments to the Privy Council, with the council tacitly conceding, in return, that colonial law need not always be identical to English law. Although the council never explicitly declared that it would not insist on its supremacy and its requirement that colonial law be consistent with English law, in practice it compromised, accommodated colonial law and imperial policy, and did not enforce its supremacy when important British interests were not at stake.

Mary Sarah Bilder has best described mid-eighteenth-century understandings of the process of appeal to the Privy Council. Appeals, as she sees it, should not be viewed as contestations between local and imperial powers. The Privy Council was not always seeking to impose central authority and policy, and colonial courts were not always striving to protect their autonomy. On the contrary, Bilder suggests, the main goal of the imperial jurisdictional structure was to provide justice to individual litigants. The Privy Council, she explains, served as a neutral arbiter of internal conflicts in cases of disagreement among Rhode Island decision makers.

Bilder also notes that the Privy Council and local courts displayed considerable respect for each other. When litigants in *Freebody v. Brenton*, for

instance, complained that a Rhode Island court thought itself "under no obligation to pay any obedience to the authority of Great Britain" and thus had
failed to obey a Privy Council order, the council backed off from confronta-
tion, merely asking the Rhode Island judges to explain what they had done.
The judges explained that although they had an "obligation of duty and respect" to the Privy Council's "right . . . of hearing and determining all matter
of appeal," they were not mere inferior officers who simply executed orders,
but judges obligated to exercise judgment in obedience to the "laws, customs
and usages of the country" under which they held their commissions. They
argued that they thus had authority to apply Privy Council orders loosely as
long as they complied with "the most substantial part and essentials" of those
orders. At the same time, they concluded that their duty to local interests
would "never be the least impediment to the most entire and ready obedience
to his royal will and pleasure signified to us either as judges of the superior
court of his loyal colony of Rhode Island, or as faithful subjects to the best of
Princes."[16]

Summary

Examination of Privy Council appeals and of practices of governance in South
Carolina, Pennsylvania, Virginia, and New England shows that by 1750 Britain
and its colonies had constructed a remarkable structure of imperial governance—
a structure that left local communities free to govern themselves while simultaneously respecting the jurisdiction of central officials. From the perspective of
mid-century, those who had created the governance structure could be proud of
their accomplishment and optimistic about the capacity of the structure and of
the empire it governed to endure over time. They had no reason to predict that
a mere quarter of a century later, both the structure and the empire would be
coming apart.

Of course, the governance structure of the mid-eighteenth-century British
empire did not function perfectly. No governance structure ever does. There
were disputes, conflicts, and tensions in every colony. And in two places to
which it is necessary to turn next—North Carolina and northern New York—
government often failed to function at all.

North Carolina

In the late 1720s, as shown in chapter 9, North Carolina's judicial system fell
apart. North Carolina then became a royal colony, and in 1731 a new royal

governor, George Burrington, arrived with the task of restoring legal order. He succeeded only minimally.

Burrington began by cleaning house, removing all members of the General Court from office. One of those he removed was Chief Justice Christopher Gale, the most distinguished lawyer in North Carolina's history up to that time. Despite Gale's accomplishments, his political activities probably necessitated his removal. But Burrington found it difficult to replace Gale. He first appointed William Smith, but Smith held office for only fifty days before resigning and leaving for England. Then the governor tried to appoint John Lovick, who had served on the proprietary General Court, but that appointment never took effect. Burrington's next choice was John Palin, who had been an assistant judge during the proprietary period, but Palin served only briefly and then resigned because of illness. Finally, Burrington settled on William Little, who had been attorney general in the Everard years. Opponents, however, found Little and the four assistant judges whom Burrington appointed unskilled in the law, and eventually the Provincial Assembly, in response to a speech by the governor, accused Little and his assistants of a perversion of justice. Soon thereafter, William Smith, who had returned to the colony, again assumed the post of chief justice.

In a strikingly partisan move, Burrington raised to the council two of his former friends and supporters during the time of the Everard governorship at the end of the proprietary era—John Ashe, the lawyer who had represented him on indictments before the General Court, and Edmond Porter, who had led the opposition to Governor Everard after Burrington's departure for England. But he quickly broke with them. About a year after his arrival in North Carolina, Burrington induced the Council, by a 4–3 vote, to suspend Porter from the council and from his post as judge of the Admiralty Court. And when Burrington seized for his personal use two horses belonging to Ashe and Ashe filed an action in the General Court, Burrington argued that as governor he could not be sued in North Carolina but only in England, and the court accepted his argument. Then, the governor procured an indictment against Ashe for criminal defamation, and the court ordered his arrest, although following an initial hearing the prosecution was dropped.

Opponents accused Burrington of seeking to influence the judiciary and the legal profession in favor of his friends and against his enemies. One of his edicts required attorneys, other than those already admitted to practice in England, to obtain Burrington's license to practice. The court used this edict to deny members of the popular party, such as Edward Moseley, who was plainly a competent attorney, the privilege of practicing law. When Moseley, despite his dismissal from the bar, nonetheless defended some individuals indicted at Burrington's behest, the governor had him arrested, although the General Court promptly released him on habeas corpus.

The bias and partisanship of the Burrington administration and, perhaps, of its judges, following upon that of Governor Everard, plagued North Carolina and undermined the development of law and the legal profession for decades thereafter. Some twenty years later, the General Assembly reminded the then governor and council that "the time [was] still within the memory of some of the members of this House" when men were "admitted to practice as Attorneys or Lawyers" who were "not properly qualified for that business . . . with no rec-ommendation, capacity, or ability than that of being obsequious tools of a bad administration," whereas "others, ancient practitioners of good character, known integrity, and knowledge in the law ha[d] been obstructed in their business or practice for no other reason than that they or their clients . . . ha[d] incurred the displeasure of the Chief Magistrate."[17]

Still, the royal government did experience gradual, partial success in resettling the courts and restoring order. Especially important were the actions of Burrington's long-term successor as governor, Gabriel Johnston, who sought to put an end to past animosities and to build an inclusive administration by achieving a reconciliation with Burrington's opponents. But North Carolina's extensive size remained a problem, and the General Court proved unable to ad-minister law effectively in areas distant from the colony's capital. As a practical matter, litigants and witnesses found it nearly impossible to travel to court from most parts of the colony, and not only civil but even criminal cases from those parts could not be adjudicated.

As early as 1731, both the General Assembly and the council had prepared legislation to establish circuit courts in the northeast, central, and southeast segments of the colony. Both bills, however, raised a difficult issue: Who would ride circuit or otherwise staff the courts? Governor Burrington was of the view that the assistant judges on the General Court possessed the same power to hear and adjudicate cases that the chief justice possessed, but several members of the council, including the incumbent chief justice, thought that only the chief jus-tice possessed judicial power; the assistants, in their view, had power only to inform and advise.

Perhaps because of this disagreement, it was not until 1737/38 that legisla-tion creating circuit courts was enacted, along with legislation abolishing the colonywide office of provost marshal and replacing it with locally appointed sheriffs for each county. The circuit courts, held only by the chief justice, then began to conduct trials under a nisi prius system and to report cases back to the full General Court meeting in Edenton on the Albemarle, where all initial actions had to be filed. Extant records suggest that the burden that circuit ri-ding placed on the chief justice and the court clerk was so heavy either that the circuit courts met only infrequently and heard few cases or that their proceed-ings were irregularly recorded. In either case, it seems, the circuit courts were relatively ineffective in bringing law and justice to more remote parts of North Carolina.

The legislature sought to remedy this situation in 1746, when it passed a new law altering the 1737/38 act. But the 1746 act only made matters worse. Although it did provide separate clerks for each circuit branch of the General Court, it did nothing to lighten the excessive burden that the earlier act had imposed on the chief justice when it confirmed that he alone could hold circuit courts. Its most significant change was to move the seat of the General Court from Edenton, in the northeast corner of the colony, to New Bern, which was more centrally located and thus more accessible to litigants and witnesses.

With the departure of the General Court from Edenton, the somewhat fragile legal profession that had grown up in the town atrophied. The quality of the judges and lawyers staffing the General Court also appears to have declined, and the clerk's office at Edenton lost a large part of its work and therefore its fees, and it too apparently atrophied. It does not appear that effective clerical and professional institutions to replace the old ones at Edenton developed either in New Bern or in the locations designated for holding circuit courts. Following the passage of the 1746 act, minutes of the General Court's sittings exist only for three terms, two in 1749 and one in 1751. Either the court did not meet in most of the terms when it was scheduled to meet or its sittings were lackadaisically recorded and its records carelessly deposited. Professional sophistication and care were similarly absent at the level of the county courts—local bodies that had replaced the old precinct courts.

In any event, especially in the decade after 1746, the judicial system lost its effectiveness and left North Carolina in turmoil. As one visitor observed, in many locales there was "perfect anarchy."

> Crimes [were] of frequent occurrence, such as murder, robbery, etc. But the criminals [could] not be brought to justice. The citizens [did] not appear as jurors, and if court [was] held to decide such criminal matters no one [was] present. If anyone [was] imprisoned the prison [was] broken open and no justice administered. In short most matters [were] decided by blows.[18]

Something had to be done. Accordingly, the legislature in 1754 adopted a law directing a Supreme Court to sit in five different locations, where it could be held either by the chief justice or, in his absence, by any two other justices. The new Supreme Court was not a nisi prius court; writs were to be filed, proceedings commenced, and judgments rendered in the locale where a given branch of the court met, not in Edenton or New Bern. Each branch also had its own clerk, who was under specific instructions about how to keep both docket books and permanent record books and who relied on local sheriffs to carry out service of process and execution of judgments. The legislature also created county courts.

The new Supreme Court appears to have functioned effectively in Edenton and New Bern, where sittings occurred regularly and where the judiciary obtained plenary control over the lawfinding power of juries. Proceedings in the Wilmington court, especially those of a regulatory and criminal nature, were similar, but far fewer civil actions were filed in Wilmington than in either Edenton or New Bern, and in fact, no civil cases were recorded in the court minutes between October 1764 and November 1768. And, as will appear in chapter 15, matters were chaotic on North Carolina's western frontier.

Northern New York

Beginning no later than the 1750s, colonial authorities in New York had great difficulty in maintaining order and enforcing the law in northern parts of the colony. Only one-third of Albany County criminal cases, for example, resulted in conviction; some 60 percent disappeared from judicial dockets for want of processing. And as early as the 1750s, a series of rent strikes began in the Taconic region on the border between New York and New England. These strikes left much of that region in open rebellion.

Problems in the Taconic arose out of the imprecision of borders. The eastern boundaries of the great Hudson River patroonships were uncertain, as were the boundaries between New York and the New England colonies of Connecticut and Massachusetts. As a result, it was unclear whether residents in a large stretch of territory, most of whom had emigrated from New England, occupied their land as tenants of the Hudson River patroons or as fee simple owners with titles derived through grants from one of the New England colonies, through purchase from Native Americans, or through adverse possession, that is, squatting. In 1751, violence broke out between the patroons and local New York authorities seeking to enforce the patroons' rights, on the one hand, and the New England emigrants and their supporters in Massachusetts, on the other. The violence continued until 1757, when the Board of Trade in England finally fixed the boundary between New York and Massachusetts. Those east of the boundary obtained their fee simple titles. Those west of the boundary officially became tenants, although conflict continued and sometimes turned into violence as patroon landlords sought to enforce their rights and the tenants resisted.

The Taconic rent strikes made it clear that law was unenforceable in New York except by local people on local terms. Law was not what the governor or even the Assembly by statute commanded; law was what local people, either jurors or trial judges beholden to local constituencies, declared the law to be and were able to enforce. New York's peripheries remained ungovernable from the center. In places like Long Island's Suffolk County, where the Puritan presence influenced legal institutions, law enforcement was efficient. On the contrary, the law in Albany and the regions to its north was ineffective, as the large size and thin population of the northern counties, along with the harshness of their climate, made enforcement difficult.

Explaining Law's Failure

How can the failure of law enforcement in much of mid-eighteenth-century North Carolina and most parts of upstate New York be explained? What made North Carolina and upstate New York different from New York City and Long Island and from Pennsylvania, South Carolina, southern New England, and Virginia?

The most important difference was geographic size. North Carolina and New York were large colonies. Until 1746, the North Carolina General Court sat only in Edenton, over 80 miles from New Bern and over 170 miles from Wilmington; even after the court moved to New Bern in 1746, major population centers remained 80 miles away. New York was even larger; Albany is some 150 miles north of New York City, and many of the outlying areas in which the law went unenforced were even more distant from the capital city. By comparison, the three southern New England colonies were tiny: the greatest distance between county seats to be traversed before the creation of Berkshire County in 1761 was between Boston and Northhampton, the county seat of Hampshire County—a total of some 90 miles. Until the 1770s, South Carolina was a tiny polity centered around Charleston. Although Pennsylvania today is a large state, it remained a small colony into the 1740s: Lancaster, the most distant county seat was only about 70 miles from Philadelphia, and Reading, the second most distant, was only some 50 miles away. Even York, which is west of the Susquehanna River and became the seat of York County in 1749 was only 30 miles beyond Lancaster.

Except in occasional locations such as the South Carolina frontier, where small units of British army regulars assisted in law enforcement, eighteenth-century government lacked a military force or a mobile bureaucracy. Its enforcement power was limited to the distance that some part-time official could travel from and back to his home in a day. Under eighteenth-century conditions, these distances were short. As a result, it was much easier to enforce the law in small colonies than it was in large ones.

Virginia was the exception. It was a geographically large colony—the largest colony of all—and it enforced law effectively. What made Virginia's legal system so strong whereas North Carolina's was so weak?

The answer lies in the structure of the judiciary. Judicial power in Virginia was localized. The colony was governed by county courts presided over by judges who were men of wealth and standing, who controlled the economic life of their counties, and on whom ordinary residents were dependent. There was a colonywide General Court with exclusive jurisdiction over major felony cases, concurrent jurisdiction over major civil cases, and broad appellate jurisdiction. But the real power of the General Court appears to have been limited. County courts ignored its mandates at times and, on the whole, decided by themselves most litigation that mattered. They constituted the governments of Virginia, and each one governed its county effectively, just as colonywide courts in small colonies governed their localities effectively.

In North Carolina, by contrast, precinct courts had limited jurisdiction. The General Court was the principal mechanism of governance. In the late seventeenth and early eighteenth centuries, when North Carolina was a small colony centered around the Albemarle Sound, the General Court could govern effectively. As the colony grew larger in the mid-eighteenth century, new institutions were needed, but the legislature was slow to establish them. When circuit courts were created in 1737–38 and again in 1746, a single chief justice was charged with staffing all the circuits; he was overwhelmed, and law and order collapsed. Only after 1754, when the legislature created a separate Supreme Court for each region of the colony and county courts modeled after those of Virginia, did law enforcement begin to recover, at least in the two most densely settled regions of the east.

A comparison between Manhattan, where law was enforced with reasonable effectiveness, and upstate New York, where law and order collapsed, reveals similar phenomena. Merchants and their lawyer allies controlled the courts in New York City. They also controlled the city's economy, and ordinary residents were dependent on them. The merchants and lawyers used their economic power to control the outcome of litigation and to enforce judgments. In upstate New York, on the other hand, there was a gap between the governing class and ordinary people—a gap that had the effect of placing those who sought to govern in a separate society from those whom they wished to govern. In the Mohawk Valley, for example, the most powerful man was William Johnson, the superintendent of Indian affairs. Johnson's wealth, however, was based on his relations with the Iroquois and gave him little influence over the small farmers who were beginning to settle the region. Likewise, in Vermont and in the Taconic region to the south, most families had migrated from New England, sometimes held land titles based on grants from New Englanders, and looked to their old communities for sustenance rather than to Hudson Valley notables or other New York landlords. As a result, the New York elite had little capacity to coerce or otherwise govern the people around them.

Four other factors also may have contributed to undermining the law in North Carolina and northern New York. The first was ethnic diversity. New England was settled by Puritan Englishmen and remained ethnically homogeneous throughout the eighteenth century. Virginia was settled by Anglican Englishmen and, at least to the east of the Shenandoah Valley, remained equally homogeneous. South Carolina had more ethnic diversity even in its eastern core, especially with the settlement of Huguenots, but its population in the region surrounding Charleston, like New England's and Virginia's, was mainly English. Pennsylvania was more diverse, with large numbers of German and Scottish immigrants, but its Quaker Englishmen remained in firm control, and German and Scottish immigrants were dispersed to the far frontier.

New York was diverse. Founded by the Dutch and conquered by Anglican English, it also was subject to substantial immigration from New England Puritans to the east. Throughout the eighteenth century, the three groups vied with one another for power, influence, and ultimately control. North Carolina was settled by similarly diverse groups of people—Anglican English in the east and Protestant dissenters from Pennsylvania, many of German background, in the west. Ethnically and religiously diverse people are more difficult to govern than people who share a common language, a common culture, and common political norms.

The pattern of land titles was a second factor contributing to chaos in the Taconic region of New York. As discussed earlier, much of the difficulty in the Taconic resulted when settlers from New England, who claimed title under grants from the New England colonies, confronted New York patroons, who claimed title to the same land under old Dutch and English New York grants.

A third factor that may have influenced the ability of elites to govern the eighteenth-century colonies was the structure of the legal profession. Virginia had a significant number of judges and lawyers who had been educated at the Inns of Court, and Charleston, New York City, Philadelphia, and by the middle of the eighteenth century, Boston, all had learned bars, with lawyers from Philadelphia and Boston traveling with judges to outlying counties and thereby spreading their learning throughout their colonies.

Learned lawyers probably helped in securing enforcement of the law. New York lawyers, in contrast, did not travel to the far northern reaches of the colony. Their absence from the Mohawk Valley and the Taconic may well have undercut law enforcement in those locales. North Carolina, in turn, had a weak profession. As shown above, the fledgling bar in Edenton was gravely undermined by the transfer of the capital to New Bern. North Carolina lawyers thereafter could provide little help in enforcing the law.

Misgovernance may have been a final factor undermining the law. The legal system worked well in New England and colonies such as South Carolina and Virginia when imperial officials paid heed to colonial interests, such as partible inheritance, sound regulation of Indian trade, and governance by local elites having knowledge of local conditions. The imperial system worked well when the center compromised with the periphery. By contrast, when governors like Richard Everard and George Burrington politicized the judiciary, the legal system collapsed. On the other hand, colonywide politics cannot explain the weakness of law in northern New York because the same politics left the law strong in New York City and elsewhere in the colony's south.

The same four factors that may have contributed to the failure of law in North Carolina and northern New York in the mid-eighteenth century undermined the ties binding Britain to its other continental North American colonies in the years to come. Misgovernance by British officials surely played a role, as did the legal profession's loyalty to the common law and its distrust of legislation. America's ethnic and religious diversity also contributed in complex ways to the coming of the Revolution. Above all, when the ties binding Britain and its colonies began to come apart, the lack of a bureaucracy and an army together with the local nature of power left British authorities with little on which they could rely to hold the empire together.

13

Weakening the Bonds of Empire

As shown in chapter 12, officials of the Crown both in Britain and in the colonies, on the one hand, and colonial leaders, on the other, tended to pursue a policy of accommodation and compromise and to treat each other with mutual respect during the first half of the eighteenth century. As a result, most colonial constitutions and governments functioned tolerably well. But with the *Zenger* case in New York in 1735, change began to occur. Memorable conflicts broke out between Crown officials and colonial figures. Lawyers who represented the colonial leaders played a decisive role in every one of the conflicts, with the result that the position of lawyers in colonial government and politics began to change. Many lawyers ceased to be what they had been—agents of the Crown who used the prestige of appointed office to build a practice through which they prevailed on subjects to pay debts and otherwise obey the law. Some lawyers, instead, coalesced to form a profession that articulated and disseminated legal and constitutional arguments designed to limit the power of Parliament and the king.

Before the details are examined, however, it is essential to be clear about what lawyers did and did not do. Lawyers did not cause the American Revolution; they did not know a revolution was coming, nor did they seek to bring one about. What lawyers did was represent individuals and interests opposed to policies of Parliament and the Crown in the same fashion that lawyers today represent clients and their interests. In the process, lawyers developed arguments in support of the supremacy of local, common law and of the duty of judges to maintain that supremacy. As representatives of what developed into the Revolutionary cause, lawyers also found themselves in positions of public leadership, and when the Revolutionary cause emerged victorious, members of the profession maintained the leadership role that had earlier been thrust upon them. As a result, American lawyers continue to this day to exercise a leadership role unique among world governments.

New York and the *Zenger* Case

According to Gouverneur Morris, a Revolutionary leader and thoughtful Revolutionary observer, "The trial of [John Peter] Zenger in 1735 was the germ . . . of that liberty which subsequently revolutionized America."[1] The *Zenger* case marked the beginning of a new era—an early step in a process leading up to the American Revolution and American independence.

The *Zenger* case arose from a new form of politics carried on in the print media and spread up and down the Atlantic coast in the decades that followed. *Zenger* began a process of removing politics from localities and relocating it on a continental scale. More important, the case marked the beginning of a new relationship between lawyers and society. Recall from chapter 4 that Charles II had brought the common law and lawyers to America to serve as enforcers of law and Crown policy in place of bureaucrats and military officers that the monarchy had no money to pay. From their arrival in the mid-seventeenth century up to the *Zenger* case, lawyers had not assumed an organized role in opposition to Crown policies; what opposition occurred had come mainly from clergymen, ethnic and religious minorities, and the poor. But in *Zenger* a significant segment of the legal profession in New York joined forces against an official of the Crown. And in a highly publicized case, the lawyers won. Many lawyers thereafter continued to work at times for the opposition, assuming a role of opposition leadership that ultimately carried the bar into revolution.

The *Zenger* case arose indirectly out of the death in 1731 of Governor John Montgomerie, whose uneventful administration had lasted for only three years. Between Montgomerie's death and the arrival of his successor, William Cosby, over a year later, Council President Rip Van Dam had served as acting governor and had enjoyed the salary and other emoluments of office. When Cosby arrived, he claimed that half of that money was his, but Van Dam refused to pay. Cosby thereupon decided to sue.

A problem Cosby faced was to choose a court in which to sue. The Supreme Court with its trial by jury was likely to favor Van Dam, a popular New Yorker, and therefore Cosby decided to sue in equity. He could not sue in the Court of Chancery, however, because he was the chancellor and could not be judge in his own case.

Cosby invented a solution. He promulgated an ordinance conferring equity jurisdiction on the exchequer division of the Supreme Court and brought suit there. However, Lewis Morris, who was chief justice of the Supreme Court, objected to this use of prerogative power by Cosby to advance his personal interest, held that the exchequer division of the Supreme Court lacked jurisdiction, and dismissed Cosby's suit. Cosby then raised the stakes by dismissing

Morris from office—a dismissal that provoked a debate in the colonial assembly about the constitutionality of prerogative equity.

Cosby made matters even worse, if that was possible, when he entertained a suit in his own chancery court challenging the title of a group of his political opponents to a large tract of land along the New York-Connecticut border. Cosby's opponents, led by Lewis Morris, Rip Van Dam, and a lawyer named James Alexander, among others, responded by anonymously founding a newspaper, the *New York Weekly Journal*. They hired John Peter Zenger, a recent German immigrant, to print the paper, and they began a newspaper campaign vehemently denouncing Cosby.

The dispute between Cosby and his opponents, as outlined so far, was not ideological. It was about money and factional politics, and like all disputes between factions about money, it could have been settled by compromise. But Cosby was unwilling to give up his personal financial goals and insisted on using his gubernatorial powers to circumvent ordinary legal procedures. His opponents responded by turning to a political technology, the print media, which had functioned for decades in England but was new to New York, to lambaste the governor.

Cosby's turn to equity failed to produce the victory he sought, and the vehement denunciations of his administration in the opposition newspaper, the *New York Weekly Journal*, continued. Still the possibility of compromise remained. But Cosby unwisely rejected it and decided instead to prosecute the printer of the *Journal*, John Peter Zenger, the only person publicly connected with the newspaper, for seditious libel. Once Cosby made this decision, the possibility of compromise disappeared and pivotal ideological stakes emerged. Either Zenger would be found guilty, opposition would be silenced, and authoritarian government, it was feared, would be inaugurated, or Zenger would be found not guilty and open, competitive, pluralist—ultimately democratic—politics would be legitimated.

For Cosby to succeed in silencing opposition, it was necessary for him to continue his policy of circumventing ordinary legal procedures. He now had to circumvent the ordinary criminal process, in particular, the power of the jury. Cosby began effectively enough by having Zenger arrested on a special warrant of the Governor's Council rather than by ordinary legal process. He next tried to induce a grand jury to indict Zenger, but it refused, and Cosby had to proceed by having the attorney general file an information in lieu of an indictment. Still, the petit jury remained ahead, and Cosby needed to get around it.

His plan was to have the attorney general argue that the jury had power only to return a verdict on the narrow question of whether Zenger had actually published the allegedly libelous words—a matter that Zenger conceded. A second, more substantive issue—whether the words constituted a libel—was, according to the attorney general, a question of law solely for the court. On the other side, Andrew Hamilton, Zenger's lawyer, argued that the jury should return a general verdict of not guilty, finding in the process that because Zenger's words were true they did not amount to a libel.

A new chief justice, James DeLancey, pressured by the governor but loyal to the legal profession, equivocated, instructing the jury that "as [the] facts or words in the information are confessed the only thing that can come before you is whether the words as set forth in the information make a libel. And that is a matter of law, no doubt which you *may* leave to the court." He then read from a charge in an earlier English case in which a jury had been instructed "to consider whether the words tended to beget an ill opinion of the government" and thereby amounted to a libel.[2] As the chief justice in his instructions had left it open for them to do, the jurors accepted Hamilton's argument, decided as a matter of law that Zenger's words did not constitute a libel, and returned a general verdict of not guilty.

What was the significance of the *Zenger* case, beyond being a crushing defeat for Governor Cosby, who died soon after? New Yorkers cheered the jury's verdict as a great victory for liberty, and the entire British world was made aware of the case by a pamphlet entitled *A Brief Narrative of the Case and Trial of John Peter Zenger*, published in 1736 by James Alexander, one of Zenger's lawyers.

Alexander's narrative summarized all the arguments in the case but focused on Andrew Hamilton's two main points. The first was that freedom of the press was the primary bulwark of a free society and that treating truth as a defense to any libel prosecution was essential to preserving that freedom. Hamilton's second main point was about the power of the jury. Hamilton "insist[ed] that where matter of law [was] complicated with matter of fact, the jury" had "at least as good a right" in a seditious libel case as in any other "to determine both."[3] The chief justice had implicitly agreed to this view when he left jurors free to decide whether the *Journal*'s words constituted a libel rather than limiting the jurors to the only issue that the attorney general thought they should decide—the issue of publication, which had been conceded by the defense.

The *Zenger* case was not a precedent that bound subsequent courts to follow what it had done. The case did not establish, as a matter of law, that truth was a defense. But it cast doubt on what had been largely accepted doctrine in New York until that time—that juries decided the facts and judges decided the law. It made the politically conscious class—the men, that is, who would sit on juries—aware of their power to ignore judges' instructions on the law and made the agents of the Crown aware of the impossibility of circumventing the jury's, and hence the people's, opinions on the law.

It is difficult to connect the *Zenger* case directly to subsequent developments leading to the American Revolution. But it does appear that the verdict of not guilty set limits on royal government in the American colonies and in that sense constituted a germ of revolution. James Alexander's *Brief Narrative* was republished fifteen times between 1736 and the end of the eighteenth century, including once in London. Although the case did not bring an end to seditious libel prosecutions in England or to prosecutions on behalf of legislative bodies in America, it did chill the capacity of British officials in the colonies to bring such cases.

In its immediate aftermath, for example, the *Zenger* case made it possible for a Philadelphia printer named Benjamin Franklin to publish a 1741 speech by a former justice of the peace in Lancaster County, who had been removed from office because he had joined the opposition to the colony's administration. Two decades later, in the 1760s, the *Zenger* case left colonial opponents of parliamentary policies similarly free to excoriate Parliament in the press. It also spread the message that juries should have power to determine law as well as fact, thereby encouraging juries to assume greater power in the legal system and, perhaps, limiting the willingness of judges to rein juries in. Increased jury power, of course, limits the power of central government officials to enforce their view of the law.

But, as suggested at the outset, the most important impact of the *Zenger* case may have been to mark the entry of lawyers into opposition politics. Of course, lawyers previously had assumed political roles but mainly in support of rather than opposition to the Crown. In *Zenger*, a significant group of lawyers joined in confronting an official of the Crown. They won, thereby instructing future opponents of British authority about how lawyers could assist them. *Zenger*, in short, created potential alliances between the bar and other American political elites and encouraged members of the bar to think about how they could serve those elites.

Virginia and the *Parson's Cause*

Parallel development in the role of lawyers and the power of juries occurred in mid- eighteenth-century Virginia, culminating in the *Parson's Cause* in 1763.

In the first half of the eighteenth century the legal profession in Virginia was comparatively weak. Lawyers who practiced in the General Court were not permitted to practice in county courts, and vice versa, and county court lawyers tended to practice only in their own county and in immediately adjacent ones. Lawyers thus did not perform the role that they play today and that they played in several other colonies—namely, of transmitting legal knowledge from high courts to lower courts and among the various lower courts. County benches, in fact, often contained men learned in the law who possessed independent knowledge of what the law required. In Virginia, it appears, gentlemen justices, some of whom practiced before the very courts on which they sat, had sufficient confidence to determine the law by themselves. The bar was not a colonywide profession ready and able to defend individuals against the Crown; instead, lawyers were a part of local governments, ready and able to help those governments keep local subjects in tow.

Moreover, the work of the bar consisted mainly of debt collection litigation. Of course, Virginia lawyers at times represented Virginia creditors. But the ultimate source of credit and the ultimate creditors were in Britain, and therefore, in an important sense, lawyers who earned their living collecting debts were representatives of British interests. They were not naturally the allies of local elites, who themselves often were deeply in debt.

But the clientele of the bar began to change when in 1752 Governor Robert Dinwiddie in pursuit of his gubernatorial instructions demanded payment of a fee for sealing patents granting land. In late seventeenth- and early eighteenth-century Virginia, land distribution policy was a highly contested issue. By 1710, however, the great planters had won the contest, and the Crown had acquiesced in the practice of granting virgin lands almost exclusively to leading planters. The planters then developed extensive land speculation schemes, on which they became dependent as they strove to maintain the economic status quo. Indeed, land speculation became so important to maintaining the status quo that leading Virginians became highly sensitive to any threats to it.

Dinwiddie's demand accordingly raised a storm. Although fees for sealing patents were common in other colonies, they had not been paid in Virginia for several decades. Moreover, the fee demanded by Dinwiddie—roughly the same as the price of a cow—was not a trivial one. Such a fee would have had its greatest impact on people seeking small grants and on speculators seeking a large number of grants—speculators who often were members either of the Governor's Council or of the House of Burgesses.

Opponents of the fee did not protest against it on economic grounds, however. Instead, they turned to a lawyer for legal and constitutional argument: the House of Burgesses retained Peyton Randolph, who had been educated at the Inns of Court and was only in his early thirties, to travel to England and, for the substantial fee of £2,500, to argue their cause before the Privy Council. Here parallels with the *Zenger* case emerge. Although there is no dispositive evidence, it may be that the Burgesses appointed Randolph because they were aware of the significant role that Zenger's lawyers had played in advancing colonial constitutional rights and hoped that Randolph could do the same for them. Certainly a parallel to the *Zenger* case occurred when Dinwiddie, behaving in the same retributive fashion as Cosby had with Lewis Morris, promptly removed Randolph from his post as the colony's attorney general.

In essence, the Burgesses' argument before the Privy Council made two points: (1) that by agreeing earlier to issue land patents without charging any fee, the Crown had established a precedent from which it could not now depart; and (2) that the fee amounted to a tax and that no tax could be levied in Virginia without the consent of the House of Burgesses. In 1755 the Privy Council rejected both arguments and upheld Dinwiddie's right to collect the fee. At the same time, however, the Privy Council brokered a compromise by which it made some concessions to the Burgesses. It exempted from the fee patents filed before Dinwiddie's announcement of the fee, grants of fewer than one hundred acres, and grants of land west of the Alleghany Mountains. As a result, few grants remained that were covered by the fee. Virginians accordingly celebrated what they counted as a victory; they also were pleased when the Privy Council, acknowledging the right of the Burgesses to appeal directly to the council, ordered Dinwiddie to restore Randolph to the office of attorney general. Dinwiddie likewise compromised and consented to the colony's payment of Randolph's £2,500 legal fee.

The importance of the dispute over Dinwiddie's demand for a fee for issuing land grants lay less in the substance of the dispute than in the habits of mind that it helped to create. The three-year-long conflict between Dinwiddie and the Burgesses established important patterns of thought that channeled future Virginia resistance to British demands.

At its root, the dispute was about an economic matter of central importance to Virginia's great planters—their access to new land on favorable terms. They could not tolerate the possibility that Crown officials might alter the land bargain worked out at the beginning of the century, a bargain on which their economic security depended. The planters argued, however, not on economic but on legal and constitutional grounds. Their belief that they had triumphed on those grounds acculturated them to turn to lawyers and constitutional argument when, within a decade, new conflicts with Great Britain arose.

The role that law and the constitution played in obstructing Dinwiddie's demands also made the interests of the bar congruent with the interests of planters. The two groups had not necessarily shared interests when debt collection had been the main task of Virginia law and lawyers; then, lawyers and planters often had been at odds. But once the great planters conceived of lawyers as protectors of the constitutional, and thus the economic, structure of Virginia society, their alliance tightened. Lawyers became important figures in the inner circle that dominated Virginia life. Lawyers enjoyed substantial gains as a result of their alliance with planter elites. Between 1750 and 1775, the power of the profession rose, and the power of the General Court over county courts and the power of judges over juries slowly declined. The growth of the profession's power manifested itself, for example, in a flowering of formalism, which, in turn, further augmented the bar's power. The main consequence of formalism's growth was to decrease judicial discretion and hence the degree of judicial control over the processing of litigation. This weakening of judges is clearest when the role of formalism is examined in the mid-eighteenth-century Virginia criminal process, where conformity with legal niceties increasingly came to matter. Other changes in the mid-eighteenth century similarly altered the relationship between the bench and the bar, strengthening lawyers and weakening lay judges, however slightly. The most important change occurred when men seeking to practice as attorneys were required to pass an examination administered by an examiner learned in the law. Although local courts retained power to grant leave to practice in individual cases and to recommend men for examination, judges lost the final say about who could practice law. The legislature also succeeded in regulating attorneys' fees, thereby depriving local judges of that power. These changes weakened local courts at least marginally. Another change was the increasing presence of law books in the colony, which made it easier for attorneys to cite precedents rather than rely on a common-sense conception of justice.

Judges of the General Court lost even more power than did county court judges. The county courts continued to be self-perpetuating bodies that informed the governor whom he should appoint. The county courts thereby preserved their independence from central authorities and at times, as was seen in chapter 12, even refused to obey orders from the governor and the General Court.

All courts, in turn, lost authority over juries. Of course, judges continued practices that, as seen in chapter 9, they had developed earlier in the eighteenth century. They policed procedures followed by juries during their deliberations, enjoined enforcement of common law judgments, ruled on the admissibility of evidence, and preserved objections to jury rulings by way of bills of exceptions. They set aside verdicts and granted new trials when juries returned verdicts contrary to the evidence. On occasion, judges also continued to penetrate beyond the rubric of contrary to evidence, which implicitly meant that a jury had disobeyed the law, and explicitly set aside verdicts as contrary to law.

Nonetheless, despite the power of judges to reject jury verdicts, at least some lawyers, perhaps as a result of their knowledge of the *Zenger* case, were prepared to argue that general verdicts were immune from judicial control. And for whatever reason, courts at times stayed their hand and did not exert their full power over juries. A 1769 case, *Doe v. Anderson*,[4] which grew out of a title dispute to three plantations and some 600 acres of land, probably typifies how cases were routinely tried. At issue was the admissibility of a deposition taken some sixteen years earlier and a copy of an alleged original survey, certified as a true copy by the proprietor's alleged agent. Plaintiff's attorney objected to the admission of oral testimony needed to authenticate the documents and also to the quality of the documents as hearsay.

But the court admitted them without instructing the jury about the weight it should give them, thereby leaving the entire outcome of the case in the jury's hands. Similarly, in a 1752 case, *Patton v. Shann*,[5] a court refused a defendant's request to direct the jury that special damages had not been proved and instead sent the jury out without direction.

Judges, in short, showed only a limited willingness to police juries. *Riddle v. Stodghill*,[6] a 1751 action of trespass for an assault, is particularly illuminating. Initially, in *Riddle*, the jury returned a verdict for the defendant, but the court, finding the verdict contrary to the evidence, directed the jury to reconsider. The jury did reconsider and returned a plaintiff's verdict for one penny damages— technically but not in practical impact different from the initial verdict rejected by the bench. Nonetheless, the court, for reasons the record fails to explicate, accepted the new verdict and entered judgment thereon. Perhaps the court was satisfied with an apparent compromise. Perhaps it appreciated that its real power to police juries was limited. Perhaps there were underlying facts that the record fails to reveal.

Several years later a new issue of constitutional dimension came to the fore and led a jury to behave exactly as the jury in *Riddle v. Stodghill* had behaved. Again the court stayed its hand. Virginia legislation in 1696, which over the years had been slightly amended, set the annual salary of clergymen at 16,000 pounds of tobacco, which at the then price of 10s. per hundred pounds gave a salary of approximately £80 sterling per year. In 1755, the House of Burgesses, fearing that a drought would lead to a tobacco shortage and a spike in its price, gave local bodies the option of paying all salaries in cash rather than in tobacco, at a rate of two pennies per pound of tobacco. When approved by the council and the governor, this act, which remained in force only for ten months, gave clergymen an annual salary of approximately £130. Anticipating that tobacco prices might rise above two pennies per pound, some clergymen were unhappy, but when prices topped out at the two penny rate they did nothing.

A second drought, with the accompanying concern about rising tobacco prices, led to the adoption in 1758 of a second Two Penny Act, this time with a one-year duration. When prices in fact rose to six pennies per pound, which would have produced annual salaries of £400, the clergy memorialized the Privy Council to disallow the legislation. The council did disapprove the legislation in the summer of 1759, but official word of the disapproval did not reach Virginia until over a year after passage of the 1758 act, by which time the act already had expired.

Nonetheless, several ministers brought separate suits to recover back pay for the difference during the year the act was in effect between the two pennies per pound of tobacco they received and the six pennies per pound market price. The legal issue in the cases was whether the Privy Council's disallowance became effective only on the date when official notice was received in Virginia, in which case the ministers lost, or whether the Two Penny Act was void ab initio, in which case the clergy was entitled to its back pay. In the first two suits, one minister won and one lost.

A third suit, known to historians as the *Parson's Cause*,[7] was filed in Hanover County. Here the court ruled as a matter of law that the Two Penny Act was void ab initio and summoned a jury of inquiry to calculate the damages to which the plaintiff minister was entitled. The defendant vestry then retained Patrick Henry, the son of the County Court's presiding justice, to represent it. In addressing the jury, Henry, whom opposing counsel accused of "treason," ignored the issue of damages and addressed directly the merits of his father's ruling of law. Henry called the Two Penny Act "a good law ... of general utility" that "could not, consistently with the original compact between King and people, ... be annulled." In Henry's view, "a King, by disallowing Acts of this salutary nature, from being the father of his people, degenerate[d] into a Tyrant, and forfeit[ed] all right to his subjects' obedience." The jury, like the one in *Riddle v. Stodghill*, agreed and effectively nullified the court's ruling of law by returning a verdict of one penny damages. When the plaintiff moved to set aside the verdict as contrary to the evidence, the court overruled the motion.

Some present in the courtroom may have wondered why Henry adopted so extreme a position. Some suspected he was seeking popularity. But there also may have been a legal reason. Writing some fifteen years later in his *Notes on Virginia*, Thomas Jefferson observed that although juries typically decided only the facts and took their law from the court,

> this division of the subject lies within their discretion only. And if the question relate[s] to any point of public liberty, or if it be one of those in which the judges may be suspected of bias, the jury undertake to decide both law and fact.[8]

Henry, that is, may have needed to argue his case as one concerning public liberty in order to deny lawfinding power to the court and to confer such power instead on the jury.

Knox v. Daniel,[9] a case from 1768, is consistent with this interpretation of Jefferson's understanding. There the jury returned a verdict for £75 damages on finding that the defendant "maliciously and unjustly to vex, injure and oppress" the plaintiff "without any just or reasonable cause" had him bound over to an examining court on suspicion of felony. The defendant moved in arrest of judgment on the ground, among others, that the jurors had improperly separated and taken meals at their own expense between the time they began receiving evidence and the time they returned their verdict. Indeed, the defendant implied that the jurors changed their verdict after separating. Normally this allegation would have led to rejection of a jury's verdict, but in *Knox* it did not. Perhaps the court deferred to the jury because it did not credit the defendant's factual claims. But the case may have been one in which the jury had ignored standard black-letter law in order to protect a subject's liberty, and the court, recognizing the jury's superior authority, tolerated its doing so.

Oldum v. Allerton,[10] a 1739 case of which Jefferson also was probably aware, likewise fits with what he wrote in *Notes on Virginia*. Although *Oldum* focused on a different issue, the immunity of judges from suit, the argument of counsel reported in the case made the same distinction as that presented in Jefferson's *Notes*—between ordinary litigation, where judges should enjoy immunity, and matters of judicial bias or threats to the liberty of the subject, where they should not. Counsel made the standard argument that "human nature is too depraved to depend altogether upon the virtue & integrity of the judge[.] Power is apt to intoxicate & spoil the best tempers. . . . Fences against arbitrary power should be kept up." At the same time, counsel recognized the "hardship" that would be imposed on judges by subjecting them to suit on account of their judgments. But he continued that judges were "always very tenderly dealt with by the jury in their damages if it appears to be a mere mistake in judgment," but that jurors made judges "smart for it in damages" when there were "any marks of violence or oppression o[r] partiality or passion . . . as indeed they ought."

We can best make sense of Jefferson's *Notes on Virginia* and the cases just discussed if we start with the proposition that early eighteenth-century judicial practices of good conscience, good reason, and justice were being transformed in the 1760s and 1770s by lawyers like Jefferson into a more formal and mechanical body of legal knowledge and legal rules. Gentlemen justices such as Patrick Henry's father had maintained control of their localities by avoiding appearances of oppression or partiality; they understood that if they behaved badly, their underlings in one way or another might make them smart. As Virginia's legal profession moved to the fore in the second half of the century, however, lawyers like Jefferson no longer were satisfied that judges would practice good conscience and maintain appearances lest the people somehow sanction them; the lawyers strove to articulate rules with which they could bind the judges. Accordingly *Notes on Virginia* spelled out as a rule what previously had been only a tendency—namely, that judges should not merely respect jury freedom in cases of public significance but that they had no power whatsoever to set aside a jury verdict in a case of constitutional magnitude.

In short, in the years leading up to the American Revolution, the law in Virginia developed in much the same fashion that the law in New York had developed. Judges, the only officials of government who directly touched the lives of the people, lost power and authority. Lawyers, many of whom increasingly found themselves allied with local leaders in opposition to British authorities, gained strength and prestige. As a result, the ties binding a loyal colony like Virginia to the Crown grew weaker.

South Carolina: A Placeman as Chief Justice

As in New York and Virginia, many members of the local bench and bar in South Carolina came to be allied with local elites against placemen sent over from Britain to govern the colony. A significant difference, however, was that the process was not gradual there as it was in Virginia: the turning of the local bench and bar occurred almost overnight in response to an appointee whom locals could not bring themselves to respect.

As shown in chapter 12, South Carolina lawyers prided themselves on their English education, their English learning, and their English manners. Members of the bench and bar thought of themselves as the intellectual equals of all but the most eminent lawyers in Britain with whom they had studied at the Inns of Court. In the 1760 case of *Watson v. Williams*,[11] in particular, they demonstrated their legal knowledge and analytical skill. They also displayed their power over the colonial legislature, even while denying that they possessed such power, and they gave a lesson to the Privy Council about why the council should defer to South Carolinians in giving meaning to South Carolina law. Thus, it was not surprising that South Carolina lawyers turned on an English placeman who was neither as smart nor as well educated as they were.

Watson v. Williams offered the South Carolina Court of Common Pleas an opportunity to hold a statute enacted by the South Carolina legislature unconstitutional and void as violative of the colony's charter, which the court understood to be one of the foundations of the colony's constitution. The charter provision alleged to have been violated prohibited the legislature from passing laws repugnant to the laws of England; the local statute in question required administrators to pay creditors of a decedent equally, whereas the common law permitted them to prefer some creditors over others. It was conceded that English courts could not hold an act of Parliament unconstitutional, and it was therefore urged that a colonial court could not invalidate an act of a colonial legislature either.

But counsel who opposed enforcement of the colonial act nonetheless argued for a declaration of unconstitutionality. He observed that the Privy Council could hold a colonial statute void if a colonial legislature exceeded the bounds of its charter in enacting a law, and he urged the South Carolina court to rule as the Privy Council would, rather than face the burden of having its judgment reversed on the ground that the South Carolina act established a rule that the common law did not permit. Alternatively, counsel contended that even if the court did not invalidate the South Carolina statute, it should construe it literally rather than equitably in a fashion that would not apply to the administrator in the pending case and would thereby render the issue of unconstitutionality moot.

The Court of Common Pleas gave three responses in an extensive opinion by Associate Justice James Michie. He had opposed enactment of the law when he had been a legislator, but he had no difficulty reaching the opposite result on the bench.

First, the court gave the statute a broad and equitable construction that resulted in its being applicable in the pending case rather than the limited construction urged by counsel.

Second, the court held that although a colonial legislature could not enact a law repugnant to the law of England, it could adopt statutes modifying that law. Its holding rested on the fact that parliamentary enactments which had not been incorporated into the common law did not apply in the colonies unless a colony was specifically named in the act or Parliament otherwise so specified. Thus, a colonial statute contrary to most parliamentary legislation would not be repugnant to English law, since the English statute had no force for purposes of colonial law.

But what if a colonial statute were contrary to the common law? Here the court held that colonial legislatures needed the power to modify the common law and noted that the Privy Council frequently had upheld their power to do so. Otherwise, because Parliament almost never legislated for the colonies, the common law would become a sort of constitutional law beyond legislative revision no matter what mischiefs it might cause.

Colonial legislatures, in short, would behave unconstitutionally if they tried to abrogate the common law, but they could modify that law—an imprecise but critical distinction. The court therefore ruled the South Carolina legislation a modification, not an abrogation, of the common law, and thus not repugnant to English law. Accordingly, the statute was not unconstitutional as beyond the legislature's power.

Third, the court, adopting a familiar line of English legal authority, declared that even if the act were repugnant and unconstitutional, the court could not grant relief:

> For if this Court has a power of judging whether the laws which the General Assembly may make are void or not, they have a power superior to the General Assembly. . . . [T]his would be for the courts jus dare & not dicere. . . . [I]f this Court has a power to adjudge our laws to be void, . . . everything will be left to precarious & arbitrary will & pleasure.

Only a colonial legislature "in the first & his Majesty in his Privy Council in the last instance were the judges" of repugnancy and hence unconstitutionality.

Justice Michie's nine-page opinion for a unanimous court in *Watson v. Williams*, with citations to English authorities, the laws of other colonies, and Privy Council practice, was remarkable for its learning and wisdom. It reached the right result: colonial legislatures needed power to enact statutes modifying the common law in order to keep abreast of changing conditions on the ground. But it contained an analytical inconsistency, reflective, in turn, of the analytical inconsistency of the imperial constitution.

Justice Michie stated in dictum the common English view that courts could not declare legislative acts void. This dictum could have resolved the *Watson* case fully. But because the dictum would have left the Privy Council free to invalidate the South Carolina statute, Michie did not allow it to determine the case. Rather, he addressed at length the scope of the South Carolina act and the issue of whether it merely modified English law or was repugnant to it.

Important considerations required him to do so. Like the United States Supreme Court today, the Privy Council needed help from inferior courts in interpreting provincial laws; the council lacked the resources it would have needed to determine the intended meaning of those laws. Undoubtedly, the South Carolina court also wished to signal to the Privy Council the view of local elites and the local bar that the South Carolina statute constituted a beneficial modification of the common law that the council ought not to override. Adjudicating the meaning and validity of the statute, however, necessarily implied that the court had power to hold it unconstitutional or at least to limit its meaning in order to avoid constitutional difficulties. What, otherwise, was the point of drawing the line between modification and repugnancy and determining on which side of the line this statute fell? Herein lay the opinion's inconsistency.

It was the nascent structure of federalism in the eighteenth-century British empire that forced the court into this inconsistency. As long as colonial judgments were subject to review by the Privy Council—and exempting them from review would have made colonial legislatures and judiciaries independent sovereigns rather than dependent participants in the imperial system—colonial judges had to address issues that might subsequently be decided by the Privy Council. Judges could not ignore issues merely because cases might never go up to the council, or might go up on inadequate records. *Watson v. Williams*, in fact, never was appealed. Someone had to decide in ongoing litigation in the first instance whether a colonial statute was repugnant to the law of England and therefore void, and only colonial judges could do it.

Thus, colonial courts needed to have jurisdiction to address repugnancy issues, although the South Carolina court refused to exercise it. At times, courts had to be superior to colonial legislatures. Colonial courts had to display their

superior knowledge of colonial conditions and, in consequence of their supe-
riority, suggest to the Privy Council, as *Watson v. Williams* did, how best to decide cases arising in the colonies. At the same time, judges had to follow English
precedent and deny that they possessed power to declare legislation unconstitutional. *Watson v. Williams* did both brilliantly, as the South Carolina profession
undoubtedly recognized.

The profession's awareness of its judges' brilliance was evident the next year in
the treatment it accorded to Charles Shinner, who arrived in the colony in 1761
following his appointment by the Crown as the colony's new chief justice. In
the words of the local press, Shinner was an "Irishman of the lowest class" who,
unlike many members of the Charleston bar, had not received his education
at the Inns of Court. Shinner's knowledge of law was so limited that he found
it necessary to bring two "valuable and sensible Gentlemen of the Law" with
him to provide the legal expertise that he himself lacked. Even with the help of
these gentlemen, however, Shinner's courtroom was still the scene of "disputes,
altercations, and debates betwixt him, the barristers, and the crown officers."[12]
The judges and lawyers of Charleston could not work with and defer to a man
who, unlike them, had not attained the same level of professionalism as the many
able English lawyers with whom they had studied at the Inns of Court. Indeed,
Shinner was so "contemptible in the Eyes of the Carolinians" that he was not
even invited to join the prestigious St. Cecilia Society, a music and concert society of which nearly every judge and lawyer in Charleston was a member.[13] Like
many lawyers in New York and Virginia, many members of the South Carolina
profession thus began to line up against the authority of Britain and the Crown.

Creole Constitutionalism in New York and Pennsylvania

Not only were colonial lawyers beginning by the mid-eighteenth century to find
themselves at times in positions averse to British interests; they also were beginning to develop constitutional arguments suggesting that colonial institutions
enjoyed and ought to enjoy some sort of equality with and independence from
the institutions of Great Britain. No one, of course, proposed to secede from the
British empire. Early proposals for American equality and independence were
tentative and incomplete. Nonetheless, colonial lawyers were beginning to think
and write about various ways in which the constitutional relationship between
Britain and its colonies might be restructured.

One body of thought arose in New York less than two decades after the
Zenger case. By 1750, Connecticut, Massachusetts, and Virginia all had founded
colleges, and many New Yorkers thought that New York ought to have a college

as well. But religion was an issue. William Livingston, an attorney and provincial booster, argued for a non-sectarian Protestant school, whereas Samuel Seabury, an Anglican minister, argued for an Anglican academy. The religious issue was related, in turn, to a question about how a college should be established. Livingston proposed that the New York legislature should adopt an act of incorporation creating the college, but, as Seabury pointed out, at common law only the king could create a corporation. In the end, the governor, as agent of the king, created the college—King's College—as an Anglican entity with Seabury as president.

The debate over the college spawned a larger debate over the power of the New York legislature and its relation to Parliament. A group of New York lawyers, whom Daniel Hulsebosch has labeled creoles, developed a theory that the New York legislature and New York's courts were the equals of Parliament and English courts. Although these lawyers conceded some unspecified degree of power to Parliament and other British institutions to regulate imperial concerns, they increasingly thought of New York's legislature and its courts as effectively sovereign in regard to New York's internal affairs. For these creole lawyers, the New York legislature was the peer and equal of Parliament—it possessed power to govern New York just as Parliament governed Great Britain. They also urged that New York's courts ultimately should determine what constituted the law of New York.

Meanwhile, the Pennsylvania Supreme Court, as shown in chapter 12, perhaps without full awareness of the theorizing of the New Yorkers, was putting creole constitutionalism into practice in Pennsylvania by refusing frequently to apply English law. In short, by the third quarter of the eighteenth century, lawyers and judges in New York, Pennsylvania, and South Carolina had begun to reexamine the constitutional relationship of their colonies to governing authorities in Great Britain. New York lawyers had written that Britain was without power to oversee their colony's internal affairs; Pennsylvania courts had felt free to reject common law doctrines and to ignore acts of Parliament that interfered with the implementation of local policies; and the South Carolina case of *Watson v. Williams* had explained to the Privy Council why it should uphold colonial law that differed from the common law. These analyses all were embryonic, and all three colonies, recognizing the ultimate authority of the Privy Council, never suggested that the colonies should secede from the British empire. Nonetheless, American lawyers had begun to advance radical arguments awaiting further clarification.

Massachusetts and Writs of Assistance

Then, in 1761, a young Massachusetts attorney took the next and ultimate step and brought clarification to the analysis. Going beyond *Watson v. Williams*, he

argued that an act of Parliament contrary to the common law, like an act of a colonial legislature, could be unconstitutional, null and void, and of no effect. He
also stated explicitly that a colonial court ought not give effect to such a statute.
With that lawyer's argument, according to another young lawyer at the time,
John Adams, "the child Independence was born."[14]

The young lawyer who made the argument was James Otis Jr., and the case in
which he made it was *Paxton's Case.*[15] The case arose when Charles Paxton, the
surveyor of customs at Boston, applied for writs of assistance to which parliamentary legislation entitled him. The writs would have given Paxton and other
officials, without any further application to a court, the right to enter any premises during the daytime and seize any contraband found; the writs became effective on the day of issuance and remained effective until six months after the
death of the sovereign in whose name they were issued. Past precedent existed
for the issuance of such writs. All the old writs had expired, however, six months
after the death of George II in 1760, requiring the issuance of new writs.

A number of Boston merchants opposed issuance of the new writs, and they
retained Otis and Oxenbridge Thacher to represent them. Thacher offered an un-
remarkable argument, leaving it to the young Otis to forge out of old precedents
a new constitutional position. Otis, in a familiar approach, maintained that the
parliamentary legislation authorizing writs of assistance was unconstitutional.
But then he added a new twist, saying that the Massachusetts Superior Court—
a court lower in the imperial hierarchy than the High Court of Parliament—
should treat Parliament's legislation as void and having no effect and as therefore
giving the Massachusetts court no authority to issue the requested writs.

Otis distilled the main thrust of his argument into a single paragraph:

> As to acts of Parliament, an act against the constitution is void: an act
> against natural equity is void: and if an act of Parliament should be
> made, in the very words of this petition, it would be void. The execu-
> tive courts must pass such acts into disuse.—8 Rep. 118, from Viner.—
> Reason of the common law to control an act of Parliament.[16]

This argument went beyond what the South Carolina court had said in *Watson
v. Williams* in two respects. First, in addition to urging that a colonial court
could determine the constitutionality of legislation, Otis explicitly urged the
court to hold an unconstitutional act null and void and to pass it into disuse.
Second, in *Watson v. Williams*, a colonial court was asked to pass upon the constitutionality of a colonial legislative act; in *Paxton's Case*, a colonial court was
passing on the constitutionality of an act of Parliament. For Otis, however, this
distinction made no difference. Like the creole constitutionalists of New York,
Otis saw Parliament as simply another legislature, and one that possessed no

greater intrinsic power than a colonial legislature. Like all other legislatures, it had no power to enact a law that was contrary to the constitution. Rejecting the view adopted by the South Carolina Court of Common Pleas that courts have no power to invalidate legislation, Otis urged the Massachusetts court to hold Parliament's legislation unconstitutional and to refuse to enforce it, as the Pennsylvania court had effectively done in connection with the arrests of British military personnel for debt.

Many of Otis's contemporaries found his argument confused and incoherent. So too have most subsequent historians. For Otis, however, there was no confusion. The maxim that Parliament had no right to violate higher law and in the process abuse its powers was familiar to all. Many constitutional thinkers agreed that statutes contrary to natural equity were unconstitutional. And local courts and juries in America, as the cases discussed in this and earlier chapters have shown, had assumed vast power to determine what law should be enforced and how to enforce it. Courts in Pennsylvania had declined to give effect to acts of Parliament. A South Carolina court had claimed that its legislature had authority to modify, although not to abrogate, the common law; New York lawyers had claimed that its legislature could ignore the common law rule that only the Crown could create a corporation; and the Pennsylvania court had rejected the common law rule that a bond was valid even in the absence of consideration. The *Zenger* case, the *Parson's Cause*, and Massachusetts law as far back as 1672 had lodged such lawfinding power in the hands of jurors rather than judges. Otis was simply reporting the practices on the ground with which he was familiar.

Of course, the Massachusetts court rejected Otis's invitation to hold parliamentary legislation unconstitutional. It is also unclear how widely Otis's argument circulated among the public. It was published in the Boston press but may not have reached other colonies. Three years later, however, in 1764 Otis repeated the argument in an appendix to his pamphlet, *The Rights of the British Colonies Asserted and Proved*. The appendix, which was transmitted by the Massachusetts assembly to the colony's agent in London, was initially published in Boston as part of the pamphlet and was reprinted in London and at least three more times in the colonies during the next two years. In the appendix, Otis asked whether the power of Parliament

> is not circumscribed within some equitable and reasonable bounds. 'Tis hoped it will not be considered as a new doctrine that even the authority of the Parliament of *Great Britain* is circumscribed by certain bounds which if exceeded their acts become those of mere *power* without *right*, and consequently void. . . . That *acts against the fundamental principles of the British constitution are void*. . . . It is contrary to

reason that the supreme power should have the right to alter the constitution. This would imply . . . that those who are invested with power to protect the people and support their rights and liberties have a right to make slaves of them. This is not very remote from a flat contradiction.[17]

By so asking a colonial court to invalidate Parliament's legislation, Otis implicitly joined forces with the creole constitutional theorizers of colonial New York, although there were two minor differences in their thinking. First, Otis was more explicit than the New Yorkers in urging that courts had the duty to invalidate unconstitutional legislation; unconstitutionality for Otis was not an issue for political posturing only but for judicial activism as well. Second, the New Yorkers had argued that parliamentary legislation regulating colonial affairs was invalid because Parliament had no jurisdiction over the colonies except perhaps to regulate imperial trade and foreign relations. Otis, by contrast, recognized Parliament's sovereignty over the colonies, but he sought to limit its power by principles of natural equity that no legislature could transgress. But, in the end, Otis's argument, like that of the New Yorkers, radically undermined the powers of Parliament and other imperial authorities: it left ultimate authority to determine law in the hands of local colonial authorities. It thus constituted a first step toward a declaration of independence.

What pointed even more strongly toward independence, at least in Massachusetts, was that the local authorities who determined the law were not judges, but juries. At the time of *Paxton's Case* the lawfinding power of juries in the Bay Colony had been established for nearly a century. That power was dramatically reaffirmed in 1761, the year of *Paxton's Case*, in *Erving v. Cradock*,[18] another politically salient piece of litigation.

Erving v. Craddock arose when a Massachusetts shipowner brought a common law writ against a customs officer who had seized his vessel and obtained its condemnation in a Vice Admiralty Court on a charge of smuggling. The five judges on the Massachusetts Superior Court unanimously instructed the jury that the admiralty decree of condemnation was res judicata and a bar to the common law trespass suit. But the jury ignored its instructions and returned a substantial damage verdict for the shipowner. The jury returned that verdict to punish the customs collector and thereby deter him and other royal officials from interfering with Massachusetts shipping in the future. Both the court and the colonial administration nonetheless understood that the verdict was binding. Thus, when the judges, as required under Massachusetts practice, declined to set the verdict aside, the practical effect of the jury verdict was to nullify enforcement of Parliament's Navigation Acts in the Bay Colony—to treat the Navigation Acts as effectively unconstitutional. Law and the constitution in Massachusetts, as Otis had argued, was what local people, not Parliament, declared.

Summary

Lawyers and the common law had been brought to English North America in the seventeenth century to uphold the property rights and thereby to protect the religious liberty of victims of religious persecution, as well as to assist the Crown in governing its colonies cheaply. No one at the time contemplated that the legal profession would develop into a focal point of opposition to royal and parliamentary government. But that is what happened. Beginning with the *Zenger* case, individuals with political, economic, or ideological interests challenged by Crown officials began to hire lawyers to represent them, and those lawyers did what lawyers always do: they made legal arguments about why their clients' particular interests should prevail. Those arguments were grounded partly in the common law, partly in the lawfinding power of juries, and more generally in the power of American localities to determine their own law for themselves.

By the early 1760s, a smattering of lawyers had transformed their various arguments into a more general constitutional bulwark in defense of colonial liberty against parliamentary legislation and the authority of the Crown. This constitutional bulwark probably had compelling meaning for some of the lawyers. Just as there are lawyers today who care more about defending their views of the law than their clients' interests and who seek out clients through whom they can advance their views, so too such lawyers may have existed around 1760. For other lawyers, however, and for most clients, the constitutional bulwark of liberty was not a motivating force but only an abstraction—nothing more than an array of legal arguments that they could call on to defend particular economic, political, and ideological interests when those interests required defense. The bulwark was a merely theoretical one, which, although occasionally accepted by judges or juries, had not been adopted by the colonial political mainstream, which remained loyal to the British empire. Americans did not yet want to secede from the empire, and no court had yet sanctioned independence or even begun to behave independently, outside the context of a handful of individual cases.

Still the theoretical argument was in place, and respected lawyers had advanced it both in court and in public debate. They had argued that common law precedent determined the procedure for the resolution of all issues of constitutionalism and law; that colonial courts, even local trial courts, and colonial juries had final power to determine the meaning and substance of law and the constitution; and that Parliament and colonial legislatures had no power to overturn that colonial, common law constitution. Colonial rights, in this radical view, were fixed in place, beyond the power of legislative change. The child Independence had, indeed, been born. All that was needed were events that would transform this radical theoretical argument advanced by a few legal theorizers and accepted by occasional judges and juries in random cases into an on-the-ground constitutional position that a substantial majority of the American people was prepared to accept, either because people believed in it or because they saw it as a way to advance other underlying interests.

14

Testing the Bonds of Empire

Between 1763 and 1766, Parliament, British officials in London, and British officials in America triggered the events that pushed colonial Americans to test the bonds of empire. Those events forced Americans to examine their interests and beliefs and to think, in particular, about the substance and structure of the colonial constitution. The more the people thought, the more they came to agree that James Otis and earlier lawyers had elaborated the constitution to which they were committed and which best advanced the public interest. Once Americans began to think in constitutional terms, they saw that they were not prepared to surrender their de facto independence; the common law, localist basis of that independence; and the prosperous lives that de facto independence had facilitated. At the same time, they were not yet prepared to sever their ties with the empire.

Britain meanwhile had developed an alternative constitution—a constitution of parliamentary sovereignty and supremacy. But few British officials had ever thought through what parliamentary supremacy required on the ground for the governance of America. By the 1760s, American constitutional thinkers had come to appreciate how self-government, in practice, required American leaders to behave. The British, in contrast, remained committed to outmoded, century-old practices of government on the cheap, unwilling to invest in new approaches that might have brought them success.

Britain's difficulty was that it never was willing to devote substantial resources to the governance of America. Initially, in the 1660s, the Crown had sought to govern through the use of lawyers aided only by a tiny army and little bureaucracy. That approach worked adequately when colonials were poor, lawyers were few, and the lawyers were dependent on the Crown for patronage that could be translated into income. Lawyers then could be relied on to remain loyal to the Crown and to keep under control the clients to whom they provided services.

By the 1730s, however, some Americans had begun to acquire wealth, and the legal profession had begun to grow. As the profession grew, the Crown lacked sufficient patronage to support all of it, and some lawyers began to work for wealthy clients whose interests, at least at times, were at odds with the interests of Britain. Those lawyers then developed constitutional theories based on the common law and familiar localist norms and practices, under which they and their clients could govern their communities. Over time, lawyers with a local clientele slowly gained wealth, stature, and power and by the 1760s had become the dominant force in the profession.

Imperial officials such as Cadwallader Colden and Sir William Johnson had a plan to reverse this trend—the creation of a salaried imperial bureaucracy. A loyal bureaucracy that provided service to the people and in the process kept the people under control might have worked. In addition, the use of British military force, on land and at sea, to further rather than obstruct colonial interests, as had been done during the Seven Years War and even earlier on the South Carolina trading frontier, might have made colonials dependent on the military and generated loyalty on their part. But Crown officials in London paid no attention, and Parliament never would appropriate the necessary money. Its aim during the 1760s was to extract money from America to retire debt accumulated during the Seven Years War, not to spend money improving the well-being of the colonies.

The Proclamation of 1763

Americans had loyally supported Britain's efforts in the Seven Years War to conquer France's North American possessions, in part, because they had expected Britain's victory to open the Ohio Valley to settlement. But they were sorely disappointed by the Proclamation of 1763, which barred all settlement west of the Appalachians. Although British mercantile interests seeking to maintain trading relationships with Ohio Valley Indians undoubtedly lobbied officials in London, the main concern behind the proclamation was financial: the ministry feared that opening the west to European settlement would lead to Native American attacks on the settlers, which, in turn, would compel Britain to use military force, potentially at significant expense, to protect the settlers.

Britain's policy of preserving the trans-Appalachian west for Native Americans hit especially hard in Virginia. Virginia's great planters always were in desperate need of new land so as to maintain their economic hegemony, and for nearly a century they had a deal: in return for periodic grants of western lands from the Virginia government, the great planters had supported Crown policies, including mercantilist policies for marketing tobacco. Relying on the deal, the planters both before and during the Seven Years War had sunk significant amounts of capital into speculative schemes in the Ohio Valley. Nothing better demonstrates how badly the great planters needed the western land in which they were speculating than their continual efforts urging the Crown to rescind the proclamation. The ultimate disappointment of Virginians and other Americans came in 1774, when the British ministry, in a conscious effort to discourage western speculation and settlement, drafted the Quebec Act to incorporate into the Roman Catholic province of Quebec much of the land Virginians had hoped to exploit.

Britain's policy of discouraging western speculation and settlement did not lead Virginians directly to revolution. But it tended in that direction. The policy made it more difficult for Virginia planters to pay debts to British creditors and to abide by long-accepted arrangements, such as those sanctioned by the Navigation Acts requiring that all Virginia tobacco be marketed through Great Britain. It led notable Virginians, such as Arthur Lee and George Washington, to suppose that the ministry was "antiamerican" [sic] and had a "malignant disposition to American[s]."[1] They and the group of legal thinkers associated with them then did what litigants and lawyers typically do in the context of an interest-group conflict: they developed theoretical legal arguments in support of their economic positions. In the process, they translated, and thereby escalated, their battle over land, tobacco marketing, and debt into a constitutional controversy that called into question long-standing assumptions about the relationship of Virginia to Great Britain.

When, before the middle of the century, Virginia's great planters understood that they had cut a deal with the Crown that gave them land in return for their acceptance of mercantilist policies, they could both cope with the economic consequences of the deal and see themselves as equal participants in a consensual process of governance. It did not matter that they were not represented in Parliament as long as they participated in other ways in the lawmaking process and could live with the material output of that process. But when the Crown and Parliament claimed supreme power and by proclamation and legislation changed fundamental rules that had been in place for decades, Virginians feared both for their economic well-being and for the loss of their liberty and power. Their economic and constitutional interests in opposing British policy became congruent, and although the Proclamation of 1763 did not instantly result in revolutionary activity, it did undermine important bonds of affinity and trust.

The Stamp Act

The Stamp Act, by contrast, produced immediate radical activity. The 1765 act of Parliament required the use of stamped paper for documents necessary for clearing ships from harbors, for land grants and deeds, for certain sorts of contracts and debt instruments, for court papers, and for pamphlets and newspapers. This stamped paper had to be purchased from the government and therefore amounted to a tax on the transactions for which its use was required. According to Claire Priest, these taxes were intended to have and, if enforced, would have had a negative impact on colonial economic activity. In particular, according to Priest, British proponents of the taxes sought to reduce litigation, thereby diminishing the compensation of the legal profession; to decrease the number of real estate transactions, thereby limiting land speculation; and to raise the cost of publishing newspapers and pamphlets, thereby stifling political opposition to the Crown and its policies. The act also would have imposed additional costs on merchants.

Lawyers, the landed class, merchants, and the press vehemently opposed Parliament's imposition of taxes such as these that cut into their livelihoods. Based on habits of thought developed over the decades since the *Zenger* case, they turned, however, not to economic arguments but mainly to legal and constitutional ones.

A vast literature quickly emerged about the Stamp Act's unconstitutionality. In Boston and Newport, Rhode Island, mobs rioted and destroyed property to force the resignation of the men who had been appointed to distribute the stamped paper. The threat of riots from New Hampshire to Georgia forced all the other stamp distributors to resign or flee from the colony for which they had been appointed. As a result, no one was willing or able to put the Stamp Act into execution in the thirteen colonies that eventually joined in the American Revolution.

The Stamp Act crisis has been the subject of significant historical writing to which little new can be added. But the legal and constitutional unfolding of the crisis on the ground has been somewhat ignored. In particular, historians have failed to examine the arguments of courts and lawyers during the Stamp Act crisis in the context of the earlier constitutional analysis discussed in chapter 13. When this material is examined in its totality, a deeper understanding of the role of courts and the law and of emerging constitutionalism surfaces.

The issue that confronted courts was whether to remain open and process pleas and other documents filed on unstamped paper or to close until stamps became available. On the one hand, it was urged that processing unstamped documents would violate the act of Parliament. A number of arguments were presented, on the other hand, in support of the courts' remaining open. One of these was the need to uphold law and order by maintaining the visibility of courts. Another was that Parliament never intended to close the courts and that because all stamp distributors had resigned and stamps were unavailable, remaining open would not violate the intent of Parliament.

But the main argument in support of remaining open was the unconstitutionality of the Stamp Act. James Otis's pamphlet on the rights of the British colonies in America had circulated widely in the previous year, and the argument about unconstitutionality was present on its face. A law against the constitution and natural equity that violated the rights of Englishmen, said Otis, was null and void and of no effect. Such a law need not be obeyed, and courts were obligated to put it into disuse. It followed that because stamps were unavailable, enforcement of the Stamp Act would impede the right of access to courts—a right of constitutional magnitude—and thus the requirement of filing court documents on stamped paper was unconstitutional.

Lawyers up and down the Atlantic coast advanced this argument during the fall, winter, and spring of 1765–66. Many courts rejected the argument. But others accepted it, challenged the power of Parliament by ruling its act unconstitutional and therefore void, and thus remained open for business without stamps. We can never know for sure why those who accepted the argument did so: perhaps they truly believed the argument; perhaps their acceptance advanced some other interest. What we can know with certainty is that every acceptance made the argument of unconstitutionality more credible and brought it increasingly into the mainstream of American constitutional thinking.

The Court of Common Pleas and the Probate Court of Suffolk County, Massachusetts, which sat in Boston, were among the first to remain open, with the Court of Common Pleas holding its scheduled regular session in early January 1766. After hearing arguments from John Adams that the Stamp Act was "utterly void, and of no binding force upon us" and from James Otis "that there are limits, beyond which if Parliaments go, their acts bind not," the Governor's Council had left the decision of whether to remain open in the hands of the courts themselves; and in consultation with the Boston town meeting and in an apparent challenge to the power of Parliament, the courts decided to continue operating.[2]

When the Massachusetts House of Representatives met later in the same month, it took the same approach and adopted a resolution, by a vote of 81 to 5, directing all courts, especially the Superior Court, to remain open. The council, the legislature's upper house, declined to concur, but it inquired whether the justices of the Superior Court would hold their regular session in March. The justices responded that they would hear cases if circumstances remained unchanged, and the court did, in fact, hear a case at its March session that had been filed before the effective date of the Stamp Act and had been continued to a future court session. By that time, rumors of the act's repeal already were circulating, and other pending business and new business were postponed. Meanwhile, all the lower courts remained open.

News about the riots and other events in Boston and about the arguments against the Stamp Act and against parliamentary claims of sovereign power leading up to those events spread throughout the colonies via Benjamin Edes's often incendiary *Boston Gazette.*

The purpose of the *Gazette* was always clear: to incite other colonies to rise up with Massachusetts in defense of American liberty against what the *Gazette* called Parliament's oppression. The *Gazette* was not alone; other newspapers in major colonial towns, which, of course, had a direct pecuniary interest in the Stamp Act's repeal, soon joined it. In this context, the contribution of the *Zenger* case to the American Revolution becomes clear. British officials did not bring a single prosecution against any newspaper that harassed them in their efforts to enforce the Stamp Act; the role of the jury in the *Zenger* case had left Crown officials unable to obtain seditious libel convictions. All pressures on the press came from the Stamp Act's opponents, who even threatened mob action against newspapers that did not support their cause. As a result, the overwhelming weight of propaganda and colonial public opinion demanded repeal of the act.

Propaganda and public opinion had their greatest impact in eastern New England. A second colony that kept all its courts open without interruption throughout the conflict over the Stamp Act was Rhode Island. There the courts acted at least in part in response to a resolution of the colonial legislature that promised to indemnify all judges and other officials for any damages suffered as a result of their disregard of the act. One small blip occurred when the king's attorney, who also had been appointed and then resigned as stamp distributor, failed to appear at the Superior Court's sitting. Taking note of his absence, the court appointed the corresponding secretary of the Providence Sons of Liberty, the leader of Rhode Island's resistance to the Stamp Act, in his place.

New Hampshire was a third colony where the courts remained open. When the Superior Court adjourned its August 1765 session in October 1765, before the effective date of the Stamp Act, it directed that a grand jury and a venire of petit jurors be summoned for its next regular session, in February 1766. When the court reopened in February, however, stamps were required on court documents, and the court clerk refused to accept documents that did not bear them. The judges immediately responded with the following order:

> The Justices considering the necessity and expediency for the preserva-
> tion of the peace and good order of the Province of holding this court
> and . . . having business done as usual and no stamped paper to be had
> in this Province, do order and command the clerk of this court to issue
> all writs, processes and copies as usual, without stamped paper.[3]

Passing on the constitutionality of the Stamp Act without explicitly using the words "unconstitutional" and "void," the justices thereby kept the Superior

Court open and the clerk protected from liability for using unstamped paper. Meanwhile New Hampshire's lower courts had continued to function.

The most contentious conflict over the Stamp Act occurred within a divided Court of Common Pleas in Charleston, South Carolina. At the court's first meeting after the effective date of the act, in November 1765, Chief Justice Charles Shinner, the Irishman for whom the local profession, as shown in chapter 13, had no respect, sat alone without the presence of any associate justices and "being of opinion that no business can [be] proceeded upon until such stamped paper can be procured," adjourned the November 1765 term.[4]

At the next term, in February 1766, however, matters began to come to a head. Thomas Bee, the attorney for the plaintiff in the case of *Jordan v. Law*,[5] informed the court that he had served a rule to plead on John Rutledge, the defendant's attorney, and that the time for pleading had long expired. Attorney Bee then moved for judgment,

> to which Mr. Rutledge said he had no manner of objection. Mr. Manigault of counsel with the plaintiff then spoke very fully in support of the motion as did also Mr. Pinckney, Mr. Parsons and Mr. Rutledge who though not concerned for the plaintiff in this particular cause said they were concerned as counsel in a great variety of causes of a similar nature.

Only the province's attorney general spoke in opposition to Bee's motion. In view of the "particular circumstances which they [were] now in and the steps" then being taken "to obtain a repeal of the Stamp Act," the court was "unanimously of opinion . . . that no positive determination be given upon the point, but that the same be postponed until the next" term.

At the April 1766 term, Bee again moved for judgment. The nub of Bee's argument was that Magna Carta declared it a wrong "to delay or deny justice to the subject," and that because of the impossibility of obtaining stamps, the Stamp Act had that effect. Accepting this argument, the Court of Common Pleas, by a 4–1 vote, ordered that judgment be entered. The majority also directed that "the process of this Court be issued out in the usual manner by any person who shall require and apply for the same, that there may no longer be a complaint that justice is either denied or delayed."[6] Chief Justice Shinner dissented. His view, in essence, was that it was not as a matter of law impossible to obtain stamps: the same people who were petitioning the judges to keep the courts open had also conspired with others to make stamps unavailable. "No man," he concluded, should "avail himself of his own wrong," and he as a judge could not "deny the legislative power of King, Lords and Commons of Great Britain over

the colonies in America." Shinner, in his words, "revere[d] our happy constitution" and was unwilling "to transgress in any instance against a fundamental rule
of law."[7]

A month later, when Common Pleas met again, Justice Lowndes filed an
opinion on behalf of the four-judge majority. The majority had hoped that the
chief justice would withdraw his dissent and not "set . . . up the judgment of one
judge in opposition to that of the rest of the whole bench, thereby inverting the
well-known order of judicial determinations, and establishing . . . a precedent
that the minority shall conclude the majority." But Shinner did not withdraw
it, and indeed, he went further and directed the officers and ministers of the
court to obey his ruling rather than that of the majority. Therefore the majority
thought it necessary to file a ten-page opinion recording its reasoning.[8]

The foundation of the majority's reasoning was a finding that because of the
unavailability of stamped paper, compliance with the Stamp Act was impossible.
The majority was unwilling to "presume[]," as had the chief justice, "that the
suitors of this Court [were] instrumental in causing the necessity which ha[d]
been so prejudicial to themselves." It continued:

> Whatever cause this may be owing to, the effect and consequences
> are the same; if no business is to be done without stamp paper, and
> it is absolutely impossible for the Court to procure stamp paper, the
> inference is, that the Stamp Act in such an exigency would oblige the
> Courts of Law to be shut up, all business to be remitted and the admin-
> istration of law and justice to be suspended. Can it be presumed that
> Parliament meant any such thing or is there one word in the act from
> the first to the last page of it that gives the least countenance to such an
> interpretation[?] Could the Parliament intend by this law to abrogate
> and repeal all precedent acts of Parliament, to unhinge the constitution
> of the colonies, to unloose the hands of violence and oppression, to in-
> troduce anarchy and confusion among us, and to reduce us to a state of
> outlawry? For to be without law, and to want the means of dispensing
> the law is one and the same thing. Yet all these consequences unavoid-
> ably result from the position that no business can be done at all events,
> without stamp paper.

In view of "the impossibility . . . of complying with the act," the majority
concluded that, at least as it was construed by the chief justice, the Stamp Act
was inapplicable. Because "no power [could] oblige to impossibilities," the court,
with an obvious but unstated reference to *Bonham's Case*, concluded that the
act "enjoin[ed] a thing impossible to be performed" and was therefore "repugnant and against reason and common right, [and] my Lord Coke says is void."[9]

The majority thereby directed the court to ignore the Stamp Act and proceed without stamped paper.

Having answered the chief justice, the majority next turned to the court's clerk. From the outset, the clerk, Dougal Campbell, had sided with the chief justice; in April 1766, he had "humbly begged leave to decline paying obedience to the direction[s] of this Court" to enter the judgment in *Jordan v. Law*. "From particular tenderness and indulgence on account of his hitherto dutiful and dili-gent behavior in office," however, the court did not punish Campbell and merely appointed a replacement, William Mason, as acting clerk.[10]

Apparently Campbell did not permit Mason to act in his stead. In his view, "the Stamp Act did not allow him to pay obedience to the directions of the Court." Accordingly, Campbell refused both to enter the judgment in *Jordan v. Law* and to issue writs. He also refused to issue a venire to summon a jury for the May 1766 term. Collectively his acts resulted in "the prevention of justice, and in all probability the total loss of many just demands."[11]

The chief justice spoke in Campbell's behalf and then "quitted the bench." Thereupon the court expressed its shock at the clerk's behavior, which it found "inconsistent with and repugnant to the very idea of that subordination which as a ministerial officer he owe[d] to the Court" and a "total inversion of all law, order, decency, and decorum." It found Campbell guilty of "endeavoring to wrest from the Court, (to whom of right it appertains to construe the laws), their proper jurisdiction" and fined him £100. Upon learning from Campbell that the chief justice was still refusing to sign or seal writs, the court also appointed the senior associate justice, Robert Pringle, to act in the chief justice's place.[12]

By the spring of 1766, in short, the Stamp Act had produced a dissolution of the bonds of subordination and authority in South Carolina. Charlestonians, acting on a claim that the act was unconstitutional, had prevented royal officials from distributing stamps and thus from enforcing the act. The majority of the Court of Common Pleas, concluding that the act together with the unavailability of stamps had resulted in an unconstitutional closure of the courts, declined to obey the law. Meanwhile, the chief justice and the court clerk, concluding that their duty required obedience to Parliament, refused to execute the judgment of the court. Where, as a result, did authority lie other than in the coercive power of whoever could bring such power to bear? Certainly, authority no longer lay in customary patterns of subordination. As one historian has observed, the crisis "seriously jeopardized the connection between Britain and the colonies," and thereafter "each side became increasingly suspicious of the other."[13]

With Parliament's repeal of the Stamp Act, South Carolina officials tried, with some success, to restore cooperation between supporters and opponents of the act and with it subordination and authority. An important step was for the clerk, Dougal Campbell, to make his peace. In a petition to the court, he pleaded that he was "unfeignedly sorry for his having incurred the censure and displeasure of this Honorable Court." He "humbly beg[ged] leave to assure your Honors" that no other event in his life had "ever occasioned him more real concern and uneasiness" and asked that his conduct "not be construed into any intended contempt or disrespect." Noting that as a result of the closure of the courts he had received no fees or other income and thus could not pay his fine, he petitioned the court "to regard his circumstances with an eye of tenderness and compassion." The court, "being of opinion that the clerk's late conduct proceeded rather from an error in judgment rather than any contempt or want of respect for the authority of the Court," reduced his fine to £10. Several months later the Privy Council remitted the fine entirely.[14]

So far, we have examined four colonies—Massachusetts, Rhode Island, New Hampshire, and South Carolina—in which courts remained open because the Stamp Act was either explicitly or implicitly held unconstitutional. In two others—Delaware and Maryland—courts also were open. In Delaware, a grand jury refused to return any criminal indictments, which could be prosecuted under the Stamp Act without use of stamped paper, until the civil courts, where stamps were required, reopened as well; the civil courts accordingly reopened. In Maryland, county courts remained open without requiring stamps as early as November 1765, when the Stamp Act first went into effect; the central courts reopened under pressure from the Sons of Liberty at the beginning of April 1766.

In New York some of the judges of the Courts of Common Pleas, apparently in response to a resolution by attorneys to do business without stamps, proposed to open the courts in January 1766. They drew up a memorial and presented it to the governor to be recorded in the minutes of the council. The governor, however, refused to entertain it and warned the judges that they would lose their seats on the council as well as on the bench if they opened the courts. Thus, despite the implicit view of judges that the Stamp Act was unconstitutionally null and void and that they should process cases without stamps, the New York courts remained closed.

The highest courts of all the other colonies remained closed as well, but in four of those colonies—New Jersey, North Carolina, Pennsylvania, and Virginia— some county courts remained open. In Virginia, at least one leading lawyer was concerned that closing the local courts might lead people to think that law and order would not be maintained; he also argued that Parliament had no authority to pass the Stamp Act and that the act was therefore null and void and of no effect. Some county courts went even further. When the judges of Accomac County opened court, they warned "that any attorney neglecting to carry on his business in court, under pretence of wanting stamps, should have his suits dismissed."[15] And the judges of neighboring Northampton County responded as follows to an inquiry from its nonjudicial officers whether they would incur any penalties for keeping the court open without using stamped paper:

> The said court unanimously declared it to be their opinion that the said act did not bind, affect, or concern the inhabitants of this colony, inasmuch as they conceive the same to be unconstitutional, and that the said several officers may proceed in the execution of their respective offices, without incurring any penalty by means thereof.[16]

In short, the radical argument of James Otis in the *Writs of Assistance Case* in 1761 had become mainstream four years later following Parliament's enactment of the Stamp Act. In Massachusetts, South Carolina, Virginia, and undoubtedly elsewhere, lawyers were arguing that acts of Parliament against natural equity and the fundamental principles of the constitution were null and void and that courts should invalidate them and give them no effect. Moreover, judges in the same three colonies, as well as in New York and elsewhere, often on a local, county level, had accepted the argument. The argument, in turn, constituted a practical declaration of independence: it meant that local people—either county judges, local juries, or the popular, local mobs that steered them—rather than Parliament ultimately determined what constituted law.

The Declaratory Act

Parliament responded with the Declaratory Act. At the same time that it repealed the Stamp Act, it declared that

> all resolutions, votes, orders, and proceedings, in any of the said colonies or plantations, whereby the power and authority of the parliament of *Great Britain*, to make laws and statutes . . . is denied, or drawn into question, are, and are hereby declared to be, utterly null and void to all intents and purposes whatsoever.

Parliament further declared that

> the said colonies and plantations in *America* have been, are, and of right ought to be, subordinate unto, and dependent upon the imperial crown and parliament of *Great Britain* . . . [which] had, hath, and of right ought to have, full power and authority to make laws and statutes of sufficient force and validity to bind the colonies and people of *America*, subjects of the crown of *Great Britain*, in all cases whatsoever.[17]

Thus, both sides by 1766 had stated their legal and constitutional arguments. Parliament had declared itself supreme and sovereign; had announced that the North American colonies were subordinate to it; and had proclaimed its power to make law for those colonies in all cases whatsoever. American legal and constitutional thinkers and a number of American judges, in contrast, understood that law emerged organically out of the communities it governed, enforced by local courts and local people who rose out of and were responsible to their communities. The parliamentary constitution was one of centralized, ultimately coercive power; the American constitution, arising out of a century of local self-rule under the common law, was one of radical decentralization of power and local autonomy.

Thus, the two opposing constitutions—the one of parliamentary supremacy and the other of local autonomy—had been elaborated. Americans, however, did not want full independence and severance of their ties with the British empire, and British officials were not inclined to press their claims of supremacy with vigor. For nearly a decade the two sides coexisted in an uneasy truce.

15

Severing the Ties of Empire

For the next decade, both sides maintained their constitutional positions but made no determined efforts to enforce them. Many skirmishes between imperial and other central authorities, on the one hand, and local interests, on the other, did occur between 1766 and 1773, and they continued the process that the Stamp Act had begun of undermining the rule of law, existing axioms of authority, and thus the foundations of imperial power. But until Parliament reacted fiercely to the dumping of tea in Boston harbor, a truce remained in place.

The Period of Truce

Others have written about Parliament's efforts to tax the American colonies between 1766 and 1773 and about American resistance to those efforts, and this is not the place to repeat what they have said. The goal here is narrower—to focus on a series of discrete, disconnected happenings in the courts during the late 1760s and early 1770s, many of which political historians have largely ignored. In the interest of comprehensiveness, it is necessary first to take some note of certain events producing reverberations in the realm of law that occurred, sometimes even before 1765 or outside the courts.

Riots and Rebellions

Four colonies—Pennsylvania, New York, and North and South Carolina—suffered major civil strife during the 1760s and early 1770s. The strife in Pennsylvania occurred first, even before the passage of the Stamp Act. It ended in a fashion that illustrates how the British imperial system at times could still function effectively.

Pennsylvania

The end of the Seven Years War in 1763 did not bring peace with all Native American nations. In particular, the Ottawas under their chief, Pontiac, continued to attack frontier settlements. Even after the attacks had subsided, frontiersmen remained angry and were searching for retribution. One mob of some fifty frontiersmen living in the vicinity of the Pennsylvania town of Paxton began to get that revenge on December 14, 1763, when they murdered six unarmed Christian Indians. Two weeks later, an even larger mob killed fourteen more peaceful Indians.

Next, the mob, which has come to be known as the Paxton Boys, headed for Philadelphia, seeking to kill other Native Americans along the way as well as whites who were protecting them. The mob began to gain support from other Scotch-Irish Presbyterian and German Protestant frontiersmen who were angry at the malapportionment of Pennsylvania's Quaker-dominated legislature and at its persistent refusal to appropriate money they requested for frontier defense. As the Paxton Boys moved east and eventually reached Germantown, only a few miles outside Philadelphia, the mob grew to some 250 men. Civil strife threatened.

Governor John Penn responded effectively. Seeking to form an alliance with Presbyterian and German interests against the Quaker majority in the legislature that was obstructing his administration, he opted for compromise. He sent a delegation from Philadelphia to meet with the Paxton Boys, offering them immunity from prosecution and an opportunity for their leaders to present their demands to the legislature. The mob accepted his offer, broke up, and went home.

Several facts about the Paxton affair are noteworthy. The first is that the pursuit of ordinary politics induced rival leaders to compromise and to avoid violent conflict. The second is that their compromise did not resolve core political issues: Philadelphia-area Quakers retained the dominance in the malapportioned Pennsylvania legislature to which their numbers did not entitle them and continued to deny frontier counties the level of appropriations for defense that the frontiersmen wanted. Meanwhile, the Presbyterian-German alliance created by Penn persisted in its demands for legislative reapportionment and frontier defense—demands that were finally met with the overthrow of Quaker rule during the American Revolution. Compromise, in short, brought only temporary peace by pushing resolution of real conflict into the future. The third fact is that the law was not enforced, perhaps because a growing localist structure of power in Pennsylvania precluded enforcement. Governor Penn bought peace by not prosecuting the Paxton Boys for the murder and mayhem they had committed.

South Carolina

Another colony where central authorities caved in to local forces of rebellion was South Carolina. Trouble began in that colony in 1766, when a crime wave featuring thefts, assaults, and even kidnappings of young women broke out in newly settled frontier regions. The next summer witnessed a series of brutal robberies. As all of South Carolina's courts and law enforcement officials were located in Charleston, the capital, authorities were nearly powerless in the outlying areas. They were able to capture only a few criminals, and even those who were apprehended rarely received severe punishment.

As a result, local people took the law into their own hands and over several months in the fall of 1767 organized some 1,000 men into a vigilante group to pursue and punish criminals. They called themselves Regulators. When the governor issued a proclamation ordering them to disperse, they ignored it. Instead, they sent a list of demands to the provincial assembly, the main one being an entreaty for the establishment of county courts in the regions beyond Charleston and the selection of sheriffs for each county to replace the colonywide provost marshal. Meanwhile, they continued to ignore the authority of the courts sitting in Charleston.

The government in Charleston caved in. In 1769 the legislature enacted a new circuit court act that established six districts outside Charleston, provided for gubernatorial appointment of sheriffs in Charleston and each of those districts, and stipulated that the justices of Common Pleas and General Sessions would hold a joint session of those courts in each of the six districts twice each year. The courts began meeting in the fall of 1772. Thus South Carolina, like Pennsylvania, did put down a rebellion, but only by recognizing the realities of local power and meeting the demands of the rebels.

New York

New York authorities were less successful than those of Pennsylvania and South Carolina in dealing with the lawlessness and rebellion confronting them. The "impression one gains from the records of criminal courts for the period after the French and Indian War," to quote the only slightly exaggerated language of Julius Goebel, "is one of a general and nearly continuous state of riot throughout the province."[1] One Albany sheriff, for instance, reported that when he tried to make an arrest, the defendant

> seized a pistol, swore he would blow my brains out, and so kept me
> from further prosecuting the arrest, uttering all the time the most

violent oaths and other abusive language against me. It is impossible for me to execute my office.[2]

Throughout the colony, prosecutors found themselves confronting witnesses who would not testify for the prosecution and trials requiring cancellation on account of a sheriff's inability to summon a jury. There was even a case in 1772 in which a man was prosecuted for usurping the office of a town mayor.

These cases were minor nuisances compared to a situation in a remote region northeast of Albany, in what is now Vermont, where

a number of people . . . live[d] in open defiance of authority— pretending to appoint officers and to erect courts among themselves— executing in the most illegal and cruel manner, the high power of trying, condemning and punishing their fellow subjects.[3]

Lawlessness was equally prevalent on the Mohawk frontier, although sparseness of population meant that lawbreakers were fewer in number and less well organized.

Meanwhile, the chaos resulting from the Stamp Act crisis led directly to new outbreaks of violence in the Taconic region. Before the passage of the act, a Native American nation had appointed one Samuel Monrow as guardian of its land rights in the Taconic, and he had formed an alliance with a group of squatters, one of whose leaders was his son, Samuel Monrow Jr. In the course of litigation, the Governor and Council had ordered the arrest of Samuel Monrow Sr., who in fact was apprehended and placed in a New York City jail in March 1765. In November 1765, however, as the Stamp Act crisis was leading toward the breakdown of law and order in New York City, the squatters called a meeting of tenants in eastern Dutchess County to demand that their patroon landlords give them long-term leases at low rents. They intimidated loyal tenants, told everyone not to pay rents, and by the spring of 1766, despite the efforts of local courts, were in control of eastern Dutchess. Meanwhile, in Westchester County, immediately south of Dutchess, after a patroon landlord had used the judiciary to evict several tenants, those tenants organized a group of friends who violently put the evicted tenants back in possession of their farms, although one of the tenants and two other rioters were promptly arrested and joined Samuel Monrow Sr. in jail in New York City.

Now the Dutchess and Westchester rebels, who soon numbered 500 men, joined together to march on New York City to free the prisoners and, in case of opposition, "kick their arses as long as we think fit."[4] Governor Henry Moore ordered British regulars and the city militia to stop the marchers, who, on entering the city and observing the military, fled without a shot being fired. The

Westchester rebellion immediately collapsed, but the Dutchess rebellion did not. Governor Moore then ordered British regulars to put down the Dutchess uprising; the troops captured some sixty rebels, but at the cost of several casualties and with most of the rebels fleeing into Connecticut.

Violence had also broken out farther north. When a sheriff's posse went out to suppress it, a pitched battle occurred with casualties on both sides, and the sheriff's posse dissolved and withdrew in defeat. Governor Moore had no choice but to send about a hundred regulars to pursue the rebels; the rebels, however, refused to fight but melted into the woods and then fled to Massachusetts. Although the army captured a few rebels and restored peace, the remainder quickly returned and regained possession of their farms and control of the Taconic region once the army withdrew, as it ultimately had to do.

In short, law and order broke down in much of the New York colony in the aftermath of the Stamp Act crisis, and British officials in New York City, without a bureaucracy and with only a limited military force, could do little about it. They should have learned a lesson: namely, that their army could march around the countryside, devastate and ravage it, and capture a few rebels, but that the army could not govern, at least not without an unacceptable, long-term expenditure of resources. When the army withdrew, the rebels would return and reinstitute the only form of government that could work in colonial America—local government. It was a lesson about the realities of American law and constitutionalism that North Carolina rebels soon taught again. Although some in Britain learned the lesson, the leaders of the government did not because, as one historian has observed, "America was too important to Britain" for Britain's leaders to conceive that they could not keep it under control.[5]

North Carolina

The most troublesome rebellion occurred in North Carolina. That colony, unlike South Carolina, provided courts for its western frontier settlements, but those courts proved no more able to enforce the law than were the courts of New York or the single central court of Charleston, South Carolina.

The same legislation of 1754 that had established courts in North Carolina's east established identical courts in the west—a Supreme Court that would sit in two different locations, Hillsborough and Salisbury, and a series of county courts. In the Supreme Court, far fewer cases were filed in the west than in the east, and the cases that were filed were routine in nature and raised few significant issues. In particular, the western courts adjudicated few cases involving land titles, which in most instances had not been acquired from the North Carolina government. When the Crown purchased the Carolinas in the 1720s from their proprietors, one of the proprietors, Lord Granville, refused to sell his share and accordingly was rewarded with title to vast tracts of land in northwestern North Carolina. The Quakers, Presbyterians, and Germans who later moved down from Pennsylvania acquired their land titles mainly from Granville, not from the North Carolina colonial government, with the result that the government had no stake in defending western titles and the settlers had no reason to look to its courts for defense.

Filings in western county courts made up to some degree for the paucity of filings in the Supreme Court. But the western county courts heard only minor cases—civil suits in which monetary recoveries were small and title to land was not at issue, and criminal cases that did not involve a penalty of life or limb. In addition, the county courts displayed favoritism to residents and were hostile to outsiders. The western county courts simply did not provide forums useful to non-residents seeking to establish their title to land or to collect large debts or to Crown officials seeking to govern the frontier.

As a result, although local communities may have effectively governed themselves, the provincial government possessed limited capacity to enforce law in the west. Trouble began as early as 1759, little more than a decade after significant settlement had occurred in the Piedmont and only five years after the establishment of the Supreme Courts. Several vigilantes from Granville County seized a land agent who had been taking fees that the vigilantes claimed were illegal. After forcing him to post an alleged bond requiring a future appearance in court, the vigilantes dispersed, but when several of them were arrested and jailed, friends broke into the jail and released them. No further prosecutions occurred.

The next riot occurred in 1765, when a group of squatters in disguise attacked and beat four surveyors who, on behalf of an absentee landowner, were mapping out the land on which the squatters had settled. Governor William Tryon issued a proclamation calling for the identification and prosecution of the squatters, but nothing happened. In the same year, a schoolteacher was sued for a small debt and responded by writing "An Address to the People of Granville County," in which he pilloried lawyers, court clerks, and sheriffs and accused them of taking unlawful fees that increased the charges of litigation. His pamphlet led to a petition to the General Assembly, but that petition was ignored. The next year, for unstated reasons, the January term of the Rowan County Court had to be postponed; all but two theft prosecutions were continued to the April term.

Enter the North Carolina Regulators. In 1767 people in the Hillsborough vicinity had sought to create formal machinery by which protests could be conveyed to the provincial government, but officials had blocked their efforts. At the beginning of April 1768 the protesters founded the Regulator Association. A few days later a Regulator refused to pay taxes, to which the sheriff responded by seizing his horse and preparing to sell it. Fellow Regulators promptly tied up the sheriff, rescued the horse, and threatened a prominent local judge. The judge called up the local militia, but when few responded to his call, he sought help from Governor Tryon.

In July, Tryon marched into Hillsborough at the head of a militia force from three counties, but the Regulators made it plain that they still intended not to pay taxes. By September the Regulators had assembled a force of some 800 men to disrupt the forthcoming Hillsborough sitting of the Supreme Court, but Tryon had twice that number. Ultimately the Regulators went home, and the Court met.

Agitation continued for the next two years, but without violence. Then in September 1770, the Regulators burst into the Hillsborough Supreme Court session, seized and beat a lawyer, dragged the assistant attorney general and one of the judges into the street, and demolished the judge's house. Other leading citizens, including the presiding judge, fled town.

The legislature responded by enacting a statute permitting the attorney general to obtain indictments against and prosecute rioters in any Supreme Court in the colony or in a specially convened court. This legislation meant that, if Regulators could be captured, they could not count on being rescued by local friends or on protection from local juries—precisely the sort of allegedly unconstitutional deprivation of the right to trial by jury that worried Antifederalists two decades later.

Next Tryon attempted to catch the Regulators. In the spring of 1771, he gathered an army to bring the west to its knees, and on May 16, 1771, Tryon's force of 1,300 militiamen defeated 2,500 Regulators in the Battle of the Alamance. He pardoned all but a handful of leaders and spent the next two months chasing after the leaders, seizing their property, and destroying much other property along his path.

Although Tryon won a battle, he did not restore the rule of law. According to surviving colonial court records, the Salisbury Supreme Court never met after 1770 and the Hillsborough Court met only briefly in March and September 1772. Although county courts throughout the west continued to meet, they had little law enforcement capacity. Local people allowed them to function only because they offered important services to local interests, such as supervising the building of infrastructure and providing a mechanism through which local people could make a permanent record of important transactions.

But the county courts proved unable to perform major governmental functions. In Tryon County in 1770, for example, the court postponed receiving a final report from the sheriff on the annual tax collection because over one-fifth of taxpayers had "absconded out of said County or [were] insolvent."[6] In Rowan in 1770, the sheriff reported that he collected almost nothing "owing to a refractory disposition of a set of people calling themselves Regulators refusing to pay any taxes"; their refusal, in turn, produced a race to the bottom in which "many well disposed people neglect[ed] to discharge their public dues."[7] In 1769, the sheriff had reported for the tax year 1765 that out of some 2,800 taxpayers, 292 were "listed twice" or had run away, whereas another 838 were "insolvents, or insurgents, mob, or such who refuse to pay their taxes," whereas for the tax year 1766, there were 1,833 "delinquents, insolvents, insurgents, mob, or such who generally refuse to pay their taxes."[8] Conditions were so bad in Rowan County by 1769 that the man chosen as sheriff was not able to obtain a performance bond, not because "his friends . . . doubted . . . his integrity or honesty" but because of the "confused state & present disturbances together with the scarcity of circulating money."[9] Two years later, Regulators still were refusing to take the oath of allegiance in support of the colony's government.

In sum, the only thing that Tryon's victory at Alamance established was that an army with superior weapons, at least in a pitched battle, could capture and kill some of its enemies. But when the bulk of the enemies disappeared into the countryside, the army could not govern them. At most, it could wreak havoc on the countryside while the people of the countryside, to the extent they wanted government, continued to govern themselves. Like parts of upstate New York, western North Carolina in many respects already constituted an entity independent of the British empire when the American Revolution broke out in 1775–76.

The Significance of the Riots and Rebellions

But the riots and rebellions that have just been discussed did not challenge parliamentary authority directly and thus did not bring the British empire to its knees. The riots and rebellions were either conflicts between local elites and underclasses or conflicts of other kinds in which the Crown and Parliament had no direct stake and therefore made no effort to intervene. Nonetheless, the riots and rebellions undermined the rule of law and historic axioms of authority, thus weakening the foundations of imperial rule. They also should have warned authorities in London of the futility of sending armies to conquer and govern America.

Cases and Controversies

The repeal of the Stamp Act did not bring challenges to British authority to an end. On the contrary, the structure of empire continued to fray. Perhaps the breakdown of authority did not result solely from the Stamp Act. It also may have been a legacy of the Great Awakening—of its schisms and even more of its idea of the capacity of all individuals to have equal access to God, knowledge, and truth. Perhaps it was a legacy of the maturation of American society. Americans of the 1760s no longer were totally dependent on British succor; both the colonies as entities and the individuals who lived there were capable of surviving on their own. They did not have to obey. In any event, the success of resistance to the Stamp Act intensified the breakdown of authority that continued to occur in the act's aftermath.

Those in authority found it increasingly difficult to obtain obedience from the king's subjects. In South Carolina, for example, the Court of Common Pleas no longer would obey automatically the bidding of imperial authorities. When in 1767 a new customs collector tried to enforce customs regulations more strictly, he confronted mobs and an avalanche of suits by local merchants that forced him to leave the colony. His departure, in turn, led to a suit and judgment against his subordinate, which the subordinate was unable to pay. The subordinate received protection from the Court of Admiralty, but admiralty's decision led only to a pamphlet war between a leading merchant and the admiralty judge, who ultimately lost his judicial post. Similarly, when the attorney general in 1769 applied for writs of assistance on behalf of royal customs officials, the South Carolina court, in a reversal of what had been done only eight years earlier even in Massachusetts, refused to issue them. According to a contemporary treatise writer, it was "unusual for justices to grant general warrants to search all suspected places."[10] Instead, the court directed the attorney general

> to inform the Custom House Officers . . . that whenever any matter occurred in the execution of their duty that made the aid of the judges necessary they would be ready on proper, special application to give them the fullest assistance.[11]

The Crown had little choice but to acquiesce.

The Supreme Courts of Pennsylvania and New York reached similar results, and again the Crown acquiesced. Although the Pennsylvania court had routinely enforced parliamentary customs legislation before the Stamp Act, its approach after the 1765 crisis was different. When the Crown in 1769 requested the issuance of "a general warrant of assistance" on behalf of "customshouse officers," the judges, upon

> considering the several acts of Parliament relating to this subject, . . . were unanimously of opinion that such a general warrant could not legally be granted, but that the custom house officers should apply

for warrants of assistance from time to time as special occasions should call for them.[12]

In New York, the Supreme Court granted a general writ of assistance as late as 1768 but refused to do so thereafter.

We will never know to what extent economic interests or belief in the illegality of general warrants or what combination of both motivated opposition to the issuance of the warrants. But we can know with certainty that the argument of James Otis that was rejected in 1761—that courts should refuse to enforce an act of Parliament that was inconsistent with the reason of the common law—had gained widespread judicial acceptance by the end of the decade and affected how courts thought about general writs of assistance.

Meanwhile, South Carolina judges became involved in yet another battle, resulting from a vote in the lower house of the legislature granting a gift to John Wilkes in appreciation of his support for Englishmen's rights. The vote produced several years of conflict between the lower house and the council, which was determined to prevent delivery of the gift. In 1773, a protest against the council's actions appeared in the *South Carolina Gazette*, to which the council responded by arresting its printer, Thomas Powell. Two local justices of the peace, who happened to be members of the lower house and perhaps remembered the *Zenger* case, promptly released Powell on habeas corpus, and no prosecution occurred.

The cases just discussed had little impact on the constitutional debate between Parliament and the American colonies and, in the main, were only of local significance. One of the eighteenth century's great constitutional cases, *Forsey v. Cunningham*,[13] did, however, have more important intercolonial significance.

The case arose in New York after Cunningham, in the midst of an altercation with Forsey, chased him and, when Forsey defended himself, stabbed him in the chest with a sword he had concealed beneath his clothing. Forsey commenced a civil action against Cunningham in the Supreme Court for battery, and in October 1764 the jury returned a large verdict of £1,500 in the plaintiff's favor. Cunningham determined to appeal to the Governor and Council, which sat without a jury, and ultimately, if necessary, to the Privy Council, which also sat without a jury. Cadwallader Colden, who was acting governor at the time, was eager to consider the appeal, which he saw as a means of limiting the power of juries and thereby enhancing the power of the Crown.

The difficulty for Cunningham and Colden was that no error appeared on the face of the record. The proceedings below had been legally simple: Forsey had filed his writ and declaration; Cunningham had properly pleaded the general issue and moved for a struck jury, which motion had been granted; and the case had been submitted to the jury on the evidence, not reported in the record, that the parties had presented. Cunningham's only objection was to the size of the verdict, but if he took his appeal by writ of error, that objection could not be raised because there was no error on the record in the proceedings below.

Cunningham accordingly sought to proceed by filing an appeal rather than a writ of error. The distinction was that on a writ of error, where a general verdict had been given, the merits of a case did not appear in the record and thus could not be considered by the higher court; it could consider only whether an issue of law had been decided improperly below. On an appeal, in contrast, the entire cause was open to reconsideration, both on the evidence below and on such new evidence as the litigants might present. Colden conceded that under earlier New York practice no one had ever proceeded by appeal from the Supreme Court to the Governor and Council, but he saw Cunningham's case as a device to alter this preexisting practice and thereby enhance the Crown's power to reexamine jury verdicts contrary to royal policies. Colden sought to allow an appeal in lieu of a writ of error on the technical argument that a clause in the instructions of the governor specifying the writ of error as the proper mode for proceeding to a higher court had been omitted from those instructions in 1753.

Relying on its own precedents and on its understanding that at common law in England, cases proceeded from lower to higher courts only by writ of error, the colony's Supreme Court, staffed almost entirely by members of the New York bar and thus somewhat accountable to it, denied Cunningham's appeal. On the advice of the judges and the attorney general, the council agreed and also denied the appeal, over Colden's dissent. In 1765, Cunningham next sought leave from the Privy Council to appeal to it. The council denied leave but at the same time directed Colden to allow an appeal from the Supreme Court to the Court of Appeal, presumably the Governor and Council, in New York.

Colden thereupon issued a writ of appeal to the Supreme Court, but the court declined to obey the writ on the grounds that the attorney seeking to appeal had not been properly retained, that it had no power to assign counsel to proceed in a court over which it lacked jurisdiction, and that, in any event, it had received no proper writ directing it to send up the record. There matters rested until November 1765, when a new governor arrived with new instructions restoring the language omitted from the 1753 instructions and confining appeals to the Governor and Council to cases of error only. Colden's effort to free New York's appellate courts from the power of local juries accordingly failed and left jurors with power to determine law as well as fact unless a trial judge, in the exercise of his unreviewable discretion, tried to use one of the procedural mechanisms at his command to stop them.

Forsey v. Cunningham, with its potential for undermining jury power, had repercussions throughout the colonies with the publication of a widely circulated pamphlet, similar to Alexander's *Brief Narrative* in the *Zenger* case. Even in

Pennsylvania, where judges in the mid-eighteenth century were declaring that it was "a settled rule, that courts of law determine law; a jury facts ... upon which maxim every security depends in an English country," the press was at the same time urging jurors to stand firm in protecting their claim of lawfinding power and thus local self-rule.[14]

With such anti-authoritarianism in the air and with the fabric of empire becoming frayed, British officials and their colonial opponents nonetheless worked hard to maintain civility, mutual deference, the tradition of compromise that had accompanied them, and thus the empire itself. *Forsey v. Cunningham* provides an example. Cadwallader Colden, the acting governor, had come close to winning his effort to strengthen imperial authority when the Privy Council directed the New York Supreme Court to allow an appeal to the Governor and Council. But the British ministry snatched victory from his hands when, in effect, they overruled the Privy Council and sent out a new governor with the old instructions to allow appeals in cases of error only. Perhaps those authorities were incompetent and did not understand how the old instructions weakened the Crown. But it seems more likely they were acting to preserve traditional legal rules promoting the accommodation and compromise by which the empire had successfully been governed for three-quarters of a century.

Freebody v. Brenton, discussed in chapter 12, provides another example. For some fifteen years, going back to the late 1750s, the Rhode Island courts and the Privy Council had worked to decide the *Freebody* case in a manner that preserved mutual legal respect. Old patterns of mutual forbearance, of giving everyone a full hearing, and ultimately of compromise persisted on the part of the Privy Council as late as 1772.

Colonials likewise did not press too hard. Consider, for example, the defense of Captain Thomas Preston by John Adams, Josiah Quincy Jr., and Robert Auchmuty. Preston, it was alleged, had ordered his troops to fire the shots that had killed civilians in the Boston Massacre. Adams was as loyal as anyone to the Revolutionary cause. But he understood that the law on which the empire rested—the law that in 1770 he still hoped could preserve the empire and avert independence—entitled Preston to a vigorous defense, and Adams gave Preston that defense.

Preston was entitled to challenge peremptorily up to twenty talesmen on the jury panel selected by the towns of Suffolk County, and Adams participated in the challenge of nineteen of them—nineteen men who, if left on the jury, almost certainly would have found Preston guilty. Adams undoubtedly knew that the county sheriff, Stephen Greenleaf, a confirmed loyalist, would go out on the street and replace those talesmen with loyalist jurors who would vote, as they did, to acquit Preston. It was not a matter of a jury giving Preston a fair hearing on the issue of whether he had ordered the shooting; it was a matter of

Preston taking advantage of a legal technicality to avoid punishment for what most people of Massachusetts deemed murder. But the law entitled Preston to that advantage, and as of 1770 John Adams still believed in law as the glue that could hold the empire together.

Toward Independence

Imperial law broke down in December 1773, when a group of Bostonians in disguise dumped tea into Boston harbor, and Parliament abandoned all restraint, made no effort to punish only the guilty, and, in the view of most Americans, punished all of America by passing the Coercive Acts, which Americans dubbed the Intolerable Acts. The political and military path that led first to Lexington and Concord, next to Bunker Hill, and ultimately to the Declaration of Independence has been well trodden by other historians, and I have nothing to add. We can, however, focus on some legal developments that occurred along the path to independence—developments that reveal a great deal about the common law, localist constitution that Americans were defending.

The first and most important developments occurred in Massachusetts. They were a product of the Massachusetts Government Act, one of the Intolerable Acts. Three provisions of that act deprived the people of the Bay Colony of control over local government and thus struck at the heart of the colonial constitution. Under the colony's 1691 charter, judges, sheriffs, and other officers of the courts were appointed by the governor with the approval of the upper house of the legislature, in the election of which the lower house had the dominant say; under the Massachussetts Government Act, the Crown's appointed governor would choose those officers by himself. The second provision permitted towns to meet to elect town officials and representatives to the General Court but prohibited town meetings for any other purpose without the prior written approval of the governor.

The third provision was the most important for the law. Instead of having jurors chosen by town meetings, the Massachusetts Government Act provided for the selection of jurors by sheriffs, who, in turn, were appointed by the governor. One need only compare the outcome of *Erving v. Cradock* with that in *Rex v. Preston* to appreciate how this third provision took ultimate control of the legal system out of the hands of Massachusetts towns and put it into the hands of the royal administration. In *Erving*, discussed in chapter 13, town-selected jurors subjected a royal customs official to a large damage judgment for seizing a ship on a charge of smuggling. In *Rex v. Preston*, one of the Boston Massacre cases, a jury chosen by a sheriff acquitted Captain Preston of charges of murdering several local civilians.

In response to the Intolerable Acts, a Worcester County convention in August 1774 urged "every town in the province, to meet and adopt some wise, prudent, and spirited measures, in order to prevent the execution of these most alarming acts of parliament, respecting our constitution." A town meeting held the next week in Pittsfield agreed that "the people . . . [should] utterly refuse the least submission to . . . these injurious, oppressive, and unconstitutional acts" by demanding "that the courts of justice immediately cease." As a result of such demands, the courts were shut down in most Massachusetts counties. Relying, in effect, on James Otis's argument in the *Writs of Assistance Case*, some of the judges even conceded that they had agreed to close the courts "on account of the unconstitutional act of the British parliament, respecting the administration of justice in this province." Courts remained open in only three counties—Suffolk, where the British occupation army protected the judges in their sittings, and Essex and Cumberland, where the judges agreed to sit and function under the provisions of the 1691 charter rather than under the Massachusetts Government Act. Town meetings also ignored the Massachusetts Government Act and continued to function and maintain order under the 1691 charter.[15]

In neighboring Rhode Island, some unidentified radicals had burned a British schooner, the *Gaspee*, off the coast of Narraganset Bay even before the destruction of the tea in Boston. While British authorities were considering how to repond to the burning, the Rhode Island Superior Court was drafting its explanation for the judgment that it had rendered in *Freebody v. Brenton*. The court's model remained one of mutual respect and compromise. The judges strove to acknowledge the Privy Council's authority while simultaneously maintaining their own independence. They conceded that they had an "obligation of duty and respect" to the Privy Council's "right . . . of hearing and determining all matter of appeal." At the same time, they argued, as Pennsylvania's judges had been maintaining for several decades, that they were not inferior servants who merely executed orders, but "judges, under a peculiar constitution," with a duty of "making or giving judgment." They had taken an oath to uphold Rhode Island's "modes of practice, laws & customs" which were "not in any essential point whatever repugnant to the laws of Great Britain," but simply different. The judges asked the council to respect their oath and duty and not to require "literal execution" of its order, but merely "near compliance" with "the most substantial part" of its decree. They ended by declaring that the parties had had "justice done them" by the Rhode Island court in the *Freebody* case and that "injustice would issue" if the Privy Council did not affirm the Rhode Island judgment.[16]

By the time the Privy Council replied in June 1774, no arrests had yet been made in the *Gaspee* burning, the tea had been dumped into Boston harbor, Parliament had passed the Intolerable Acts, and the Privy Council had lost patience. Instead of ending its order with its customary request that the lower court "govern themselves accordingly," the council "peremptorily order[ed], require[d] and command[ed]" the Rhode Island Court to "comply punctually," "forthwith and without delay," to "yield due obedience," and to put the Privy Council's order "literally into execution."[17]

From there the pattern of disrespect spread. After the filing of one more appeal to the Privy Council by the collector of customs in 1775, the Rhode Island legislature repealed its act permitting such appeals. The Privy Council then reversed the judgment against the collector. In June 1776 Rhode Island struck the king's name from its charter.

The Intolerable Acts produced a similar breakdown of mutual respect and willingness to compromise in Virginia. In 1769, for example, many Virginians had joined other colonists in a boycott of imported British goods that aimed to pressure British merchants to urge Parliament to repeal the Townshend duties. The Virginians had refused, however, to take the further step of pressuring the merchants by withholding exports of tobacco. But after Parliament passed the Quebec Act and the other Intolerable Acts in 1774, Virginia did join a boycott that included a ban on tobacco exports.

The ban, however, created a problem. Without income from the sale of their tobacco, Virginia planters had no money with which to pay debts to British creditors. Thus, non-exportation required the enactment of legislation to stop debt collection, which, in turn, would further pressure Parliament to repeal the Intolerable Acts. Such legislation, though, appeared certain to be met with a gubernatorial veto.

But Lord Dunmore, the royal governor, inadvertently came to the rescue. Under Virginia law, various fees paid to court officers were set by statute, and the statute setting those fees had expired in April 1774. Renewal of the fee bill thus was on the legislature's agenda at its May 1774 session. But before the legislature could act, Governor Dunmore dissolved the House of Burgesses when it approved a resolution condemning Parliament's closure of the Port of Boston. Historians dispute whether the Burgesses intentionally postponed consideration of the fee bill in the expectation that they would be dissolved or whether failure to enact the bill before dissolution was a mere accident.

Whatever the intention of the legislature, the law, lawyers, and courts, in alliance with the economic interests of the planters, now entered the picture. At a rump session of the burgesses in Raleigh Tavern the day after dissolution, the issue arose of how the courts should deal with the failure to enact the fee bill. Some thought they should stay open and establish fees by themselves; others thought that in the absence of statutory fees, the courts were required to close. An intermediate position was that courts should remain open for criminal prosecutions, administration of estates, and recording of documents but should not hear debt cases or civil suits more generally.

Demonstrating their independence from the General Court as well as from the authority of the Crown, the county justices did what most of the former burgesses wanted: in most counties, they remained open but heard few debt or other civil cases. Through local legal interpretation rather than a legislative act, the local judiciary thereby put maximum pressure on Parliament to repeal the Intolerable Acts. And there was nothing that the governor and the General Court could do in response, although the General Court itself, over which the governor presided, tried to remain open. But it too was forced to suspend its sessions when the small group of attorneys who practiced before it organized a boycott, which litigants and witnesses later joined. Local institutions on the ground overwhelmed what little power the central government of Virginia possessed.

The turn of Virginians to lawyers in the summer of 1774, following habits of mind that had grown up over the previous quarter century, effectively demonstrated their independence from royal authority and from the colony's central government. Local courts, with their self-perpetuating membership, went about business as usual, except that they declined to hear the category of cases—those involving debt collection—that British authorities most wanted them to hear. But although they acted independently, most Virginians were by no means ready to declare independence formally, even as tensions continued to mount through the autumn and winter of 1774–75.

Then, in April 1775, Governor Dunmore took two steps that pushed Virginians to open rebellion. On April 21, apparently out of fear that he and other senior officials were threatened with bodily harm, Dunmore ordered the colony's supply of gunpowder removed from the Williamsburg Powder Magazine and placed on board a royal naval vessel. The next day he quietly warned the speaker of the House of Burgesses that if any senior British official was harmed, he would proclaim freedom for slaves. Several weeks later Dunmore himself fled Williamsburg and began raising an army to defend Britain's interests. At first, he welcomed slaves to join his forces by quietly promising them freedom; later, in November 1775, he issued a formal proclamation stating that he would free any slaves who joined. The threat of a slave revolt pushed Virginians nearly unanimously in the direction of independence. As a result, beginning in the spring of 1776, courts began to appoint officials such as sheriffs "pursuant to an ordinance of convention" rather than on a commission from the royal governor.[18]

Except in Massachusetts, where courts in all but the three counties noted above were closed down by revolutionary forces, nearly all courts in the new American states remained open. Most colonial judges, with the exception of occasional Loyalists who left the bench and a few others, remained on the courts and continued to conduct business as they had for several decades. The one change that occurred in all of the courts, pursuant to a May 1776 resolution of the Continental Congress, was that they ceased meeting under the authority of George III and began meeting under new authority. In a remarkable display of localism, for example, the judges of Delaware, who formerly had sat in the name of the king, reconstituted themselves in August 1776 as the "Justices of the Government of New Castle, Kent & Sussex"—the three counties contained within the old colony.[19]

The Connecticut Superior Court provides another example. By the winter of 1775–76, the people of Connecticut were choosing sides in the impending struggle for American independence. Those who refused to acknowledge the authority of the king and Parliament were in control of the institutions of local government, and they used that control to bring criminal prosecutions against pro-British members of the community who would not obey them, using such charges as sedition, passing sensitive information to British authorities, and enlisting in British military service. As late as February 1776, however, these prosecutions were still being brought in the name of the king; it was only in June 1776 that the courts hearing the charges were convened by special order of their chief judges and that prosecutions were brought in the name of the grand jury of the county. What was most significant was that at least occasional individuals, for reasons left unstated in the court records, were found not guilty of the offenses charged; it seems that those in control of the Revolutionary legal system still sought to maintain some bonds of community and justice.

The continued use of old legal tools, albeit for new purposes, occurred as well in the mid-1770s in South Carolina. Recall, as seen in chapter 12, that a traditional power of grand juries in that colony had been to present the grievances of the community. In the April 1776 term, the grand jury presented its grievances as it always had. But the grievances no longer were about local matters to which the justices of General Sessions had responded in the past. Now the grievances were about constitutional politics. The people had come to understand that the "powers of government . . . were originally derived from themselves for the protection of their rights."[20] They no longer were prepared to accept what had been obvious only sixteen years earlier—that the "plantations [were] limited and dependent governments" under the sway of Parliament and the king and Privy Council.[21] "Tho ever submissive to the just mandates of legal authority," South Carolinians now found "intolerable to the spirit of a people born and nurtured in the arms of freedom . . . the unjust, evil and diabolical acts of the British Parliament."[22]

Why did the people of South Carolina complain to the Court of General Sessions about the acts of the British Parliament? The answer is that General Sessions had always been the entity to which people had complained. It was the entity of government that had always interacted with the people, and with the dissolution of the imperial system in the spring of 1776, it remained the entity of interaction.

The criminal prosecutions in Connecticut and the presentation of grievances in South Carolina illustrate that the coming of the American Revolution placed new demands on government but did not alter the institutions of government that had always responded to the society's demands. Local courts had long been the principal institutions through which colonial government had functioned, and those same local courts, staffed by the same local elites, remained the principal institutions of revolutionary government. The coming of the Revolution did not immediately transfer power from one class of rulers to another, nor did it immediately transform the institutions, mechanisms, and procedures through which those rulers governed. But it did place new demands on the law, and over time, the need to respond to those demands would change everything.

16

A Historian's Postscript

When the War for Independence broke out in 1775–76, significant legal and constitutional doctrines and practices that have endured throughout the American Republic's history already were in place. Although the nation's legal and constitutional system would, of course, change over time, much would remain intact, as the following examples suggest.

The centrality of the common law in the American legal order is one matter that has remained unchanged; in the words of John Bannister Gibson, an important early nineteenth-century judge, the common law has penetrated "so essentially into the composition of our social institutions as to be inseparable from them."[1] At the same time, the legal profession that administers the common law continues to enjoy great stature and to wield vast power. Legal rules protecting private ownership of land and other means of production together with freedom of contract likewise have remained at the foundation of the American economy. At the same time, government has continued to subsidize, stimulate, and regulate the market to promote economic growth and, at times, to spread the benefits of that growth among large segments of the community, although, of course, innumerable specific rules of property, contract, and regulation differ today from the rules of 1776. The law of religion similarly has changed, albeit in directions in which it had already been evolving—in the nineteenth century toward a generic Protestant faith and in the twentieth to an informal Judeo-Christian establishment.

Another constant has been the coercive power of local government. Few Americans today can avoid interactions with state and local governments, which in addition to overseeing the police, control the education bureaucracy, the motor vehicle bureau, building and housing departments, and health departments. Of course, the scope of federal power has undergone change, but on the whole the national government continues to exert its power through wealth transfers—through collecting taxes and distributing welfare benefits and other forms of largesse—rather than through direct coercion. And the law of federalism—the mechanisms for maintaining a balance between the state and federal governments—can also be traced back to the eighteenth-century Privy Council and to a small number of prerogative courts that, like today's federal district courts, exercised original jurisdiction over cases of a specialized nature.

How did these patterns of law and constitutionalism develop and why have they persisted? As the preceding pages have indicated, kings, government ministers, and Parliament played major roles in creating the institutions and practices that were in place by 1776. Parliament, as shown in Part II, left two Stuart kings, Charles II and James II, penurious, and the kings responded by imposing the common law and the legal profession on the American colonies as the vehicles through which the Crown could govern at little expense. In contrast, as Part III recounted, William III and his successors, who were less concerned than Charles II and James II with enhancing the monarch's power, although they continued to insist on reception of the common law, did not stand in the way of local governments in the colonies accumulating substantial power within the common law system.

Unlike his predecessors, William III was concerned with supporting colonial Protestants in the practice of their religion; as a result, he put an end to Roman Catholic governance of Maryland, and he and his Parliaments enacted legislation discriminating against Catholics and protecting the religious freedom of all Protestants. Finally, as Part IV showed, George III, his ministers, and Parliaments, made a series of imprudent decisions that prompted American lawyers to explicate the tacit constitutional rules under which they lived—an explication that resulted in the elaboration of such doctrines as judicial review of the constitutionality of legislation. In short, kings, ministers, and Parliament played a substantial role in creating the colonial constitutional order that was in place in the mid-eighteenth century.

That constitutional order emerged, however, not only from the policies of leaders but also from demands made by those who were governed. Although some of the early settlers of Massachusetts, such as John Winthrop, were gentlemen of stature, most settlers were ordinary people. Their demand that the law be publicized so that they could know how they were required to behave forced such leaders as Winthrop to enact codes and to leave discretion to interpret those codes in the hands of representatives of the people, sitting either as jurors or as elected legislators. Similarly, large numbers of often ordinary people resisted the policies of George III, his ministers, and Parliament, and thereby preserved the power of local self-government as a key element of American constitutionalism.

Often the forces underlying legal development were quite complex. Consider, for example, early Virginia. The colony needed immigrant settlers, but Dale's *Lawes* together with the Virginia Company's ownership of all property discouraged potential settlers from migrating. In 1619 and the years following, as shown in chapter 1, elite leaders of the company privatized property and established self-government under the common law; they acted, of course, in pursuit of their own interest in preserving the company and making it profitable, but also in response to pressures from ordinary people whom they were striving to encourage to migrate. Several years later, Virginia likewise adopted common law doctrines of debtor and creditor under pressure from ordinary Virginians seeking to borrow capital and from ordinary London merchants prepared to advance loans as long as repayment was assured.

These few examples, as well as many others in the preceding pages, suggest that students of legal history striving to understand how law comes into being and how it functions need to pay attention to policies pursued by elite leaders, who often possess plenary power to declare what is law, as well as some power to enforce it. But it is also necessary to pay attention to the demands of ordinary people who must be willing to obey the law voluntarily in order to have it function cheaply and effectively, and to attend as well to structural conditions, of the sort dictated, for example, by markets, that often control how both leaders and ordinary people can behave. In conclusion, the history and functioning of America's legal and constitutional order is a complex one that can be understood only through an appreciation of the policies of leaders, the demands of common people, and a knowledge of hard facts that often limited what both could do.

NOTES

Introduction

1. Woodrow Wilson to J. H. Kennard, Nov. 18, 1884, quoted in Hugh Hawkins, *Pioneer: A History of the Johns Hopkins University, 1874–1889* (Ithaca, N.Y.: Cornell University Press, 1960), 283; Bernard Bailyn, *The Origins of American Politics* (New York: Knopf, 1965), vii.
2. A major topic that, because of time constraints, this book does not address is the extent to which other British colonies, such as Nova Scotia and the Atlantic and Caribbean islands, developed along patterns similar to those of the thirteen colonies that became the United States. A particularly intriguing question, which lack of time precludes studying, is why only thirteen of Britain's more than twenty colonies rebelled in the 1770s.

Chapter 1

1. David H. Flaherty, ed., *For the Colony in Virginea Brittania: Lawes Divine, Morall and Martiall, etc.* (Charlottesville: University of Virginia Press, 1969), 17–19. Spelling and punctuation have been modernized in all quotations.
2. Flaherty, *Lawes*, 19.
3. A Briefe Declaration of the Plantation of Virginia, in *Journals of the House of Burgesses of Virginia, 1619–1658/59*, ed. H. R. McIlwaine (Richmond, Va.: Colonial Press, 1915), 28, 36.
4. Statement of Hamer, Va. Gen. Ct. 1624, in *Minutes of the Council and General Court of Colonial Virginia*, 2nd ed., ed. R. B. McIlwaine (Richmond: Virginia State Library, 1979), 31.
5. Francis Moryson and Henry Randolph, eds., *The Laws of Virginia Now in Force* (London, 1662), 2.
6. Inhabitants v. Cololough, Northumberland County Va. Ct. Oct. 20, 1658 (microfilm in Library of Virginia).
7. Rex v. Epps, Va. Gen. Ct. 1626/27, in *Minutes of General Court*, 140–42, 148.
8. Rex v. Walker, Northampton County Va. Ct. Jan. 28, 1645/46, in *County Court Records of Accomack-Northampton, Virginia, 1640–1645*, ed. Susie Ames (Charlottesville: University Press of Virginia, 1973), 340.
9. Confession of Willmote, Northampton County Va. Ct. 1649, in *Northampton County Virginia Record Book: Orders, Deed, Wills, 1645–1651*, ed. Howard Mackey (Rockport, Me.: Picton Press, 2000), 347. The case has been the subject of a book by John R. Pagan, *Anne Orthwood's Bastard: Sex and Law in Early Virginia* (New York: Oxford University Press, 2003).
10. Laws of Feb. 17, 1644/45, Act XIV, in *The Statutes at Large; Being a Collection of all the Laws of Virginia from the First Session of the Legislature in the Year 1619*, ed. William W. Hening (New York: R. & W. & G. Bartow, 1823), 1: 296.
11. Rubin v. Dirrickson, Northampton County Va. Ct. 1643, in *Records of Accomack-Northampton, 1640–1645*, 288.

12. Deposition of William Munns, Northampton County Va. Ct. 1644/45, in *Records of Accomack-Northampton, 1640–1645*, 405–6.
13. Laws of Feb. 17, 1644/45, Act XV, in Hening, *Statutes*, 1: 296.
14. Resolution of Va. General Ct., Dec. 4, 1627, in *Minutes of General Court*, 483.
15. Order re Debts, Va. Gen. Ct. 1627, in *Minutes of General Court*, 483.
16. Act Concerning Religion, 1648, in *Archives of Maryland*, 72 vols. (Baltimore: Maryland Historical Society, 1883–1972), 1: 244–47.
17. Proprietary v. Fitzherbert, Md. Prov. Ct. 1658-1661/62, in *Md. Archives*, 41: 144, 566.
18. Complaint of Lewis, Md. Prov. Ct. 1638, in *Md. Archives*, 4: 35.
19. Robinson v. Wennam, Charles County Md. Ct. 1661, in *Md. Archives*, 53: 133.
20. Stratton v. Turner, Md. Prov. Ct. 1659, in *Md. Archives*, 41: 291, *reversing* Stratton v. Turner, Charles County Md. Ct. 1658/59, *Md. Archives*, 53: 30, 37 (jury verdict for Stratton on same evidence as on appeal).
21. Cornwallis v. Gerrard, Md. Prov. Ct. 1653/54, in *Md. Archives*, 10: 341.
22. Quigley v. Delaroche, Md. Prov. Ct. 1676, in *Md. Archives*, 56: 347.
23. England v. Slye, Md. Prov. Ct. 1680/81, in *Md. Archives*, 59: 320 (argument of counsel).

Chapter 2

1. John Winthrop, "A Model of Christian Charity" (1630), in Collections of the Massachusetts Historical Society, 3d ser., 7 (Boston, 1838), 31, 33–34, 46.
2. John Cotton, *An Exposition upon the Thirteenth Chapter of the Revelation* (London: Livewel, Chapman, 1655), 71–73.
3. Winthrop, "Model of Christian Charity," 34.
4. Gardiner v. Nevard, Middlesex County Mass. Ct. June 15, 1675, and Dec. 19, 1676 (microfilm in possession of Utah Genealogical Society).
5. Colony v. Ledra, Mass. Ct. Asst. 1660/61, in *Records of the Court of Assistants of the Colony of Massachusetts Bay, 1630–1692*, 3 vols. (Boston: Suffolk County, 1901–1926), 3: 93–94.
6. Colony v. Woodman, Ipswich Mass. Quarterly Ct. 1669, in *Records and Files of the Quarterly Courts of Essex County*, 8 vols. (Salem, Mass.: Essex Institute, 1911-1921); 4: 122–23.
7. Colony v. Woodman, Ipswich Mass. Quarterly Ct. 1671, in *Records of Essex*, 4: 350–51.
8. Colony v. Gilbert, Ipswich Mass. Quarterly Ct. 1671, in 1921, 4: 122–23.
9. Mansfield v. Hathorne and Longley v. Hathorne, Essex County Mass. Ct. 1663, in *Records of Essex*, 3: 24, 29. On the affirmance by the Court of Assistants, *see* Mark DeWolfe Howe, ed., *Readings in American Legal History* (Cambridge, Mass.: Harvard University Press, 1949), 137.
10. *See* Giddings v. Brown, Essex County Mass. Ct. 1657, in Mark DeWolfe Howe, *Readings in American Legal History*, 232.
11. Colony v. Marshall, Suffolk County Mass. Ct. 1671/72, in *Records of the Suffolk County Court, 1671–1680*, 2 vols. (Boston: Colony Society of Massachusetts, 1933), 1: 86.
12. The Body of Liberties of 1641, in Edwin Powers, *Crime and Punishment in Early Massachusetts, 1620–1692: A Documentary History* (Boston: Beacon Press, 1966), 533, 536.
13. The *Book of the General Lawes and Libertyes Concerning the Inhabitants of the Massachusetts* (Cambridge, Mass., 1648), ed. Richard S. Dunn (San Marino, Calif.: Huntington Library, 1998), 23.
14. Order re Judicial Laws, New Haven Gen. Ct. 1644, in *Records of the Colony and Plantation of New Haven*, 3 vols. (Hartford, Conn.: Case, Tiffany & Co., 1857–1858) 1: 130.
15. Order re Sabbath, New Haven Gen. Ct. 1647/48, in *New Haven Colony Records*, I: 358.
16. Act of June 6, 1655, in *Records of the Colony of New Plymouth*, ed. Nathaniel B. Shurtleff, 12 vols. (Boston, Mass.: William White, 1855–1861), 11: 64.
17. Laws of September 29, 1658, in *Records of Plymouth*, 11:100.
18. Order for Day of Fasting and Humiliation," Ply. Gen. Ct. 1658, in *Records of Plymouth*, 3: 151.
19. Will of Tomson, Conn. Magis. Ct. 1656, in *Records of the Particular Court of Connecticut, 1639–1663* (Hartford: Connecticut Historical Society, 1928), 163.
20. Colony v. Marsh, New Haven Magis. Ct. 1645, in *New Haven Colony Records*, I: 180.
21. Complaint against Train Band of Scituate, Ply. Gen. Ct. 1655, in *Records of the Colony of New Plymouth*, ed. Nathaniel Shurtleff, 12 vols. (Boston, Mass.: William White, 1855–1861), 3: 89.

22. John D. Cushing ed., *The Earliest Acts and Laws of the Colony of Rhode Island and Providence Plantations, 1640–1719* (Wilmington, Del.: Michael Glazier, 1977), 5, 12.

23. Colony v. Parent, R.I. Ct. Trials 1658, in *Rhode Island Court Records: Records of the Court of Trials of the Colony of Providence Plantations 1647–1670*, 2 vols. (Providence: Rhode Island Historical Society, 1920–1922), 1: 44.

24. Hollister v. Church of Wethersfield, Conn. Gen. Ct. 1658/59, in *The Public Records of the Colony of Connecticut*, 15 vols. (Hartford, Conn.: Brown & Parsons, 1850–1858), 1: 330.

25. Peirson v. Cowper, New Haven Magis. Ct. 1658, in *New Haven Colony Records*, III: 270.

Chapter 3

1. The Humble Remonstrance and Petition of the Colonies and Villages in this New Netherland Province, New Netherland Council 1653, in *New York Historical Manuscripts: Dutch: Volume V, Council Minutes, 1652–1654*, ed. Charles T. Gehring (Baltimore: Genealogical Publishing, 1983), 91, 92; Petition of Representatives of Villages of . . . New Netherland Council 1653, in *Council Minutes, 1652–1654*, 100; Fiscal v. Rendelman, New Netherland Council 1652, in *Council Minutes, 1652–1654*, 56.

2. Aertsz v. Adriaensz, Rensselaer New Neth. Patroon Ct. 1649, in *Minutes of the Court of Rensselaerswyck, 1648–1652*, ed. A. J. F. van Laer (Albany: University of the State of New York, 1922), 65.

3. Order Establishing Inferior Courts, New Amsterdam Burgomasters Ct. 1654, in *Records of New Amsterdam from 1653 to 1674*, ed. Berthold Fernow (New York: Knickerbocker Press, 1897), 1: 173.

4. Schout v. Cornelissen, New Amsterdam Burgomasters Ct. 1662, in *Records of New Amsterdam*, 4: 68.

5. Commissary v. Jansen, Fort Orange N. Neth. Inferior Ct. 1660, in *Minutes of the Court of Fort Orange and Beverwyck, 1652–1656*, ed. A. J. F. van Laer (Albany: University of State of New York, 1920), 2: 281.

6. Ebbingh v. Sleght, Kingston N. Neth. Ordinary Ct. Mar. 1662 (microfilm in possession of Queens Library, Jamaica, N.Y.).

7. Schout v. de la Sina, New Amsterdam Burgomasters Ct. 1655, in *Records of New Amsterdam*, 1: 290, 291.

8. Remonstrance of Inhabitants of Flushing (1658), in *Documents Relating to the Colonial History of the State of New York: Colonial Documents* (Albany, N.Y.: Weed, Parsons, 1883), 14: 402.

9. In William S. Pelletreau, ed., *The First Book of Records of the Town of Southampton* (Sag Harbor, N.Y.: John H. Hunt, 1874), 1: 18.

10. Helm v. Oelsen, Upland Ct. 1676/77 and 1677, in *The Record of the Court at Upland, in Pennsylvania, 1676–1681* (Philadelphia, Pa.: Joseph Mitchell, 1954), 47, 53–54.

11. Mortense v. Staecke, Upland Ct. 1676/77, in *Record of Upland Court*, 47.

Chapter 4

1. The First Charter of Massachusetts, March 4, 1629, in Documents of American History, 1, 10th ed., ed. Henry Steele Commager and Milton Cantor (Englewood Cliffs, N.J.: Prentice Hall, 1988), 16.

2. The Charter of Maryland, June 20, 1632, in Commager and Cantor, *Documents*, 1: 21.

3. Charter for the Province of Pennsylvania, 1681, in *The Federal and State Constitutions, Colonial Charters, and Other Organic Laws of the States, Territories, and Colonies Now or Heretofore Forming the United States of America*, 7 vols., ed. Francis N. Thorpe (Washington, D.C.: Government Printing Office, 1909), 5: 3035.

4. Protest of Schout and Commissaries, Kingston N.Y. Ordinary Ct. Feb. 1665 (microfilm in possession of Queens Library, Jamaica, N.Y.).

5. Duke of York's Laws, in *The Colonial Laws of New York from the Year 1664 to the Revolution* (Albany: James B. Lyon, 1894), 1: 6, 42–45 (emphasis added).

6. The King to the Governor of the Massachusetts Bay, June 28, 1662, in *Calendar of State Papers, Colonial Series, America and West Indies, 1661–1668*, ed. W. Noel Sainsbury (London: Longman, 1880), 93, 94.

7. Copy of a Paper Endorsed Mr. E.R's. Narrative Sept. 20th and Octo. 12th 1676, in *A Collection of Original Papers Relative to the History of the Colony of Massachusetts Bay*, ed. Thomas Hutchinson (Boston: Thomas and John Fleet, 1769), 477, 481–82.

8. Mark DeWolfe Howe and Louis F. Eaton, "The Supreme Judicial Power in the Colony of Massachusetts Bay," *New England Quarterly*, 20 (1947), 291, 305 (quoting the oaths), 308 (quoting a report of the clergy), 311 (quoting the argument of the magistrates), 306.

9. Bushell's Case, 124 Eng. Rep. 1006 (Com. Pleas 1670).

10. Randolph v. Hutchinson, Mass. Ct. Asst. 1680, in *Records of the Court of Assistants of the Colony of Massachusetts Bay, 1630–1692*, 3 vols. (Boston: Suffolk County, 1901–1926), 1: 168.

11. King v. Ralph, Fairfield Co. Conn. Super. Ct. Feb. 1766 (manuscript in possession of Connecticut State Library).

12. Return of Whitman, R.I. Ct. Trials 1662/63, in *Rhode Island Court Records: Records of the Court of Trials of the Colony of Providence Plantations, 1647–1670*, 2 vols. (Providence: Rhode Island Historical Society, 1920–1922), 2: 15–16.

Chapter 5

1. Charge of Mompesson, C.J., in Queen v. Makemie, N.Y. Sup. Ct. 1707, *quoted in* Julius Goebel, Jr. and T. Raymond Naughton, *Law Enforcement in Colonial New York: A Study in Criminal Procedure (1664–1776)*, (New York: Commonwealth Fund, 1944), 666.

2. Petition of Sandor, Ulster Co. N.Y. Gen. Sess. Ct. May 1745 (microfilm in possession of Queens Library, Jamaica, N.Y.).

3. *Quoted in* Philip Ranlet, *Enemies of the Bay Colony: Puritan Massachusetts and Its Foes*, 2nd ed. (Lanham, Md.: University Press of America, 2006), 177.

4. 124 Eng. Rep. 1006 (Com. Pleas 1670).

5. Savage v. Menzeis, Suffolk Co. Mass. Com. Pleas Ct. April 2, 1728 (microfilm in possession of Utah Genealogical Society).

6. Hall v. Armstrong, Worcester Co. Mass. Super. Ct. Sept. 19, 1733 (microfilm in possession of Utah Genealogical Society).

Chapter 6

1. Order re By-Laws, Northampton County Va. Ct. 1665, in *Northampton County Virginia Record Book, 1664–1674*, ed. Howard Mackey (Rockport, Me.: Picton Press, 2003), 19.

2. Order re Shires, Va. Gen. Ct. 1634, in *Minutes of the Council and General Court of Colonial Virginia*, 2nd ed., ed. R. B. McIlwaine (Richmond: Virginia State Library, 1979), 481.

3. Colony v. Cornwallis, Md. Prov. Ct. 1643/44, in *Archives of Maryland*, 72 vols. (Baltimore: Maryland Historical Society, 1883–1972), 4: 249.

4. Clocker v. Gwyther, Md. Prov. Ct. 1659/60, in *Md. Archives*, 41: 368.

5. Halfhead v. Nicculgutt, Md. Prov. Ct. 1664, in *Md. Archives*, 49: 237.

6. Information against Robins, Northampton County Va. Ct. Aug. 30, 1687 (microfilm in possession of Utah Genealogical Society).

7. *Quoted in* Edwin B. Bronner, *William Penn's "Holy Experiment": The Founding of Pennsylvania, 1681–1701* (Philadelphia, Pa.: Temple University Press, 1962), 10–11 (emphasis in original).

8. The Concessions and Agreements of West New Jersey, chs. 13, 16 (1676/77), in Aaron Leaming and Jacob Spicer, *The Grants, Concessions, and Original Constitutions of the Province of New Jersey* (Philadelphia, 1752; reprinted Somerville, N.J., 1881), 382, 393, 394.

9. Concessions and Agreements, ch. 39, p. 407.

10. Concessions and Agreements, chs. 17, 19, pp. 395–97.

11. *Quoted in* Preston W. Edsall, "Introduction," in *Journal of the Courts of Common Right and Chancery of East New Jersey, 1683–1702*, ed. Preston W. Edsall (Philadelphia, Pa.: American Legal History Society, 1937), 123.

12. Lords Proprietors v. Berry, E. Jersey Common Right Ct. 1684, in *Journal of the Courts of Common Right*, 187.
13. Discussed in Edsall, "Introduction," 103–5.
14. Discussed in Edsall, "Introduction," 96–101, 105.
15. Discussed in Edsall, "Introduction," 105–8.
16. Refusal of Fretwell, N.J. Sup. Ct. Burlington November 1715 (manuscript in possession of New Jersey State Archives).
17. Rex v. Brown, N.J. Sup. Ct. Burlington August 1725 (manuscript in possession of New Jersey State Archives).
18. The Fundamental Constitutions of Carolina, secs. 64, 72, 73, 86–101 (July 21, 1669), in *North Carolina Charters and Constitutions, 1578–1698*, ed. Mattie Erma Edwards Parker (Raleigh, N.C.: Carolina Charter Tercentenary Commission, 1963, 132.
19. *Quoted in* Anne King Gregorie, "Historical Introduction," in *Records of the Court of Chancery of South Carolina, 1671–1779*, ed. Anne King Gregorie (Washington, D.C.: American Historical Association, 1950), 3, 5; *quoted in* James Nelson Frierson, "Legal Introduction," in *Records of Chancery*, 20, 21, 25.
20. *Quoted in* James Nelson Frierson, "Legal Introduction," 20, 21, 25.
21. Nicholas Trott, Charge Delivered at S.C. General Sessions and Gaol Delivery Ct., Charleston, S.C., March 17, 1702/03, p. 8 (manuscript in possession of South Caroliniana Library, Columbia, S.C.).
22. Act of December 12, 1712, in *The Earliest Printed Laws of South Carolina, 1692–1734*, 1, ed. John D. Cushing (Wilmington, Del.: Michael Glazier, 1978), 236, 254.
23. Allen D. Chandler, ed., *The Colonial Records of the State of Georgia*, 7 (Atlanta: Franklin Printing and Publishing, 1906), 53.
24. An Act for the Better and More Effectual Preserving the Queen's Peace sec. 3, in *The Earliest Printed Laws of North Carolina, 1699–1751*, ed. John D. Cushing (Wilmington, Del.: Michael Glazier, 1977), 2: 166, 167.

Chapter 7

1. Powell v. Kroft, Chester Co. Pa. Com. Pleas Ct. Aug. 1730 (manuscript in possession of Chester County Archives).
2. Dougharty v. Lowdon, Lancaster Co. Pa. Com. Pleas Ct. Feb. 1730/31 (manuscript in possession of Lancaster Historical Society).
3. Imprisonment of Prosser, Goochland County Va. Ct. 1730, in *Goochland County Virginia Order Books, 1 & 2, 1728–1731*, ed. Ann K. Blomquist (Westminster, Md.: Heritage Books, 2007), 258. While in jail, he also refused to turn over the declaration that had been returned to him in the case he was litigating, apparently on the ground that prisoners had no duty to provide material to courts. Ultimately, Prosser made peace with the court and was permitted to continue practicing. *See* Petition of Prosser, Goochland County Va. Ct. 1730, in Blomquist, *Goochland County Order Books, 1728–1731*, 283.

Chapter 8

1. Francis Hutcheson, *A System of Moral Philosophy, in Three Books* (London, 1755) 2: 240–66, quoted in Caroline Robbins, *The Eighteenth Century Commonwealthman: Studies in the Transmission, Development and Circumstance of English Liberal Thought from the Restoration of Charles II until the War with the Thirteen Colonies* (Cambridge, Mass.: Harvard University Press, 1961), 190.
2. The discussion of *Winthrop v. Lechmere* and the cases in the following four paragraphs is based on the analysis of Joseph H. Smith, *Appeals to the Privy Council from the American Plantations* (New York: Columbia University Press, 1950), 537–77.
3. Burk v. M'Clain, 1 Harris & McHenry 236, 238 (Md. Prov. Ct. 1766).
4. "From our Yearly Meeting held at Philadelphia . . . to the several Quarterly and Monthly Meetings thereunto belonging," 1719, 12 (typescript in possession of Friends Library, Swarthmore College).

5. *Quoted in* Nancy Hathaway Steenburg, *Children and the Criminal Law in Connecticut, 1635–1855: Changing Perceptions of Childhood* (New York: Routledge, 2005), 143.
6. South Carolina Laws of 1740, *quoted in* Thomas D. Morris, *Southern Slavery and the Law, 1619–1860* (Chapel Hill: University of North Carolina Press, 1996), 342.
7. Opinion of Daniel Dulany, Dec. 16, 1767, in 1 Harris & McHenry 559, 560 (emphasis omitted).
8. Laws of 1660/61, Act XXII, in *The Statutes at Large; Being a Collection of all the Laws of Virginia From the First Session of the Legislature in the Year 1619*, ed. William W. Hening (New York: R. & W. & G. Bartow, 1823), 2: 26.
9. Opinion of Daniel Dulany, Dec. 16, 1767, in 1 Harris & McHenry 559, 561, 563 (1767).
10. King v. Mingo and Hannah, Hampshire County Mass. Ct. March 29 and April 12, 1692 (microfilm in possession of Utah Genealogical Society).
11. Petition of Jack Negro, Suffolk Co. Mass. Gen. Sess. Ct. Jan. 30, 1709/10 (microfilm in possession of Utah Genealogical Society).
12. Northampton County Va. Ct. Mar. 20, 1700/01 (typescript distributed by Antient Press).
13. Tucker v. Sweney, Randolph's Reports 39 (Va. Gen. Ct. 1730).
14. Goff v. Green, Middlesex County Mass. Ct. April 15, 1690 (microfilm in possession of Utah Genealogical Society).
15. Huntington v. Whetmore, New London Co. Conn. Super. Ct. March 26, 1751 (manuscript in possession of Connecticut State Library).
16. See Colony v. Barney, Hartford Co. Conn. Super. Ct. Sept. 6, 1743 and Nov. 15, 1743 (manuscript in possession of Connecticut State Library). The quoted language from Connecticut records in the *Barney* case is in Lawrence B. Goodheart, *The Solemn Sentence of Death: Capital Punishment in Connecticut* (Amherst: University of Massachusetts Press, 2011), 63.
17. *See* Petition of Meredith, Bucks Co. Pa. Quarter Sess. Ct. June 1762 (manuscript in possession of Bucks County Historical Society).

Chapter 9

1. *Quoted in* Wout Troost, *William III, the Stadholder-King: A Political Biography*, trans. J. C. Grayson (Aldershot: Ashgate, 2005), 293.
2. Linda Colley, *Britons: Forging the Nation, 1737–1807* (New Haven, Conn.: Yale University Press, 1992), 368.
3. Robert Molesworth, "The Translator's Preface," in Francis Hotman, *Franco-Gallia; or, An Account of the Ancient Free State of France and Most Other Parts of Europe, before the Loss of Their Liberties*. ed. Edward Valentine, trans. Robert Molesworth (London, 1721), xxxv (emphasis in original).
4. *Quoted in* Colley, *Britons*, 34.
5. *Quoted in* John Phillip Reid, *Constitutional History of the American Revolution: The Authority of Law*, 4 (Madison: University of Wisconsin Press, 1993), 56.
6. Dering v. Elliott (S.C. Ch. 1772), in *Records of the Court of Chancery of South Carolina*, ed. Anne King Gregorie (Washington, D.C.: American Historical Association, 1950), 602, 603 (argument of counsel).
7. *Quoted in* Robert M. Weir, *Colonial South Carolina: A History* (Milwood, N.Y.: KTO Press, 1983), 217.
8. King v. Lovick, N.C. Gen. Ct. 1728, in *Colonial and State Records of North Carolina*, ed. William L. Saunders (Raleigh, N.C.: P. M. Hale, 1886), 2: 832–33.
9. John Lovick to the Board, December 12, 1728, in *Colonial Records*, 3: 1.
10. King v. Smith, N.C. Gen. Ct. 1729, in *Colonial Records*, 3: 54–56.
11. Rex v. Snowden, N.C. Gen. Ct. October 1731 (microfilm reel 138.4 in possession of North Carolina State Archives).
12. Governor Burrington to the Duke of Newcastle, July 2, 1731, in *Colonial Records*, 3:192.
13. Governor Burrington to the Lords of Trade, September 4, 1731, in *Colonial Records*, 3: 202.
14. Hurst v. Dippo, 1 U.S. (1 Dallas) 20, 21 (Pa. Sup. Ct. 1774).
15. Anonymous, 1 U.S. (1 Dallas) 20 (Pa. Sup. Ct. 1773).

16. "The Englishman's Right: A Dialogue between a Barrister at Law and a Juryman," *Pennsylvania Chronicle*, Feb. 3, 1772, pp. 1, 5 (emphasis in original).

17. Massachusetts House of Representatives to Agent Bollan, December 31, 1754, and Address of New Jersey Assembly to Governor, October 18, 1754, *quoted in* Harry M. Ward, *"Unite or Die": Intercolony Relations, 1690–1763* (Port Washington, N.Y.: Kennikat Press, 1971), 16–17.

18. The case is discussed in Joseph H. Smith, *Appeals to the Privy Council from the American Plantations* (New York: Columbia University Press, 1950), 537–77.

Chapter 10

1. Rex v. Plummer, York Co. Mass. Super. Ct. June 15, 1737 (microfilm in possession of Utah Genealogical Society).

2. Rex v. Smith, Middlesex Co. Mass. Gen. Sess. Ct. March 13, 1743/44 (microfilm in possession of Utah Genealogical Society).

3. Rex v. Prescott, Middlesex Co. Mass. Gen. Sess. Ct. May 15, 1744 (microfilm in possession of Utah Genealogical Society).

4. Rex v. Fairservice, Suffolk Co. Mass. Gen. Sess. Ct. May 15, 1749 (microfilm in possession of Utah Genealogical Society).

5. Rex v. Edson, Plymouth Co. Mass. Gen. Sess. and Com. Pleas Ct. 1698, in *Plymouth Court Records, 1686–1859*, 15 vols., ed. David Thomas Konig (Wilmington, Del.: Michael Glazier, 1978–1981), 1: 226.

6. King v. Panthorn, Hampshire County Mass. Ct. March 31, 1691 (microfilm in possession of Utah Genealogical Society).

7. Rex v. Bartlett, Hampshire Co. Mass. Gen. Sess. and Com. Pleas Ct. March 2, 1735/36 (microfilm in possession of Utah Genealogical Society).

8. Pynchon v. First Parish in Springfield, Hampshire Co. Mass. Gen. Sess. and Com. Pleas Ct. May 18, 1736 (microfilm in possession of Utah Genealogical Society).

9. Pynchon v. First Parish in Springfield, Hampshire Co. Mass. Gen. Sess. and Com. Pleas Ct. May 18, 1736 (microfilm in possession of Utah Genealogical Society); Pynchon v. First Parish in Springfield, Hampshire Co. Mass. Gen. Sess. and Com. Pleas Ct. Aug. 31, 1736 (microfilm in possession of Utah Genealogical Society).

10. Rex v. Moor, Hampshire Co. Mass. Gen. Sess. and Com. Pleas Ct. Aug. 25, 1741 (microfilm in possession of Utah Genealogical Society).

11. N.H. Super Ct. March 20, 1744/45 (microfilm in possession of Utah Genealogical Society).

12. The Concessions and Agreements of . . . West New Jersey, chs. 13, 16 (1676/77), in Aaron Leaming and Jacob Spicer, *The Grants, Concessions, and Original Constitutions of the Province of New Jersey* (Philadelphia, 1752, reprinted Somerville, N.J., 1881), 393, 394.

13. The oaths are quoted in Joseph H. Smith and Philip A. Crowl, "Introduction," in *Court Records of Prince Georges County, Maryland, 1696–1699*, ed. Joseph H. Smith and Philip A. Crowl (Washington, D.C.: American Historical Association, 1964), xxiv–xxv.

14. Godwin v. Lunan, Jefferson's Reports 96 (Va. Gen. Ct. 1771).

15. Oath of Spicer, King George County Va. Ct. May 19, 1721 (typescript distributed by Antient Press).

16. Oath of Judges, Albany N.Y. Extraordinary Ct. 1669, in *Minutes of the Court of Albany, Rensselaerswyck and Schenectady, 1668–1685*, 3 vols., ed. A. L. F. VanLaer (Albany: University of the State of New York, 1926–1932), 1: 113, 114.

17. Petition of Those of Augsburg Confession, Albany N.Y. Extraordinary Ct. 1670, in *Minutes of Albany*, 1: 144.

Chapter 11

1. Regina v. Faulkner, Suffolk Co. Mass. Gen. Sess. Ct. July 1, 1707 (microfilm in possession of Utah Genealogical Society).

2. Cock v. Rambo, Philadelphia Pa. County Ct. 1685, in *Pennypacker's Colonial Cases*, 79, 82–83.

3. "From our Yearly Meeting held at Philadelphia . . . to the several Quarterly and Monthly Meetings thereunto belonging," 1719, pp. 9, 25 (typescript in Friends Library, Swarthmore College).

4. Yarnall v. Musgrove, Chester County Pa. Ct. June 1693, in *Records of the Courts of Chester County, Pennsylvania, 1681–1697* (Philadelphia, Pa.: Patterson and White, 1910), 289–91 (jury verdict in his favor for costs and 2d. damages).

5. King and Queen v. Taylor and Williamson, Chester Co. Pa. Quarter Sess. Ct. Mar. 1694/95, in *Records of the Courts of Chester*, 339.

6. Washington Parish v. Buss, Westmoreland County Va. Ct. June 24, 1713 (typescript distributed by Antient Press).

7. King v. Dye, Richmond County Va. Ct. July 4, 1728 (typescript distributed by Antient Press).

8. Matter of Bonne, Essex Co. Mass. Com. Pleas Ct. April 20, 1720 (microfilm in possession of Utah Genealogical Society) (prosecution of constable who "neglected" to be in court as was "customary").

9. *See* Colony v. Barney, Hartford Co. Conn. Super. Ct. Sept. 6, 1743 (manuscript in possession of Connecticut State Library); Lawrence B. Goodheart, *The Solemn Sentence of Death: Capital Punishment in Connecticut* (Amherst: University of Massachusetts Press, 2011), 63. The quoted language from Connecticut records is in Goodheart, *the Solemn Sentence of Death*, 63.

10. Julius Goebel Jr., and Raymond T. Naughton, *Law Enforcement in Colonial New York: A Study in Criminal Procedure (1664–1776)* (New York: Commonwealth Fund, 1944), xxv.

11. J. T. Kempe Letters, *quoted in* Goebel and Naughton, *Law Enforcement*, 607.

12. Search Warrant, Essex Co. Mass. Gen. Sess. Ct. June 27, 1710 (microfilm in possession of Utah Genealogical Society).

13. Return of Whitman, R.I. Ct. Trials 1662/63, in *Rhode Island Court Records: Records of the Court of Trials of the Colony of Providence Plantations, 1647–1670*, 2 vols. (Providence: Rhode Island Historical Society, 1920–1922), 2: 15, 16.

14. Colony v. Lewis, Conn. Ct. Assistants 1703, in *Colony of Connecticut: Minutes of Court of Assistants, 1669-1711*, ed. Helen Schatvet Ullmann (Boston, Mass.: New England Historic Genealogical Society, 2009), 339.

15. Queen v. Evans, Middlesex County Va. Ct. Feb. 16, 1712/13 (typescript distributed by Antient Press).

16. Petition of Colman, N.H. Super. Ct. Feb. 1767 (microfilm in possession of Utah Genealogical Society).

Chapter 12

1. Grievances of Grand Jury, S.C. Gen. Sess. Ct. May 1773 (microfilm in possession of South Carolina State Archives).

2. Petition of Parr, Philadelphia Co. Pa. Quarter Sess. Ct. Sept. 1767 (manuscript in possession of Philadelphia City Archives).

3. Lownes v. Price, Pa. Sup. Ct. Apr. 1742 (microfilm in Pennsylvania State Archives).

4. 1 U.S. (1 Dallas) 9 (Pa. Sup. Ct. 1764).

5. King v. Lukens, 1 U.S. (1 Dallas) 5 (Pa. Sup. Ct. 1762).

6. Petition for Sale of Hasell's Real Estate, Pa. Sup. Ct. Apr. 1769 (microfilm in Pennsylvania State Archives).

7. Confirmation of King's Road, 1 U.S. (1 Dallas) 11 (Pa. Sup. Ct. 1764).

8. Davey v. Turner, 1 U.S. (1 Dallas) 11, 13–14 (Pa. Sup. Ct. 1764).

9. Lessee of Lloyd v. Taylor, 1 U.S. (1 Dallas) 17 (Pa. Sup. Ct. 1768).

10. Lessee of Fothergill v. Stover, 1 U.S. (1 Dallas) 6, 7 (Pa. Sup. Ct. 1763).

11. Riche v. Broadfield, 1 U.S. (1 Dallas) 16–17 (Pa. Sup. Ct. 1768).

12. King v. Rapp, 1 U.S. (1 Dallas) 9 (Pa. Sup. Ct. 1764).

13. Address of Andrew Hamilton to the Pennsylvania Assembly, 1738, in *Pennypacker's Colonial Cases*, 23.

14. Dr. Mosheim, in *Pennypacker's Colonial Cases*, 24.

15. The discussion of Winthrop v. Lechmere and the cases in the following paragraph is based on the analysis of Joseph H. Smith, *Appeals to the Privy Council from the American Plantations* (New York: Columbia University Press, 1950), 537–77.

16. Quoted in Mary Sarah Bilder, *The Transatlantic Constitution: Colonial Legal Culture and the Empire* (Cambridge, Mass.: Harvard University Press, 2004), 182–84.

17. Message of General Assembly to Council, April 9, 1753, in *The Colonial Records of North Carolina*, 5, ed. William L. Saunders (Raleigh: Josephus Daniels, 1887), 70.

18. Statement of Moravian Bishop August Gottlieb Spangenberg, 1752, *quoted in* William S. Powell, *North Carolina through Four Centuries* (Chapel Hill: University of North Carolina Press, 1989), 145.

Chapter 13

1. Quoted in Livingston Rutherfurd, *John Peter Zenger: His Press, His Trial* (New York: Chelsea House, 1981), 131.

2. Charge of DeLancey, C.J., *quoted in* Julius Goebel Jr. and T. Raymond Naughton, *Law Enforcement in Colonial New York: A Study in Criminal Procedure (1664–1776)* (New York: Commonwealth Fund, 1944), 666 (emphasis added).

3. James Alexander, *A Brief Narrative of the Case and Trial of John Peter Zenger*, ed. Stanley N. Katz (Cambridge, Mass.: Harvard University Press, 1963), 91–92.

4. Doe v. Anderson, Fauquier County Va. Ct. Sept. 26, 1769 (typescript distributed by Antient Press).

5. Patten v. Shann, Augusta County Va. Ct. Nov. 17, 1752 (microfilm in possession of Utah Genealogical Society).

6. Orange County Va. Ct. Aug. 23, 1751 (typescript distributed by Antient Press).

7. Quoted in Richard R. Beeman, *Patrick Henry: A Biography* (New York: McGraw-Hill, 1974), 19.

8. Thomas Jefferson, *Notes on the State of Virginia*, ed. J. Randolph (Richmond: J. W. Randolph, 1853), 140. *See* Beeman, *Patrick Henry*, 20.

9. Fauquier County Va. Ct. Oct. 25, 1768 and June 26, 1770 (typescript distributed by Antient Press).

10. 2 Virginia Colonial Decisions 331(Va. Gen. Ct. 1739).

11. S.C. Com. Pleas Ct. Jan. 1760 (typescript in possession of South Carolina State Archives). The case has been printed in Julius Goebel Jr., ed., *Cases and Materials on the Development of Legal Institutions* (Brattleboro, Vt.: Vermont Printing Co., 1946), 285.

12. The quotations are from Charles Woodmason, *The Carolina Backcountry on the Eve of the Revolution: The Journal and Other Writings of Charles Woodmason* ed. Richard Hooker (Chapel Hill: University of North Carolina Press, 1969), 289 n.93, 292 nn.96–97, and 293 n.98.

13. Nicholas Butler, *Votaries of Apollo: The St. Cecilia Society and the Patronage of Concert Music in Charleston, South Carolina, 1766–1820* (Columbia: University of South Carolina Press, 2007), 274, 278.

14. John Adams to William Tudor, March 29, 1817, quoted in L. *Legal Papers of John Adams*, ed. Kinvin Wroth and Hiller B. Zobel (Cambridge, Mass.: Harvard University Press, 1965), 2:107.

15. Quincy 51 (Mass. Super. Ct. 1761).

16. John Adams's Report of the First Argument in February 1761 in Paxton's Case, Quincy 469, 474 (Mass. Super. Ct. 1761). The reference in the text to 8 Rep. 118 is to Sir Edward Coke's opinion in Bonham's Case, 77 Eng. Rep. 646 (Com. Pleas 1610).

17. James Otis, "The Rights of the British Colonies Asserted and Proved," in *Pamphlets of the American Revolution, 1750–1776*, ed. Bernard Bailyn and Jane N. Garrett (Cambridge, Mass.: Harvard University Press, 1965), 476–77 (emphasis in original).

18. 18 Quincy 553 (Mass. Super. Ct. 1761).

Chapter 14

1. Quoted in Woody Holton, *Forced Founders: Indians, Debtors, Slaves, and the Making of the American Revolution in Virginia* (Chapel Hill: University of North Carolina Press, 1999), 9, 32.

2. *Quoted in* Edmund S. Morgan and Helen M. Morgan, *The Stamp Act Crisis: Prologue to Revolution*, rev. ed. (New York: Collier Books, 1963), 182–83.
3. *Quoted in* Morgan and Morgan, *Stamp Act Crisis*, 227.
4. Order Adjourning Court, S.C. Com. Pleas Ct. Nov. 1765 (typescript in possession of South Carolina State Archives).
5. S.C. Com. Pleas Ct. Feb. 1766 (typescript in possession of South Carolina State Archives).
6. Jordan v. Law, S.C. Com. Pleas Ct. April 1766 (typescript in South Carolina State Archives).
7. Opinion of the Chief Justice in Jordan v. Law, S.C. Com. Pleas Ct. April 1766 (typescript in South Carolina State Archives).
8. Opinion of the Justices in Jordan v. Law, S.C. Com. Pleas Ct. May 1766 (typescript in South Carolina State Archives).
9. Opinion of the Justices in Jordan v. Law, S.C. Com. Pleas Ct. May 1766 (typescript in South Carolina State Archives). The citation to Bonham's Case is 77 Eng. Rep. 646 (K.B. 1610).
10. Jordan v. Law, S.C. Com. Pleas Ct. April 1766 (typescript in South Carolina State Archives).
11. Judgment upon the Clerk's Conduct, S.C. Com. Pleas Ct. May 1766 (typescript in possession of South Carolina State Archives).
12. Judgment upon the Clerk's Conduct, S.C. Com. Pleas Ct. May 1766 (typescript in possession of South Carolina State Archives).
13. Robert M. Weir, *Colonial South Carolina: A History* (Milwood, N.Y.: KTO Press, 1983), 299.
14. Petition of Clerk, S.C. Com. Pleas Ct. May 1766, (typescript in possession of South Carolina State Archives).
15. *Quoted in* Morgan and Morgan, *Stamp Act Crisis*, 222.
16. Motion of Clerk and Other Officers, Northampton County Va. Ct. Feb. 11, 1766 (microfilm in possession of Utah Genealogical Society).
17. Declaratory Act, 6 Geo. III, ch. 12 (1766), in *The Statutes at Large*, ed. Danby Pickering (Cambridge: John Archdeacon, 1767), 27: 19, 20 (emphasis in original).

Chapter 15

1. Julius Goebel Jr. and T. Raymond Naughton, *Law Enforcement in Colonial New York: A Study in Criminal Procedure (1664–1776)* (New York: Commonwealth Fund, 1944), 86.
2. Jacob Van Schaack to Cadwallader Colden, Dec. 31, 1760, *quoted in* Douglas Greenberg, *Crime and Law Enforcement in the Colony of New York, 1691–1776* (Ithaca, N.Y.: Cornell University Press, 1974), 159.
3. Cadwallader Colden to General Gage, Sept. 7, 1774, *quoted in* Greenberg, *Crime and Law Enforcement*, 182.
4. *Quoted in* Sung Bok Kim, *Landlord and Tenant in Colonial New York: Manorial Society, 1664–1775* (Chapel Hill: University of North Carolina Press, 1978), 388.
5. Andrew Jackson O'Shaughnessy, *The Men Who Lost America: British Leadership, the American Revolution, and the Fate of the Empire* (New Haven: Yale University Press, 2013), 355.
6. Report of Tagert, Tryon County N.C. Ct. 1770, in *Tryon County North Carolina: Minutes of the Court of Common Pleas and Quarter Sessions, 1769–1779*, ed. Brent H. Holcomb (Columbia, S.C.: SCMAR, 1994), 49.
7. Report of Allison, Rowan County N.C. Ct. 1770, in *Abstracts of the Minutes of the Court of Pleas and Quarter Sessions, Rowan County, North Carolina, 1753–1789*, 2 vols., ed. Jo White Linn (Salisbury, N.C.: privately printed, 1977–1982), 2: 114.
8. Report of Lock, Rowan County N.C. Ct. 1769, in Linn, *Rowan Minutes*, 2: 101.
9. Report of Allison, Rowan County N.C. Ct. 1769, in Linn, *Rowan Minutes*, 2: 99.
10. William Simpson, *The Practical Justice of the Peace and Parish-Officer, of his Majesty's Province of South Carolina* (Charleston: Robert Wells, 1761), 225.
11. Application of Attorney General, S.C. Com. Pleas Ct. Oct. 1769 (typescript in possession of South Carolina State Archives).
12. Motion of Attorney General, Pa. Sup. Ct. Apr. 1769 (microfilm in possession of Pennsylvania State Archives).

13. The case is most thoroughly analyzed in Joseph Henry Smith, *Appeals to the Privy Council from the American Plantations* (New York: Columbia University Press, 1950), 390–416. The following discussion is based entirely upon Smith's analysis.

14. Hurst v. Dippo, 1 U.S. (1 Dallas) 20, 21 (Pa. Sup. Ct. 1774).

15. *Quoted in* Ray Raphael, *The First American Revolution: Before Lexington and Concord* (New York: New Press, 2002), 63, 66, 135.

16. *Quoted in* Mary Sarah Bilder, *The Transatlantic Constitution: Colonial Legal Culture and the Empire* (Cambridge, Mass.: Harvard University Press, 2004), 183–84.

17. *Quoted in* Bilder, *Transatlantic Constitution,* 185.

18. Appointment of Dally, Northampton County Va. Ct. Mar. 12, 1776 (microfilm in possession of Utah Genealogical Society).

19. Opening of Kent Co. Del. Com. Pleas Ct. Aug. 1776 (microfilm in possession of Delaware State Archives).

20. Grievances of the Grand Jury, S.C. Gen. Sess. Ct. Charleston Dist. April 1776 (manuscript in possession of South Carolina State Archives).

21. Watson v. Williams, S.C. Com. Pleas Ct. Jan. 1760 (typescript in possession of South Carolina State Archives).

22. Grievances of the Grand Jury, S.C. Gen. Sess. Ct. Charleston Dist. April 1776 (manuscript in possession of South Carolina State Archives).

Chapter 16

1. Eakin v. Raub, 12 Sergeant & Rawle 330, 344, 346 (Pa. 1825) (dissenting opinion).

BIBLIOGRAPHY

This book is an abbreviated, largely unfootnoted version of William E. Nelson, *The Common Law in Colonial America*, 4 vols. (New York: Oxford University Press, 2008–2017). These volumes, in turn, were based on extensive research in colonial American court records between the dates of the earliest colonial settlements and 1776. Nearly all colonial court records have been deposited in official state or local archives. In most states, the records of both the highest colonial courts and the local courts are in the state archives, but in New York and Pennsylvania, and occasionally elsewhere, records are in the possession of local archives, local historical societies or libraries, or county court clerks. In addition, the Genealogical Society of Utah has microfilmed a large quantity of colonial courts' records; several states have microfilmed their records; and Maryland has either printed its records or made them available online. Several genealogical publishers—most notably the Antient Press, which has been acquired by Colonial Roots, 34491 Sunset Drive, Millsboro, Delaware 19966, with a website, www.colonialroots.com—have published printed or typescript editions of records, as have occasional academic publishers.

In volumes 1 through 4, I have cited the version of the records I actually used. I always used printed or typed records when they were available. My next choice was online records or microfilmed records. I traveled to archives only to examine original documents that were not available in a more convenient form. But I have cited cases in a fashion that should enable readers to find them in any format in which they are available. For example, I cited an important Virginia case as follows: Hughlett v. Schreever, Northampton County Ct. Mar. 20, 1700/01 (typescript distributed by Antient Press). The case can be found by searching the Antient Press publication for the stated county and date, or by obtaining the Utah Genealogical Society microfilm for that county and date, or in the original manuscript form in the Library of Virginia, which is the state archive in Richmond.

Most of the printed sources I used and all of the microfilm sources are on deposit at the Law Library of New York University School of Law and can be obtained through customary inter-library loan channels.

In the remainder of this bibliography, I identify for each chapter of this book the volume and chapters of the four-volume version of *The Common Law in Colonial America* from which the particular chapter was derived. I also note other sources, primarily historical monographs, of which I made substantial use in drafting the original chapters. Any scholar seeking supporting authority for any particular statement in the abbreviated volume will need to refer to the relevant chapters in the underlying four volumes, which contain extensive endnotes.

Chapter 1 was derived from volume 1, chapters 1, 2, and 6. There are no good monographs on the legal history of early seventeenth-century Virginia. I relied heavily on an article, David Thomas Konig, "'Dale's Laws' and the Non-Common Law Origins of Criminal Justice in Virginia," *American Journal of Legal History*, 26 (1982), 354. I found useful information in Kathleen M. Brown, *Good Wives, Nasty Wenches, and Anxious Patriarchs: Gender, Race, and Power in Colonial Virginia* (Chapel

Hill: University of North Carolina Press, 1998); James Horn, *A Land as God Made It: Jamestown and the Birth of America* (New York: Basic Books, 2005); James Horn, *Adapting to a New World: English Society in the Seventeenth-Century Chesapeake* (Chapel Hill: University of North Carolina Press, 1994); Richard B. Morris, *Government and Labor in Early America* (New York: Columbia University Press, 1946); Mary Beth Norton, *Founding Mothers and Fathers: Gendered Power and the Forming of American Society* (New York: Alfred A. Knopf, 1996); John R. Pagan, *Anne Orthwood's Bastard: Sex and Law in Early Virginia* (New York: Oxford University Press, 2003). Two helpful books on Maryland are Marilyn L. Geiger, *The Administration of Justice in Colonial Maryland, 1632–1689* (New York: Garland, 1987), and Bradley T. Johnson, *The Foundation of Maryland and the Origin of the Act Concerning Religion of April 21, 1649* (Baltimore: Maryland Historical Society, 1883).

Chapter 2 was derived from volume 1, chapters 3, 4, and 5. The two most important books on seventeenth-century Massachusetts law are George Lee Haskins, *Law and Authority in Early Massachusetts: A Study in Tradition and Design* (New York: Macmillan, 1960), and David Thomas Konig, *Law and Society in Puritan Massachusetts: Essex County, 1629–1692* (Chapel Hill: University of North Carolina Press, 1979). There are many other books and articles, among the most valuable of which are Daniel R. Coquillette, ed., *Law in Colonial Massachusetts, 1630–1800* (Boston: Colonial Society of Massachusetts, 1984), which contains a wealth of bibliographical information; Cornelia H. Dayton, *Women before the Bar: Gender, Law, and Society in Connecticut, 1639–1789* (Chapel Hill: University of North Carolina Press, 1995); David H. Flaherty, *Privacy in Colonial New England* (Charlottesville: University Press of Virginia, 1972); Edgar J. McManus, *Law and Liberty in Early New England: Criminal Justice and Due Process, 1620–1692* (Amherst: University of Massachusetts Press, 1993); Edwin Powers, *Crime and Punishment in Early Massachusetts, 1620–1692: A Documentary History* (Boston: Beacon Press, 1966); and Roger Thompson, *Sex in Middlesex: Popular Mores in a Massachusetts County, 1649–1699* (Amherst: University of Massachusetts Press, 1986). Joseph H. Smith, ed., *Colonial Justice in Western Massachusetts (1639–1702): The Pynchon Court Papers* (Cambridge, Mass.: Harvard University Press, 1961), contains a valuable introductory essay. A book that understands early Massachusetts law very differently from my interpretation is David Grayson Allen, *In English Ways: The Movement of Societies and the Transferal of English Local Law and Custom to Massachusetts Bay in the Seventeenth Century* (Chapel Hill: University of North Carolina Press, 1981). An early classic article that also takes an approach that differs from mine is Julius Goebel Jr., "King's Law and Local Custom in Seventeenth Century New England," *Columbia Law Review*, 31 (1931), 416. More general books include Virginia DeJohn Anderson, *New England's Generation: The Great Migration and the Formation of Society and Culture in the Seventeenth Century* (New York: Cambridge University Press, 1991); Francis J. Bremer, *The Puritan Experiment: New England Society from Bradford to Edwards*, rev. ed. (Hanover, N.H.: University Press of New England, 1995); Stephen Innes, *Creating the Commonwealth: The Economic Culture of Puritan New England* (New York: W.W. Norton, 1995). On Puritanism, in particular, I relied on James F. Cooper Jr., *Tenacious of Their Liberties: The Congregationalists in Colonial Massachusetts* (New York: Oxford University Press, 1999), especially helpful for its explanation of church government as parallel to my understanding of secular law and government; Michael P. Winship, *Creating Heretics: Militant Protestantism and Free Grace in Massachusetts, 1636–1641* (Princeton, N.J.: Princeton University Press, 2002); and, of course, on the classic work of Perry Miller, *The New England Mind: The Seventeenth Century* (New York: Macmillan, 1939), and *Errand into the Wilderness* (Cambridge, Mass.: Harvard University Press, 1956).

Readers should also refer to the sources cited in the bibliography for chapter 1.

Chapter 3 is derived from volume 2, chapters 1 and 7. There are two outstanding monographs on the history of New Netherland that contain substantial discussion of the law—Jaap Jacobs, *New Netherland: A Dutch Colony in Seventeenth-Century America* (Leiden: Brill, 2005), and Russell Shorto, *The Island at the Center of the World: The Epic Story of Dutch Manhattan and the Forgotten Colony that Shaped America* (New York: Random House, 2004).

Chapter 4 is derived from volume 2, chapters 2 and 3, and from volume 3, chapters 6 and 9. Important work on the legal history of colonial New York in general includes Daniel J. Hulsebosch, *Constituting Empire: New York and the Transformation of Constitutionalism in the Atlantic World, 1664–1830* (Chapel Hill: University of North Carolina Press, 2005); Eben Moglen, "Settling the Law: Legal Development in New York, 1664–1776" (Ph.D. diss., Yale University,

1993); and the introductory essay in Richard B. Morris, ed., *Select Cases of the Mayor's Court of New York City, 1674–1784* (Washington, D.C.: American Historical Association, 1935). Work on specific topics includes Linda Briggs Biemer, *Women and Property in Colonial New York: The Transition from Dutch to English Law, 1643–1726* (Ann Arbor, Mich.: UMI Research Press, 1983); Julius Goebel Jr. and T. Raymond Naughton, *Law Enforcement in Colonial New York: A Study in Criminal Procedure (1664–1776)* (New York: Commonwealth Fund, 1944); David E. Narrett, *Inheritance and Family Life in Colonial New York City* (Ithaca, N.Y.: Cornell University Press, 1992).

For Massachusetts, in addition to the material noted for chapter 2, above, see Francis J. Bremer, *Puritan Crisis: New England and the English Civil Wars, 1630–1670* (New York: Garland, 1989); Mark DeWolfe Howe and Louis F. Eaton, "The Supreme Judicial Power in the Colony of Massachusetts Bay," *New England Quarterly*, 20 (1947), 291. For New Hampshire, see Elwin L. Page, *Judicial Beginnings in New Hampshire, 1640–1700* (Concord: New Hampshire Historical Society, 1959).

Chapter 5 is derived from volume 2, chapter 3, and from volume 3, chapters 7 and 8. For additional reading, see the materials cited in the bibliography for chapter 4 above.

Chapter 6 is derived from volume 2, chapters 4, 5, 6, and 7 and from volume 3, chapters 1 and 3. Work on the legal history of the Quaker colonies includes Jack D. Marietta and G. S. Rowe, *Troubled Experiment: Crime and Justice in Pennsylvania, 1682–1800* (Philadelphia: University of Pennsylvania Press, 2006), and William M. Offutt Jr., *Of "Good Laws" and "Good Men": Law and Society in the Delaware Valley, 1680–1710* (Urbana: University of Illinois Press, 1995). On East Jersey, see the introduction in Preston W. Edsall, ed., *Journal of the Courts of Common Right and Chancery of East New Jersey, 1683–1702* (Philadelphia: American Legal History Society, 1937). On the general history of early Pennsylvania, see Edwin B. Bronner, *William Penn's "Holy Experiment": The Founding of Pennsylvania, 1681–1701* (Philadelphia: Temple University Press, 1962). The best work on reception of the common law in Virginia is Warren Billings, "The Transfer of English Law to Virginia, 1606–1650," in K. P. Andrews, N. P. Canny, and P. E. H. Hair, eds., *The Westward Enterprise: English Activities in Ireland, the Atlantic, and America, 1480–1650* (Detroit, Mich.: Wayne State University Press, 1979), and Warren M. Billings, "Pleading, Procedure, and Practice: The Meaning of Due Process of Law in Seventeenth Century Virginia," *Journal of Southern History*, 47 (1981), 569. No extensive work has been published on the legal history of Delaware, Georgia, Maryland, North Carolina, or South Carolina.

Chapter 7 is derived mainly from volume 4, chapter 1, although portions of the chapter come from brief discussions of the legal profession scattered throughout the first three volumes. The classic work on the history of the legal profession is Charles Warren, *A History of the American Bar* (Boston: Little, Brown, 1911). I have also relied on Gerard W. Gawalt, *The Promise of Power: The Emergence of the Legal Profession in Massachusetts, 1760–1840* (Westport, Conn.: Greenwood Press, 1979), and E. Alfred Jones, *American Members of the Inns of Court* (London: St. Catherine Press, 1924).

Chapter 8 is derived from volume 1, chapters 1, 2, 5, and 6; from volume 2, chapters 4 and 6; from volume 3, chapters 3, 5, 8, and 9; and from volume 4, chapter 3. No monographs exist surveying the law of property or the law of contract and debtor-creditor in colonial America. But see Bruce H. Mann, *Republic of Debtors: Bankruptcy in the Age of American Independence* (Cambridge, Mass.: Harvard University Press, 2002); Marylynn Salmon, *Women and the Law of Property in Early America* (Chapel Hill: University of North Carolina Press, 1986). On labor, see the classic work of Richard B. Morris, *Government and Labor in Early America* (New York: Columbia University Press, 1946). There is a vast literature on slavery. The leading books include David Brion Davis, *Inhuman Bondage: The Rise and Fall of Slavery in the New World* (New York: Oxford University Press, 2006); Eugene D. Genovese, *Roll, Jordan, Roll: The World the Slaves Made* (New York: Pantheon Books, 1974); Winthrop D. Jordan, *White over Black: American Attitudes toward the Negro, 1550–1812* (Chapel Hill: University of North Carolina Press, 1968); Allan Kulikoff, *Tobacco and Slaves: The Development of Southern Cultures in the Chesapeake, 1680–1800* (Chapel Hill: University of North Carolina Press, 1986); Edmund S. Morgan, *American Slavery, American Freedom: The Ordeal of Colonial Virginia* (New York: W.W. Norton, 1975); Kenneth Morgan, *Slavery and Servitude in Colonial North America: A Short History* (New York: New York University Press, 2001); Thomas D. Morris, *Southern Slavery and the Law, 1619–1860* (Chapel Hill: University of North Carolina Press, 1996); Lorena S. Walsh, *Motives of Honor, Pleasure, and Profit: Plantation Management in the*

Colonial Chesapeake, 1607–1763 (Chapel Hill: University of North Carolina Press, 2010). I have also relied on two important articles: Oscar Handlin and Mary F. Handlin, "Origins of the Southern Labor System," *William and Mary Quarterly*, 3d ser., 7 (1950), 199; and Russell R. Menard, "The Transformation of the Chesapeake Labor System," *Southern Studies*, 16 (1977), 355–390.

Chapter 9 is derived from volume 2, chapter 5, from the introduction to volume 3, and from volume 4, chapter 2. For most colonies, there is no significant monographic work regarding the matters discussed in the chapter. But there is important work for New England and Virginia. For New England, see Mary Sarah Bilder, *The Transatlantic Constitution: Colonial Legal Culture and the Empire* (Cambridge, Mass.: Harvard University Press, 2004); Cornelia H. Dayton, *Women before the Bar: Gender, Law, and Society in Connecticut, 1639–1789* (Chapel Hill: University of North Carolina Press, 1995); Bruce H. Mann, *Neighbors and Strangers: Law and Community in Early Connecticut* (Chapel Hill: University of North Carolina Press, 1987); William E. Nelson, *Americanization of the Common Law: The Impact of Legal Change on Massachusetts Society, 1760–1830* (Cambridge, Mass.: Harvard University Press, 1975); Elwin L. Page, *Judicial Beginnings in New Hampshire, 1640–1700* (Concord: New Hampshire Historical Society, 1959). For Virginia, see Rhys Isaac, *The Transformation of Virginia, 1740–1790* (Chapel Hill: University of North Carolina Press, 1982). On the policies of William III, see Steve Pincus, *1688: The First Modern Revolution* (New Haven, Conn.: Yale University Press, 2009); Wout Troost, *William III, the Stadholder-King: A Political Biography*, trans. J. C. Grayson (Aldershot, UK: Ashgate, 2005). On eighteenth-century British imperial policy, see Linda Colley, *Britons: Forging the Nation 1707–1837* (New Haven, Conn.: Yale University Press, 1992); Eliga H. Gould, *The Persistence of Empire: British Political Culture in the Age of the American Revolution* (Chapel Hill: University of North Carolina Press, 2000).

Chapter 10 is derived from volume 4, chapter 3, and from other discussions of the law of religion scattered throughout the first three volumes. For other sources, readers should see Sanford H. Cobb, *The Rise of Religious Liberty in America: A History* (New York: Macmillan, 1902); Thomas J. Curry, *The First Freedoms: Church and State in America to the Passage of the First Amendment* (New York: Oxford University Press, 1986); Mark Douglas McGarvie, *One Nation under Law: America's Early National Struggles to Separate Church and State* (DeKalb: Northern Illinois University Press, 2005); Mark D. McGarvie, *Law and Religion in American History: Public Values and Private Conscience* (New York: Cambridge University Press, 2016); William G. McLoughlin, *New England Dissent, 1630–1833: The Baptists and the Separation of Church and State, 1* (Cambridge, Mass.: Harvard University Press, 1971); John A. Ragosta, *Wellspring of Liberty: How Virginia's Religious Dissenters Helped Win the American Revolution and Secured Religious Liberty* (New York: Oxford University Press, 2010). See also the sources on Puritanism cited in connection with chapter 2 above.

Chapter 11 is derived from volume 1, chapter 3; from volume 2, chapters 3, 4, 5, and 6; from volume 3, chapters 4, 6, 8, and 9; and from volume 4, chapter 3. Noteworthy secondary sources include E. Digby Baltzell, *Puritan Boston and Quaker Philadelphia: Two Protestant Ethics and the Spirit of Class Authority and Leadership* (New York: Free Press, 1979); Julius Goebel Jr. and T. Raymond Naughton, *Law Enforcement in Colonial New York: A Study in Criminal Procedure (1664–1776)* (New York: Commonwealth Fund, 1944); Hendrik Hartog, *Public Property and Private Power: The Corporation of the City of New York in American Law* (Chapel Hill: University of North Carolina Press, 1983); Jack D. Marietta and G. S. Rowe, *Troubled Experiment: Crime and Justice in Pennsylvania, 1682–1800* (Philadelphia: University of Pennsylvania Press, 2006); and the introduction to Peter Charles Hoffer and William B. Scott, eds., *Criminal Proceedings in Colonial Virginia: Records of Fines, Examination of Criminals, Trials of Slaves, etc., from March 1710/1711 to 1754: Richmond County, Virginia* (Athens: University of Georgia Press, 1984).

Chapter 12 is derived from volume 4, chapters 4 and 5. Important additional sources include Mary Sarah Bilder, *The Transatlantic Constitution: Colonial Legal Culture and the Empire* (Cambridge, Mass.: Harvard University Press, 2004), John Phillip Reid, *A Better Kind of Hatchet: Law, Trade, and Diplomacy in the Cherokee Nation during the Early Years of European Contact* (University Park: Pennsylvania State University Press, 1976), and Joseph Henry Smith, *Appeals to the Privy Council from the American Plantations* (New York: Columbia University Press, 1950), an extraordinarily valuable source of accurate information on any colonial case that ultimately came before the Privy Council. On New York, see Julius Goebel Jr. and T. Raymond

Naughton, *Law Enforcement in Colonial New York: A Study in Criminal Procedure (1664–1776)* (New York: Commonwealth Fund, 1944); Douglas Greenberg, *Crime and Law Enforcement in the Colony of New York, 1691–1776* (Ithaca, N.Y.: Cornell University Press, 1974); Daniel J. Hulsebosch, *Constituting Empire: New York and the Transformation of Constitutionalism in the Atlantic World, 1664–1830* (Chapel Hill: University of North Carolina Press, 2005); Sung Bok Kim, *Landlord and Tenant in Colonial New York: Manorial Society, 1664–1775* (Chapel Hill: University of North Carolina Press, 1978).

Chapter 13 is a condensed version of volume 4, chapter 6. Important additional sources include Richard R. Beeman, *Patrick Henry: A Biography* (New York: McGraw-Hill, 1974); Daniel J. Hulsebosch, *Constituting Empire: New York and the Transformation of Constitutionalism in the Atlantic World, 1664–1830* (Chapel Hill: University of North Carolina Press, 2005); Richard Kluger, *Indelible Ink: The Trial of John Peter Zenger and the Birth of America's Free Press* (New York: W. W. Norton, 2016); Robert Douthat Meade, *Patrick Henry: Patriot in the Making* (Philadelphia: J. B. Lippincott, 1957); Livingston Rutherfurd, *John Peter Zenger: His Press, His Trial* (New York: Chelsea House, 1981); Joseph Henry Smith, *Appeals to the Privy Council from the American Plantations* (New York: Columbia University Press, 1950); M. H. Smith, *The Writs of Assistance Case* (Berkeley: University of California Press, 1978); Jack P. Greene, "The Case of the Pistole Fee: The Report of a Hearing on the Pistole Fee Dispute before the Privy Council, June 18, 1754," *Virginia Magazine of History and Biography*, 66 (1958), 399; Stanley N. Katz, "Introduction," in James Alexander, *A Brief Narrative of the Case and Trial of John Peter Zenger*, ed. Stanley N. Katz (Cambridge, Mass.: Harvard University Press, 1963); Stanley N. Katz, "The Politics of Law in Colonial America: Controversies over Chancery Courts and Equity Law in the Eighteenth Century," in *Law in American History*, ed. Donald Fleming and Bernard Bailyn (Boston: Little, Brown, 1971), 255; Glenn Curtis Smith, "The Affair of the Pistole Fee, Virginia, 1752–55," *Virginia Magazine of History and Biography*, 48 (1940), 209.

Chapter 14 is a condensed version of volume 4, chapter 7. For additional sources on the Proclamation of 1763, see T. H. Breen, *Tobacco Culture: The Mentality of the Great Tidewater Planters on the Eve of the Revolution*, 2nd ed. (Princeton, N.J.: Princeton University Press, 2001); Colin G. Calloway, *With the Stroke of a Pen: 1763 and the Transformation of North America* (New York: Oxford University Press, 2006); Patrick Griffin, *American Leviathan: Empire, Nation, and Revolutionary Frontier* (New York: Hill and Wang, 2007); Woody Holton, *Forced Founders: Indians, Debtors, Slaves and the Making of the American Revolution in Virginia* (Chapel Hill: University of North Carolina Press, 1999); L. Scott Philyaw, *Virginia's Western Visions: Political and Cultural Expansion on an Early American Frontier* (Knoxville: University of Tennessee Press, 2004); Craig Yirush, *Settlers, Liberty, and Empire: The Roots of Early American Political Theory, 1675–1775* (New York: Cambridge University Press, 2011). On the Stamp Act controversy, see Peter David Garner Thomas, *British Politics and the Stamp Act Crisis: The First Phase of the American Revolution, 1763–1767* (Oxford: Clarendon Press, 1975); Edmund S. Morgan and Helen M. Morgan, *The Stamp Act Crisis: Prologue to Revolution*, rev. ed. (New York: Collier Books, 1963); Justin duRivage and Claire Priest, "The Stamp Act and the Political Origins of American Legal and Economic Institutions," *Southern California Law Review*, 88 (2015), 875, which contains an excellent list of relevant literature; John Phillip Reid, "In an Inherited Way: English Constitutional Rights, the Stamp Act Debates, and the Coming of the American Revolution," *Southern California Law Review*, 49 (1975), 1109.

Chapter 15 is a condensed version of volume 4, chapter 8. There is a vast monographic literature on events between 1765 and 1776 culminating in the American Revolution. I have relied especially on Robert A. Becker, *Revolution, Reform, and the Politics of American Taxation, 1763–1783* (Baton Rouge: Louisiana State University Press, 1980); Mary Sarah Bilder, *The Transatlantic Constitution: Colonial Legal Culture and the Empire* (Cambridge, Mass.: Harvard University Press, 2004); Frank L. Dewey, *Thomas Jefferson: Lawyer* (Charlottesville: University Press of Virginia, 1986); Woody Holton, *Forced Founders: Indians, Debtors, Slaves and the Making of the American Revolution in Virginia* (Chapel Hill: University of North Carolina Press, 1999); Pauline Maier, *From Resistance to Revolution: Colonial Radicals and the Development of American Opposition to Britain, 1765–1776* (New York: Alfred A. Knopf, 1972); Jerrilyn Greene Marston, *King and Congress: The Transfer of Political Legitimacy, 1774–1776* (Princeton, N.J.: Princeton University Press, 1987); Andrew Jackson O'Shaughnessy, *The Men Who Lost America: British Leadership, the*

American Revolution, and the Fate of the Empire (New Haven, Conn.: Yale University Press, 2013); Ray Raphael, *The First American Revolution: Before Lexington and Concord* (New York: New Press, 2002); Peter David Garner Thomas, *The Townshend Duties Crisis: The Second Phase of the American Revolution, 1767–1773* (Oxford: Clarendon Press, 1987); Peter David Garner Thomas, *Tea Party to Independence: The Third Phase of the American Revolution, 1773–1776* (Oxford: Clarendon Press, 1993). Joseph Henry Smith, *Appeals to the Privy Council from the American Plantations* (New York: Columbia University Press, 1950), remained especially valuable. On local riots and rebellions in the 1760s and 1770s, I have relied on Richard Maxwell Brown, *The South Carolina Regulators* (Cambridge, Mass.: Harvard University Press, 1963); Julius Goebel Jr. and T. Raymond Naughton, *Law Enforcement in Colonial New York: A Study in Criminal Procedure (1664–1776)* (New York: Commonwealth Fund, 1944); Douglas Greenberg, *Crime and Law Enforcement in the Colony of New York, 1691–1776* (Ithaca, N.Y.: Cornell University Press, 1974); Sung Bok Kim, *Landlord and Tenant in Colonial New York: Manorial Society, 1664–1775* (Chapel Hill: University of North Carolina Press, 1978); Paul David Nelson, *William Tryon and the Course of Empire: A Life in British Imperial Service* (Chapel Hill: University of North Carolina Press, 1990); Brooke Hindle, "The March of the Paxton Boys," *William and Mary Quarterly*, 3d ser., 3 (1946), 461; Nathan Kazuskanich, "'Falling under the Domination Totally of Presbyterians'; The Paxton Riots and the Coming of the Revolution in Pennsylvania," in *Pennsylvania's Revolution*, ed. William Pencak (University Park: Pennsylvania State University Press, 2010), 7.

INDEX